# Screwballs, Curves
# and Knuckleheads

# Screwballs, Curves and Knuckleheads

A Father's Tips, Quips and Musings on Getting
the Most from Your Youth Baseball Experience

## By Jeffrey J. Kirst

For Parents, Players and Coaches

© 2006 Jeffrey J. Kirst

Library of Congress Control No. 2005935649

ISBN: 0-9777754-0-2

Publisher: Sierra Features, Inc. (jkirst6918@aol.com)

P.O. Box 5154, Incline Village, NV 89450.

Editor: Michael Sion, www.mikesion.com

Illustrators: Calder Chism (humorous cartoons); Reed Kirst (inset drawings)

Page designer: www.meshcreative.com

Printer: Sheridan Books, Ann Arbor, Michigan


First edition


Printed in the United States of America

# DISCLAIMER

The author is not providing legal, medical or mental-health advice. This document is not a substitute for a qualified professional. Neither the author nor publisher shall be held responsible for any litigation or sticky social situations, injuries or psychological problems allegedly resulting from the contents of this book. The reader — whether a concerned parent, beleaguered coach or desperate player — should seek the appropriate advice of a qualified professional for all legal, medical or emotional crises beyond the normal that may occur during the course of a season in youth baseball.

\* \* \*

# NOTE ON GENDER USAGE

In the interest of simplifying sentence constructions in the text, I've often used masculine forms of pronouns (he, him, his) in reference to players, coaches and officials, even though I acknowledge (and fully support!) the participation of each gender in youth baseball.

# CONTENTS

## PART III: POLITICS

## PART IV: THE CHURCH OF BASEBALL

*To:*

*My dad. He taught me to play The Game.*

*My mom. She made it possible for me to go to my practices and games,*
*cleaned my uniform and saved my baseball cards.*

*My sons. They reawakened my interest in baseball*
*as we played The Game together.*

*My wife. Her patience, encouragement and understanding let baseball*
*enter our home and become a valuable part of our lives.*

# ACKNOWLEDGMENTS

As human beings, we all have our thoughts, hopes, dreams, fears, frustrations, feelings, emotions, opinions, experiences, and observations about life and the many different things we are occupied with in our lives. Crafting some parts of all this muddle into any sort of coherent form using the 26 symbols and agreeable punctuation is a large part of what writing a book is all about. It is not an easy task. This book would still be jottings on scraps of paper in my baseball archives and an alphabet soup of ideas circulating slowly round about in my mind without the guidance of Mike Sion. His editorial assistance was invaluable to me in getting these words onto paper. His planning, organizing, information gathering and motivational help in pushing this project on to completion made it possible. I can't thank him enough for all he has done to enable me to relate some parts of The Game, which has been such an interesting and fulfilling part of my life, on to the readers of this book in hopes of helping them have the same satisfaction, warm feelings and fond memories I have had with the baseball experience. Thank you, Mike Sion. Here's more than a tip of my baseball cap to you.

The sandlot, the urban alley, the local park and the home back yard are all places where The Game is learned, played and enjoyed. However, it is important to acknowledge the contribution that formal organized youth baseball programs across the nation make to enhance the baseball experience. They provide a framework and guidelines for local volunteers to be active and participate in The Game. Millions of people get to feel the magic of baseball in a unique and positive forum that would be impossible without the support given by these organizations. Here in Reno, Nevada, the Little League Baseball,

Babe Ruth Baseball and American Legion Baseball national programs have done the behind-the-scenes organizational work that helped each of my seasons happen. Thanks are in order for what these organizations have done to make my baseball experience here a great one, and thanks are also in order to the other organizations, large and small, across the land that promote and support The Game, our baseball, Our National Pastime.

Thanks to the talented young artists Reed Kirst and Calder Chism for providing the artwork gracing these pages. Milan Sperka of MeshCreative batted a thousand in the book design.

Special thanks go to all my players, my coaches, the parents of my players, and all the other great people who were in and around the ballparks during my many days in the dugouts, treading the sidelines and sitting in the stands at our Fields of Dreams. You were, each and every one of you, bright spots in my life. It has been a joy to know you all, and I wish the best for all of you both on and off the field as our lives move forward to new challenges and opportunities. May all your at-bats in your lives be fence busters.

Others have contributed in ways great and small to help me achieve my ambition of actually writing a book. A book that might, I hope, one day give help, enlightenment and a few laughs to my fellow human beings. I am grateful to all and thank them for their attention and kindness.

# INTRODUCTION

B aseball is the great American pastime and every person in our wonderful country should have the opportunity to enjoy The Game.

For many, if not most, baseball enthusiasts, the love affair begins in childhood. It starts with fathers and sons (or fathers and daughters, or even mothers and sons or mothers and daughters) the first time they play catch together. My father's father taught him to play. My father taught me to play. I taught my sons to play. The Game transcends generations. And I know that when the time comes, my sons will teach their children to play. It is important. It is part of our culture. It makes America a better place.

Ours being a nation of innovators and entrepreneurs, it was inevitable that someone would think to tap into the armies of young sandlot players by organizing actual leagues for children, complete with teams in uniforms — and adults running the show. Thus, youth leagues took hold during the economic and population boom following World War II, and have continued in popularity (and intensity) to this day.

At the onset of a new century, Little League, Babe Ruth League and their many counterparts have woven themselves into the fabric of the typical American family's life along with school reports, music recitals, holiday gatherings, camping trips and vacations to Las Vegas or Disney World. For families whose children become involved with organized youth baseball, there is usually a big-time commitment, a roller coaster of emotions on and off the field, and lessons to learn about themselves and the rest of humankind.

In this book I have called upon my considerable experience with youth baseball to share some things with you that will make your involvement with The Game more understandable and enjoyable. This humble tome is spawned from extensive and intensive personal involvement. I played The Game as a boy and young man. I coached and managed youth-league teams as an adult. I've been an umpire. I've been a board member, officer and president of a league, and am even known amongst my friends as "The Commissioner." That's involvement! I've also been a fan of The Game at its amateur and professional levels, and a parent with four sons on youth teams. In all, I have endured more than 60 seasons of youth-league baseball — and lived to tell about it.

So, welcome to the world of screwballs, curves and knuckleheads. Youth baseball, and the recipe for surviving, thriving at, and enjoying The Game without smacking someone upside the head with a baseball bat . . . or worse!

# AUTHOR'S NOTE:
## Stepping up to the Plate

Parents end up involved with youth baseball in different ways. My initial participation was pretty common for our overworked, fast-paced American society — as a mildly curious dad checking up on his first-born's little team, after my wife had signed him up as a 6-year-old.

I couldn't have imagined, at this innocent start, what a long-term, time-consuming commitment youth baseball would end up being for the Kirst family, as each of our four sons progressed up the ranks of the different age levels between kindergarten and high school. Yes, The Game wove its way into the fabric of our lives. And here I am — all these years later — writing a book aimed at helping other parents, players — and coaches — get the most out of their participation.

Well, life is unpredictable, isn't it?

It seems funny now to think back to the beginning ...

I WAS VERY BUSY with running my business at the time when my oldest son, Reed, age 6, was signed up by his mother for his first participation in organized youth sports: Tee Ball, the introductory level of Little League Baseball, in which players bat a soft rubber ball off a waist-high tee.

Abby, my wife, had gotten a flier in the mail from the Little League in our Reno, Nevada, neighborhood, announcing sign-ups. I was all for it, because baseball had been a big part of my youth in Cincinnati. I loved The Game; and once afflicted by Baseball Fever, you're smitten for life. I'd been away from The Game for many years, though.

When I got a chance in my busy schedule, I headed out to the baseball field to see Reed's team. It was a spring evening. I parked and walked around the city recreation complex with its backstops facing each other and respective infields fanning out in opposite directions. Finally I spotted Abby, our younger sons in tow. I joined them in the bleachers and squinted and focused on the little players arrayed around the diamond wearing matching T-shirts and caps, all from a distance generally resembling each other like clones. It took me a bit of time to spot Reed — but there he was, standing unoccupied out in right field. That gave me a tiny jolt. My fond memories of youth baseball were bound up with the position I played during much of my career: catcher. As a catcher, I was always in the middle of the action. I was behind the plate when I started playing organized baseball at about age 9, and remained so through most of my time at the upper-age playing levels. I wore out two of my own catcher's mitts. Had I continued in high school (that is, had I persevered and been able to make the cut for the school squad), I might not have been able to remain as backstop, but the point is moot. I gave up baseball and focused on the swim team. But I never gave up loving The Game.

Watching my own flesh and blood out there on the field confirmed for me my bond with baseball and my abiding interest in having my boys get as much out of The Game as I had. When we got home that night I asked Reed, "How do you like baseball?"

"It's OK," he said.

"Are you learning how to do it?"

"Sort of."

Reed was happy to have his T-shirt (emblazoned with the name of the sponsor, the local waste-removal firm: Reno Disposal) and his cap. He was happy to be involved in an organized activity. He was having fun. His coach was a good guy. But I could see that if he continued in Little League to the competitive levels, he'd have to improve his skills if he were to earn spots in the fun positions: infield, maybe even pitcher . . . or catcher.

I started making some time at home to practice with him in the back yard. (After all, if you want to improve, you have to accept the fact that baseball is an everyday game. It's not enough for a competitive player to just show up at games, or games and team practices. You have to practice on your own.) We threw the ball around. First, I threw to Reed's left side, right at his glove. When he mastered that skill I threw to his right side, so he had to cross over and catch the ball. Finally, I threw straight at his chest, since he was able to defend himself by getting the glove in front of the ball before the ball could nail him.

After we got the throwing and catching down, I tossed him grounders and flies so he could learn to field. Then it was time for live hitting. I lobbed him pitches. And slowly but surely, the sport of baseball asserted itself into the regular routines of the Kirst household.

Reed did continue onto the next level of Little League: Farm division, with batters hitting against a pitching machine. Casual observation by me confirmed that the coaching ranks were filled by cronies, with playing time allotted to the kids according to the political pecking order. While I continued to work with Reed in the back yard to develop his skills, and his younger brothers began taking their turns in the drills, my best hope to gain precious playing time for my sons was to get involved with the league, somehow . . .

Their skills did improve from the backyard training, although their growing prowess had little bearing on "PT" — playing time, the currency of youth sports. While my own father hadn't coached when I was in the youth-organization and Knothole leagues back in Cincinnati, I was well familiar with "Coach's Son Syndrome." On the teams I played for, the kids who pitched, played second base and shortstop typically were the sons of the coaches. (I was lucky in getting to play catcher and be in the midst of the action, because not many players wanted to be catcher, and most people did not consider playing catcher to be a case of good luck.) So I knew how critical parental involvement at the coaching level can be to ensuring a child's opportunity for ample PT.

Reed, despite having to play lots of outfield and bat far down the order, enjoyed his youth-league experience. It is nice to be part of a team. (Indeed, he continued on through two years of high school junior varsity.) It was about five years after he started in Little League that I became involved as a coach. By this time I was able to squeeze more time away from business. Charlie, 18 months younger than Reed, was now in the Farm division and facing the pitching machine. I offered my coaching services to his team's manager and coaches. Despite a less-than-warm reception, I seized a window of opportunity: as an unofficial hitting coach working with the other nonpolitically connected kids on the team. (I recount this experience in the Part III chapter, "The Bottom Five.")

AFTER THAT DUTY AS an auxiliary coach, I worked my way into our Little League's political arena and ended up the next year as the manager (top dog) of a team in the Minor division (at that time, usually for players ages 10-12, with 11- and 12-year-olds with lesser experience or talent at this level). We were the Pirates, and both Reed, 12, and Charlie, 10, were on the roster as "coach's options." Reed certainly could have played in the Main division, but I insisted he stick with his dad and brother to ensure a productive and exciting baseball season. His previous season had been miserable, since the coaches on the team he'd been on had not been particularly interested in finding ways to dole out playing time to non-coaches' sons and make the baseball experience fulfilling.

"I'm your father," I told Reed, "and if you can't get a break from your father, you can't get a break from anybody." Although league rules forbade 12-year-olds from pitching in Minor, Reed could play any other position. And, suffice to say, his final season in Little League was full of fun, excitement — and playing time. He played third base for the most part, got up to bat 76 times and got on base with hits or walks 51 times. That's a very nice season.

I did my best, by the way, to avoid Coach's Son Syndrome and work with all the players on the team I managed. It was the right thing to do. I did my best to make every player have a good baseball experience the way I wanted my sons to have a good experience. I did my best to give everyone a chance to play his favorite position, if only for an inning or two. I did my best to allow each player to enjoy moments of glory, to create lasting good memories of The Game. (The kind of memories, incidentally, that rekindle when former youth players show up in a major league ballpark, looking out at the action, and remembering when they, too, ran down a long fly, or nabbed a grounder before they even realized it was in their glove, or slid under the catcher's mitt at home for the winning run.) And in these early years, I learned much about the youth baseball experience and how to improve my approach to The Game.

In the following years, I went on to manage or coach many more teams in spring and fall in Little League and in Babe Ruth League, and to watch my sons continue on with their high school programs. (One son, Charlie, even had the option of playing in college, but declined.) I joined the league boards and served as our Little League's president. I helped get the league's Fall Ball program going. I coached in all-stars.

In all, I've participated in more than 60 seasons of youth-league baseball with my four sons, adding up each season each boy played in, during spring and fall. I managed teams in 15 seasons, and coached numerous other seasons. I've been on the field as a manager or coach from the Little League Farm division to a few games at the American Legion level (for ages 16-19). I even was drafted into service as a field umpire for a couple American Legion games after the regular umpire stalked off after verbal altercations with coaches. Add that to the years I played myself as a boy and young man, and the decades as a fan of The Game from its lowest to highest levels, and you could say I've accumulated quite a bit of experience and useful information, as well as a mental attic stuffed with useless trivia but also memorable tales of humor, absurdity and who'd-a-thunk-its.

You can't help but develop philosophies of The Game — and life — after that many seasons wearing a baseball cap. And you can't help, as the years advance, feeling like you should share your wizen-headed wisdom with others. I realized I'd reached a turning point during the high school baseball season — a few years ago — when it was the last time I could pick up the local newspaper and read a name in the sports pages of any of the players I'd coached in the youth leagues. So my participation with The Game, other than as a fan, should now rightly be as a "sage" (or at least as a humble scribe).

EVERYTHING IN THIS BOOK — from skill-building drills to coaching strategies, explanations of politics, advice to parents, war stories, and musings on The Meaning of It All — comes from firsthand experience. There's nothing theoretical about any of it. The drills are those that work. Same with the tactics of managing a team. Same with the realities of league politics (and the sooner parents gain an understanding of those politics, the sooner they'll be able to tailor their children's experience to become as positive as possible, as I myself was able to do).

The situations I found myself in, the emotions I savored or swallowed, the triumphs and trip-ups, the dizzying elations and deflating frustrations, over the years are the same that millions of other parents, players and coaches have experienced or will experience. Including you, the reader. I'm sharing my thoughts on these many matters so that you can benefit from one who's been there, over and over, seeing history repeat itself, over and over. Often predictably. But sometimes unpredictably!

The chapters ahead will help any earnest reader to better enjoy the game of youth baseball in all its richness, drama and glory. The chance for wonderful, enduring memories begins each time the umpire behind the plate barks, "Play ball!" and a new game begins.

So take your seventh-inning stretch now. And then feel free to dig into the chapters ahead.

I'll close by wishing that your youth baseball experience will be as fulfilling as it has been for the Kirsts: Jeff, Abby, Reed, Charlie, Rew and Paul. Baseball has been good to us.

PART I

# SKILLS AND DRILLS

*The tips, tactics and techniques described in this part of the book are all based on my personal experience as a player, parent and coach.*

*These drills are simple. I claim no expertise in the finer points of The Game. I'm not selling any videotapes or DVDs or running pricey weekend camps. But I do claim repeated success with the drills explained in this part. They are time-tested, and actually work. I've seen them work, over and over, with my own eyes. What's more, these drills are FUN for young players. (Baseball is, after all, a game!)*

*Every youth-league roster has players of widely different levels of skill. The drills included here will be useful to just about any player who performs them, and any coach who employs them correctly.*

*As I say several times in this book: Baseball is an everyday game. To improve, you must practice, including at home if possible. You can't rely on miracles to happen during a game. True, just about anything can happen during a game — especially in youth baseball, where nothing is routine. But miracles, by definition, almost never occur.*

*So, practice, practice, and practice some more. The drills in this part will work for you.*

# Notes:

# What to Expect at Each Level (From Chasing Bees to Courting Scouts)

From the first introduction to organized baseball, through the high school experience, a player will probably play in several leagues. It all begins with the typical Little League divisions competing on a field with the pitching rubber 45 feet from home plate, 60-foot bases and 200-foot outfield fences. There is no leading off base for runners in Little League, and no running for first on a third-strike passed ball. But all this changes when players reach age 13 and move up to Babe Ruth (or Pony or whatever the division for this age group is called in your locale). Then the competition is on regular-sized diamonds with the rubber 60 feet, 6 inches from the plate, bases 90 feet apart, fences pushed back to 250 or 300 feet or more, and runners leading off base or racing for first after a third-strike pitch gets away from the catcher.

Here's generally what to expect in skills development at each level:

• Tee Ball. This is mostly for ages 5 and 6 (although some 4-year-olds may be approved, and some 7-year-olds may qualify). As its name implies, Tee Ball means players hit the ball off a tee — a T-shaped stand. Therefore, there are no strikeouts (although the ball isn't hit cleanly on every swing; the tee itself absorbs plenty of punishment). Also, no scores are kept. These very young players are just getting used to the concepts of rules, fundamentals and uniforms (a T-shirt and cap). A rubberized ball softer than a traditional baseball is used, as well as smaller, lighter bats, and games are usually kept to a 90-minute limit.

If you're a coach, consider it best to have no more than 15 players on your team. Use a continuous batting order so that every player has a turn at bat and feels part of the game, before the order restarts. Have all the players take the field. You can post individual players at each infield spot and send the rest into the outfield. Know that three-quarters of the players in the outfield will sit there and pick clover, chase bees or talk with each other. Try to keep them on their feet, knees bent, glove palm facing the plate, in the "ready position." But don't expect too much out of them.

Rotate all the players through the infield at some time every few games. As in regular baseball, a side is retired after making three outs, so it's helpful for you to find a good fielder to stand at the pitcher's mound, a shortstop who can field, catch and throw, and a first baseman who can catch. If you have three such players out of your 15, consider yourself lucky. You can use them the majority of the time at these positions, while rotating others in for the experience.

Even though a side is retired after three outs, a team also finishes batting in an inning after 10 players have batted. Batting can be prolonged, since there are no strikeouts. What's more, you draw a circle on an 8-foot radius around home plate, and any ball hit and stopping in that territory should be considered a foul. As for overthrows (which frequently happen), runners may advance one base. A play also is ended after a ball is back in a fielder's hand on the pitcher's mound.

Tee Ball is fun to watch. It's typically the most integrated level for the two genders. And in every game you'll see things you've never observed before in baseball! For example, don't be surprised to see a batter-runner take off for third instead of first.

Last, but not least, the big lesson for tee-ball players is to learn to BE

POSITIVE. They may be thrown out, but there's always the next time up. And a player may make a mistake, but teammates need to support him. And players shouldn't get upset when an opposing player makes a good play. Sportsmanship is essential to enjoying the experience.

• Farm. Players ages 7 to 8 (with some 6- and 9-year-olds) have a division often called Farm. This level uses the greatest technological innovation ever made for enhancing the action factor in little-kid baseball: the pitching machine. This adjustable, plug-in contraption on a three-legged stand gets young players used to swinging at live pitching without fear of being hit by a wild pitch (unless the coach mishandles the machine, of course, and the player somehow finds his way into the path of the ball). Staying in the batter's box, not bailing out, is a key skill developed at this level. So is keeping one's head on the ball, swinging level and putting the ball into play instead of striking out. (Striking out is probably the worst moment for anyone in any sport!)

At this level, players' nascent batting, fielding and throwing skills start to emerge, scores are kept, umpires are used and there typically is a postseason league tournament — so the competitive level is now raised from Tee Ball. If the league is a prosperous one with scoreboards, Farm games have a running board, which adds to the excitement.

Players have a much better grasp of the rules and strategy than do Tee Ballers, and as a season progresses it's quite gratifying to see players throw to correct bases, heed base coaches' directions — and even snag pop-ups and flies (catching is one of the last skills youngsters develop).

Games can go the full six innings of Little League, or end because of a time limit, typically two hours. An inning half ends after three outs are made or if five runs are scored (or up to eight, if a batter hits a grand slam after five runs have already come in).

A coach should put 12 or 13 players on a team and, as with Tee Ball, use a continuous batting order. Every player should also get a chance to play at least one inning in the infield each game. The umpire should be positioned at the mound. I recommend the umpire feed the pitching machine, but usually coaches handle this task — giving their players the best possible pitches at 40 mph. Regular rules hold sway at the Farm level, except that there are no called balls on pitches. If a pitch is out of the strike zone and the batter doesn't swing, it can be called a "no pitch."

A batting tip about this level: Hitters at this age often have a good swing, but cannot adjust to a pitch. Check if the swing is over or under the ball, then reposition the player forward or backward in the batter's box parallel with the plate. You'll see some VERY interesting batting stances in this division. Most memorable for me was the kid who repeatedly went up to the plate and stood right on it. He finally figured it out and moved to the side to avoid getting hit by the ball.

One other skill you can begin teaching at the Farm level: bunting. Show hitters how to keep their knuckles curled back behind the bat, and to slide the hands out properly for a solid, still stance. Make sure they know to hold the bat far from their bodies, and to keep their heads from coming over the plate (where they can get hit in the face by a foul tip). Remind them to bend their knees (a basic of all batting — indeed, all baseball skills). Teach them to "catch" the ball with the bat, to deaden the ball (instead of batting it forward, where it could end up in the pitcher's glove), and also teach them to pull the bat back from the plate if the pitch is out of the strike zone (this is extra insurance against an umpire calling the pitch a strike, maintaining the batter was swinging at it). Bunting will become an important skill as early as the Minor level, and it's also a good technique for poorer hitters to use at the

Farm level so that they can put the ball in play instead of repeatedly striking out. (My personal favorite method of teaching bunting is by using tennis balls, which eliminate the fear factor for beginners.)

When it comes to fielding, there is one ironclad rule you give to Farm outfielders: THROW IT TO SECOND BASE. The concepts of cutoff men and other intricacies are too complex for this age group. Believe me!

ONE SEASON, DURING ONE of our first practices, I walked out to my player standing in right field and asked, "What position are you playing and what are you going to do with the ball when you get it?" He answered: "I'm playing right field and when I get the ball I'm going to throw it to first base." "OK, we'll talk about that later," I said.

I walked out to center field and asked the player there: "What position are you playing and what are you going to do with the ball when you get it?" He replied: "I'm playing center field and when I get the ball I'm going to throw it to first base." "OK, we'll review that later," I said. I walked out to the left fielder — a young little guy who was standing way out in the dirt of the warning track. "What position are you playing and what are you going to do when you get the ball?" I asked. He said: "Coach, I'm playing shortstop, and I'm gonna throw the ball to first base!"

Yes, Farm is a learning experience. At this level it's good to review what position the players are playing and what they'll do with the ball when it's hit to them.

There is plenty of unique stuff to witness during Farm games. A few tears and some temper tantrums, too. (It's surprising how much those very young players want to win when they're out there on the field. An hour after the game, many of them can't remember whether they won or lost. They will remember, however, whether they did something good — scored a run, hit the ball.) For players, the frustrations with baseball begin at this level. But so do the big feelings of pride and joy, and finding some moments of glory.

• Minor. This is generally for players 10-12 (with some 9-year-olds, too). Now there is live pitching, and the very best players (or best-connected politically) have shots at making it onto their league's summertime all-star squads, particularly the 9-and-10-year-old all-stars, since the Main division players occupy the 11-and-12-year-old rosters. The point is: Minor is another step up in competitiveness from Farm. Managers want to win all the more badly at this level. Usually they're thinking ahead to landing a team at the Main level in a following season, for further glory.

The most serious, gifted or driven (by their parents) players begin to emerge at the Minor level, claiming spots high up in the batting order, and the choice positions in the field (pitcher, catcher, shortstop and second base). This is also the level at which enthusiastic parents pay for weekly batting or pitching lessons at the local batting cages. (Make no mistake about it: practice pays off!) If a player is not naturally talented, if he puts in the practice time, the player will still have great success at the Minor level, even in comparison to more talented players who don't regularly work on their games. An extra note: Learning the strike zone (which is really helped by extra batting practice) is the single most important skill a player can develop at this level, because it makes the greatest difference when facing live pitching in an actual game.

The nature of the jump in competition from Farm to Minor requires a preseason draft. Many, if not most, of the players who've signed up are still unknown to coaches at the Minor level, but already there are some "stars" who get snatched up right away. Leagues also typically have "coaches' options," meaning if you manage or coach a team, your son or daughter is on your roster.

The squad is filled up with the 10-, 11- and 12-year-olds who weren't drafted by Main teams, and by unknowns chosen more or less randomly as the draft rounds ensue.

For many coaches, play in Minor attempts to copy that in Main: live pitching for six innings, signs (including bunting) given to batters by the third-base coach, arguments (I mean, discussions) with the umpires, who call games from behind the plate. For a number of reasons, this division can be extremely difficult to have a good time in. Over my years of participation with teams in this division, and after much agonizing, I came up with a good format to use to parcel out action for all the players:

Have 12-player teams. Use the continuous batting order (all 12 players hit in order, instead of just nine players with three on the bench). Play four outfielders (that's my preference; most leagues probably won't go for that). Use live pitching for the first three innings and the pitching machine for the last three (ditto the previous parenthetical comment). I took plenty of heat from other coaches for this pitching setup when I was managing in Minor — and it's likely that if you try to institute it, you'll face stiff resistance and may not get your way — but I found my setup works. One main reason why my way is better than the traditional format is because, in the draft, all the really good older pitchers wind up on Main teams. That leaves players of lesser talent (or age) in the Minors, and very few are capable of doing an adequate job of pitching. Thus, games can become walkathons, and rarely go the full six innings because the two-hour time limit elapses. There's not enough real action. Everyone's experience suffers.

But in my preferred pitching format, there are action-filled games that are fun for large numbers of players. The pitchers with ability can still get their innings in, but then the pitching machine comes in and plenty of hitting is guaranteed. That means games are won or lost with hitting and fielding, not due to walks. It gets the baseball experience more like baseball should be. You may notice that a game under this format will take about an hour for the first three innings to finish, then conclude with a "fun-for-all" in 20 or 30 minutes, as using the pitching machine allows good hitters to hit and good fielders to have something to field.

• Main. Now the competition level is SERIOUS. Coaches compete for bragging rights in the standings and the postseason tournament. Players vie for coveted all-star spots. In the back of the minds of the most gung ho players, coaches — and parents — is the dream of making it to the Little League World Series in August in Williamsport, Pennsylvania.

Players who reach Main typically have been playing since age 5 or 6 — meaning half or more of their young lives. They've grown up as ballplayers. By this level, the less serious or able players have begun to leave baseball. Either they didn't enjoy their experiences in Minor, or didn't perform well enough for themselves or their parents to care to continue, or became interested in other sports (such as soccer) or activities (such as scouting, martial arts or musical instruments) that took precedence. A few even wanted to spend more time on their schoolwork. Some players of marginal ability or interest do continue on to Main, however. Unfortunately, they are not destined for much playing time. The hardcore parents have their budding little stars in weekly private lessons, and an earnest family may even put Junior on a traveling competitive team that plays during the months outside of Little League, and on larger fields.

Main has 12-player teams, with nine at a time in the lineup. There are substitution and returning-player rules, meaning a starting player can be put on the bench and then brought in later in the game. If the entire team shows up for a game, then three players will have to be substituted in. Usually, a league's minimum-play rule requires that every player present get a minimum of one at-bat and two innings in the field in a game, or the team forfeits. Further playing-time rules typically limit pitching to 12 innings per week per pitcher, with a rest period of a day and a game for pitchers who throw in more than one inning. There also are limits on the number of pitches a player can throw in a game (such as 65 pitches early in the season, then 80 later in the season and 90 during the postseason tournament). (League officials may claim that the pitching rules are meant to prevent players from hurting their arms, but I maintain the real reason is to keep an overpowering pitcher from dominating a league. After all, there are no limits on the number of tosses a catcher can make in a game, and the catcher throws the ball back on every pitch and also may try to gun down runners at first, second or third.)

In Main, many of the nuances of baseball, such as cutoff men in the field, and fake throws to second that instead go to the pitcher to catch a runner racing from third to home, are used. With less than two outs and the bases loaded, the infield is drawn in. There are sacrifice bunting (the third baseman keeping a watchful eye) and other tactics. The third-base coach will use a series of gestures (touching the hat, the nose, swiping an arm sleeve or pant leg) to tell the batter to hit, take, bunt, fake bunt or slash. The manager on the sidelines may send signals to the catcher to relay to the pitcher. There are fastballs, changeups and curves (though many coaches say 12-year-old arms are not ready to throw breaking stuff). The level of play can be very good — the players having honed their skills and built their knowledge to an impressive degree — and yet the diamond is still at the little size it's been since Farm division. With the number of home runs some Main players clout in a season, it seems that their age group may have outgrown the field's dimensions.

One other aspect of Main: these players are aware that they will hurt their chance to make all-stars (or to even get starts and lots of playing time on their own teams) if they don't conduct themselves with maturity. That means no tossing of helmets or bats after a strikeout or bad call by the umpire, no profanity, no temper tantrums, no back talk to coaches during a game or practice. How a player acts around the other teams' parents, coaches and kids — even standing in line at the snack bar before or after a game — can affect the player's reputation. Yes, Main is a whole new level of living for youth baseball players.

Prep. That's the term, short for "preparatory," used in my area for the 13-year-old division of Babe Ruth League. At this level the full game of baseball is played over seven innings (with, typically, a two-hour time limit). There are runners leading off, pitchers making pickoff moves or pitchouts, passed balls in play, 60 feet, 6 inches from the pitching rubber to the plate, 90 feet between bases, and outfield fences looming at least 250 feet from home. (Some locales have a mid-sized diamond as an intermediate step; but I've played on both and know it is better to just have players jump to the big field and adapt that much quicker. The adjustment may be tough, but players understand that the field will never get any bigger, only that the outfield fence will keep moving back and back and back.)

This is a tough year. All of a sudden, the veterans of Little League must adapt to the larger distances, and it's not uncommon to see the old rainbow arcs on tosses from third to first. Most pitchers find it difficult to throw effectively from this longer distance. They are not able to throw strikes consistently, and there are many walks. When it comes to batting, there is a longer run to first, and speed has become more important. What would have been solid hits to the outfield a year before are now groundouts, line-outs and pop-ups. Batting averages plunge. Welcome to the real world.

For these players a year out of Little League, their world has changed in a big way. While perhaps a handful of the players in Little League had facial hair, deep voices, great height and other signs of pubescence, in Prep there are many more man-children. Another reality of the shift up: Little Leaguers who were used to scoreboards, but only announcers when they were in all-star games or tournaments, may now, in Prep, be playing on a ballfield where there is a scorer's booth and someone at the microphone calling their names before they come to the plate.

Some leagues at this level of ball do away with the mandatory-play rule, meaning that — as in high school, college, semi-pro and professional baseball — some players sit the bench an entire game. I strongly oppose this. Teams at this level should have no more than 12 players, and every player should get at least an at-bat and a couple innings in the field each game.

Babe Ruth. (Again, other locales may have different names or affiliations for leagues for 14- and 15-year-olds.) This is a continuation of the same game as for the 13-year-olds — only the level of play is much higher because the players are stronger and have a better grasp of the game. More strategy is used: fielding shifts, cutoffs, hit-and-runs, and so on. The main thing to really watch out for is the arms of the pitchers. At this age, hurlers have the muscle power to really throw hard, but they can hurt themselves since few have the brains or experience to know when to quit. Coaches should watch for sore arms very carefully at this level. It is important.

High school. By age 16, if not before, players have usually gravitated to a high school program that runs through the spring. The players typically play year-round in city-sponsored or other affiliated leagues that tie in with high school programs for the off-season. The players in these summer and fall leagues can be up to college age. There usually are a few prospects — players whom professional scouts are watching — in these programs.

I recommend that everyone who can, play until getting out of high school. Then the player should take a scholarship to a major or junior college if offered, turn professional if drafted, or give up The Game. It is just too hard to keep playing after that, because so many people have other things to do (studies, careers, families) and it's difficult to get 18 people plus umpires and substitutes to show up in one place at a time. (An exception is city-sponsored leagues — but playing in these takes up a lot of time.) Another option, of course, is shifting into casual softball leagues.

So those are the level breakdowns of youth baseball. For parents whose child is just starting out in organized baseball, now you have a vague picture of what to expect in the years ahead.

# Getting in the Swing

.......................................................................................................................

*"They throw it and I just sock it."*

— Babe Ruth, on the art of hitting a baseball

Hitting a baseball is said to be the most difficult thing to do in all of sport. I'd have to agree with that. But . . . it is something that anyone (save those with a serious injury or physical disability) can learn to do . . . and do adequately enough to have some moments of glory.

And while hitting may be tough, it is the most rewarding thing you can do in baseball. There is nothing like that great feeling you get when you connect with the pitch solidly and watch it rocket into the air faster than you could ever throw it, then land and skip across the green outfield grass as the fielders race to chase it down and get it back into the infield. And you know that it was *you*, the power in *your* body, that sent that projectile flying.

Getting to the point where a player can have that feeling requires some doing.

Go out and buy a bat. Make it a light bat with a thin grip. And get some batting gloves. Batting gloves hadn't been invented in my day, and if there had been any wimps wearing them back then, they would have been laughed off the field. Our hands were covered with calluses from swinging wooden bats and filled with splinters. On a cold day, when you hit the ball a little off the bat's center, it was like you'd picked up a high-tension electric wire . . . such a shock and sting in your hands! But times have changed. Batting gloves are *de rigueur.*

Most youth baseball players seem to get a bat that is too heavy for them.

That's understandable. Bats are so expensive — close to $200 for a new one — that parents figure Junior can grow into it. But he'll never learn to bat well with a bat he can't swing properly. So be careful when you buy a bat that it's not too heavy. (When I was a team manager, I made sure there was one expensive, new team bat in the equipment bag for all the players to use if they didn't have a quality bat of their own.)

When you're equipped with the bat and batting gloves, you're ready to go. Don't forget the helmet when it comes time to face live pitching.

The first thing the player should do is get used to swinging the bat — both to loosen up before hitting the ball in practice, and as a necessary muscle-building exercise to be performed daily. Different muscles, in different combinations, are used for batting than are used in any regular activity. (This is easily proved. Swing a bat a number of times, then note how stiff your arms and shoulders feel the next day. Even your hips and legs may be sore, since the proper swing means turning into the ball, uncoiling the arms, twisting and following through.) The only motion close to batting is chopping down trees with an ax, and there's not much of that going on with kids these days. A good drill is to swing the bat 20 or 30 times every day. A player can augment this by tossing up an object (a plastic ball, an apple from a tree), or by watching his reflection in a mirror or picture window to ensure his form is right.

Swinging a bat every day is an easy exercise, and worth the effort in the results the player will get.

WHEN I WAS A boy in Ohio in the late 1950s and early '60s, I had a hitting game in the fall around World Series time. I'd go in the back yard where there was a walnut tree. A walnut tree has lots of nuts, and under the tree would be a harvest of green-husked walnuts that had fallen. These nuts were solid as rocks when they first fell off; but if they'd sat on the ground for a time, the outer shell would get crispy and the inside turn a mushy brown. I'd throw a walnut up with my left hand and then swing at it with the bat and see how far I could hit it. I'd hit as many walnuts as had fallen that day, then walk out and hit them back toward the tree.

There was a drawback. The more you hit, the husks would begin flying off, and the juice and smell of walnut would get all over you and the bat. If the walnuts were especially ripe, your hands would be covered with a brown stain that wouldn't come off. No matter how hard you washed, your fingers and palms would remain brown and be dyed dark down in the cracks.

One day, the school secretary called my mother and asked why I hadn't been taking baths. Due to the walnut stains, I'd looked awfully dirty to my teacher and she'd sent me to the principal's office. Cleanliness and personal hygiene were taught as a priority at the school. The principal and teacher finally relented when it became clear that my apparently filthy hands were, in fact, scrubbed clean, but would remain dirty-looking until the walnut-stained skin eventually peeled off.

The backyard batting drill wasn't limited to smacking walnuts. There were the big red Jonathan apples. Whack, whack, whack. Then I'd switch to the golden delicious apples. Whack, whack, whack. Then, for more of a challenge, the crabapple tree. Crabapples are quite a bit smaller than regular apples, meaning that hitting them is more of a challenge.

When I was worn out, I'd scrape all the applesauce, apple juice, seeds, skins and stems from my bat and hands, and head inside. Practice complete.

These days, kids don't need a bunch of fruit or nut trees to practice batting for free. They can use Wiffle Balls, plastic golf balls — even pebbles and broomsticks (but not bats with rocks, since you don't want to dent those expensive bats).

The key is to keep swinging. It builds up muscles. And it develops hand-eye coordination.

And it's fun.

# Better Batting through Tennis Balls

WHY THE USE OF TENNIS BALLS ON THE DIAMOND SHOULD BE CONFINED TO BATTING PRACTICE, NOT ACTUAL GAMES.

Tennis balls?! What do they have to do with baseball?

Plenty. Tennis balls are one of the greatest things going for improving batting. I learned this the hard way, so you'll now get to learn it the easy way.

My oldest son was having trouble hitting. He'd just started in Little League, and he just couldn't get his bat on the ball. Substitute right fielder — that was his destiny. He felt bad. I felt bad. He just wasn't getting the glory from The Game he deserved. What to do? Batting practice, of course!

I bought a couple dozen baseballs and started pitching to him in the back yard on a regular basis. Two things happened. One, I nearly killed him hitting him with the baseball so often. Even as my pitching improved, I'd still plunk him every so often. If you've ever been smacked with a baseball, you know it hurts. It's not pleasant.

The other thing that happened was that when he finally started hitting the ball, he nearly knocked the house down with each smash into the green siding. Not good.

So I determined to find some better way to teach the boy how to bat. I tried Wiffle Balls. Rag balls. A ball on a string that I would swing around my head. Finally I decided that tennis balls could be the ticket. I got three-dozen of them and started pitching. For years I'd heard that you should NEVER throw a tennis ball. They were said to be too light for the motion and cause horrific strain. Your arm would shrivel up, turn black and fall off if you threw a tennis ball. I overcame this piece of traditional baseball wisdom and started pitching the fuzzy green orbs to my son.

The first bit of good news is that when you hit Junior with a tennis ball, IT DOESN'T HURT. The next good thing is that when he hits it, his hands don't sting. Third, the ball goes a LOOOONG way when he connects. It was really tough to harm windows, doors, siding, trees, fences and other obstacles by hitting them with a batted tennis ball. Hallelujah!

Once we got the hang of hitting tennis balls, it became a real confidence builder. I could pitch inside and my son wouldn't flinch. I could throw outside and he would step out to hit. I could change speeds, throw from different angles, even lay on some curves if I did it just right. Thus, tennis balls appeared to be the way to go when it came to practicing how to hit, learning the strike zone and seeing lots of live pitching. Bunting, too, became an easier skill to learn without the fear of mashed fingers from hardballs.

I can't tell you how great it was to have figured this out! As my other sons began in The Game, they all wanted to hit tennis balls. And their hitting ability went through the roof. They now KNEW they could hit the ball.

I pitched hundreds of tennis balls to my kids and continued the system when I started coaching teams. We used tennis balls on the tee, in the soft-toss machine and in live-pitching situations. We produced some really good hitters. I'd always show a beginning hitter a baseball and a tennis ball and ask him to compare the sizes. The baseball is much larger. Then I'd tell him that if he could just get the bat on the tennis ball and foul it off, that would probably be a hit when he connected the same way with the larger baseball.

It worked! Our players were hitting the tennis balls squarely, learning their strike zones and improving dramatically. Kids who could never hit before were connecting regularly in games. Practice, practice, practice. Now, some of the coaches charged with doing the live pitching complained that pitching tennis balls would cause them to throw out their arms. My answer: "You're 40 years old. So WHAT if you throw out your arm? Your career is over. What better cause than teaching these kids to hit?" The reluctant coaches kept on throwing the tennis balls, and by and large didn't throw out their arms. My own arm got stronger and stronger. I was tossing 500 or 600 pitches at a practice with no ill

effects. After several months of this, I could scratch the top of my foot with my right hand without bending over, but those tendons and ligaments needed to be loosened up, anyway.

I collected several garbage cans full of tennis balls. Waste not, want not. The more you have, the better. That way you can pitch and pitch and pitch. Each can holds about 300 balls, and when you have a giant hoard you can just call the batters up one by one and keep pitching. Then, when the supply is littering the field, you gather them up as a team. It saves time.

There are two other benefits of tennis balls. One is that you can work in close quarters with them, because if you get hit in the back of the head with a flying tennis ball, it doesn't faze you. It doesn't hurt your shins either when a hot one comes back at you. My usual practice was setting up three batting stations a few yards apart to have coaches pitch to the players. You don't need a catcher, and the balls don't roll very far behind the batter if there's no backstop. You can set up stations on the open field.

The other benefit of tennis balls is that they don't wear out bats. These new, ultra high-tech bats made out of aircraft aluminum only have a few thousand hits in them before losing their sting and going flat, and sometimes even cracking in half. Practicing with hardballs shortens the lives of these expensive bats.

I recommend tennis balls. They are the greatest hitting tool around!

UNFORTUNATELY, THERE IS A downside. Traditional baseball enthusiasts laugh, hoot and holler when you get out the tennis balls and start hitting them all over the field. You'll suffer. You'll be ridiculed. It isn't pretty. The traditionalists cannot stand seeing a tennis ball on the diamond — or anywhere near a bat and glove. I'd be walking around the baseball park and someone would come up to me with a tennis ball and a smirk or look of disdain and say, "Here, this is yours." The traditionalists gripe about tennis balls. They whine. They moan. But I tell them all: "Too bad! Tennis balls WORK!"

If you're a coach, watch your players bat in the game and you'll see what a difference tennis balls can make. As the season progresses, fans will come up to you and say, "Jeesh, your team sure can hit. How did you draft that many good hitters? What's the secret?" I'd give them a wink and whisper: "Tennis balls." They'd get a bewildered look and walk away.

When your players stop hitting tennis balls, they'll slip right back into being mediocre hitters. Seeing the live pitching makes all the difference. If you pitched that many baseballs to them, they'd probably be better hitters, too, but they'd all be injured from being hit so many times. Out of 50 pitches thrown hard, a kid will be hit two or three times. With a baseball, they'll be setting up three feet off the plate, or will be begging not to have to hit any more. You can't go wrong with tennis balls.

As time went on and my tennis-ball drill became known around the league, I'd get late-night calls from coaches who'd become reluctant believers. "Can I borrow the tennis balls for my practice tomorrow? We've got a big game coming up." Or: "Could I have 50 tennis balls for the season? I'll give them back." I've always helped these guys out even though they were too embarrassed to let anyone know what they were doing.

Still, even the baseball gods had trouble with tennis balls, I discovered.

I finagled a practice session at Reno's minor league ballpark, Moana Stadium, for a team I was managing. I thought it would be a great thing for my players. It was a professional field. Many famous players working their way up to the majors had played on that field, including Satchel Paige, Dennis Eckersley and Dave Henderson. A friend of mine with connections had told me that my team could practice at Moana a couple times to get ready for a tournament. I was excited.

So my team got out there and warmed up. We tossed the baseball around for a while. Then I wanted everyone to get in lots of hitting, so I set up two batting-tee stations against the cyclone fence, started my coaches on live pitching with baseballs on the actual field and arranged two tennis-ball hitting stations in the outfield along the foul lines, with the batters swinging toward the outfield area. The sun was shining; not a cloud in the sky. Just beautiful baseball weather.

After 20 minutes or so, the outfield was covered with tennis balls. I had brought about 600 of them, and 450 of them were dotting the grass. Then out of nowhere, the sky clouded over. It grew dark. We could hear some thunder, and see a little lightning. I knew this was because of the tennis balls. None had ever been on this field before. The baseball gods were angry. Tradition had been broken.

I had the balls cleared from the field. Then I thought, "Nope, I'm right about tennis balls! I'll just keep pitching!" So I went back out, threw 25 pitches to the next hitter, and before I was through, the sky cleared up, the temperature rose to normal, the wind died down, and it was happy baseball weather again.

And I knew from then on, without a doubt, that tennis balls were OK to use to improve a player's hitting ability.

# Simply Hitting

I made the point in the chapter titled "Getting in the Swing" that good equipment makes a significant difference. The best equipment will really help a player. (This point was also made by the father I met of a major league player, Mark Grace, whom you'll read about in the Part IV chapter, "The Pros and I.")

One of my sons, Charlie, was doing very well on his high school team in batting average. He was hitting in the neighborhood of .500. He got a bit of ink in the local newspaper's prep sports statistics roundup. Then all of a sudden, he went into a slump. There he was, batting second in the order on a solid high school squad, expected to reach base, yet he could not buy a hit. He was still getting his bat on the ball, but the ball wasn't jumping off his bat as it had been. His coaches were puzzled.

I had an idea. I looked at his equipment and said, "Y'know, you need a new bat. This bat's dead." Indeed, it was. There are only so many hits in the lifespan of a metal bat before it goes flat. The engineering stops working in your favor.

We went down to the sporting-goods store and got Charlie a new bat. It did the trick. Now, when he hit the ball, it took off faster — and those few inches more demanded of a fielder to make a play made all the difference. Charlie was reaching base safely again on a regular basis.

Keep this in mind if you're frustrated why a batter with good technique — who has worked hard with coaches and on his own and seems to be fundamentally sound and doing everything right — can't seem to drive the ball to the right spots.

LET'S TAKE A LOOK at another basic factor in good batting: where a player sets up next to the plate. The batter looks at the plate, and then his feet, and stands where he can get the sweet part of his bat on a pitch in the strike zone, including the outside corners. Another adjustment is moving forward or backward in the box, depending on the speed of the pitcher and the batter's bat speed. A batter shifts back if he'll need more time to react; forward, if pitches are coming in slow and he doesn't want to swing too early. Moving forward in the box also opens up the whole field by giving better angles off the bat when contact is made. Kind of an open Japanese fan effect.

Each season, as a young player grows, he should shift a bit farther away from the plate, since his arms will be longer. Full-grown professional players usually have bat coverage a full foot off the outside of the plate. The youth player should simply be positioned to get the meat of the bat on the ball whether it's pitched an inch inside or outside the corners of the plate (the standard distance for strikes to be called in youth leagues). When a player looks down at the plate, he sees his toes and how far off the plate they are — not how much he's grown during the off-season. So he may need to modify foot placement dramatically from season to season as he grows.

HERE'S ANOTHER BASIC POINT about hitting:

A young player who is naturally right-handed shouldn't necessarily avoid learning to bat left-handed. The southpaw stance gives the batter an edge —

he's a step closer to first base and will get there safely more often. If a player can learn to bat left-handed, he should become a lefty hitter.

Besides having a dominant arm (and leg), a person also has a dominant eye. The batter who stands with his dominant eye closer to the pitcher (for example, right-handed if his left eye is dominant) will fare better. How can you determine which of your eyes is dominant? Simple: hold your hands up a foot or so in front of your face and make a triangle with your fingers, thumbs creating the triangle's base. Focus on an object in the near distance. Now, close one eye, then open it. Did the object remain still, or shift in focus? Try the other eye. Did the object shift? The eye whose focus kept the object still is your dominant eye. (The other eye gave you the parallax view of the object.)

Let's say a player has a dominant right eye, but is naturally right-handed. Let him try batting left-handed. If he has success, and enjoys it, encourage him. Even if he has a dominant left eye, let him try hitting lefty. If he has success, he may be ready to seize the southpaw edge.

Each of my four sons is naturally right-handed, but after trying out batting southpaw, two of them ended up hitting lefty throughout their youth-league careers.

Switch-hitting? A great skill if you can master it. But it takes a tremendous amount of time and effort to develop proficiency from both sides of the plate. I'd advise against it at the youth levels.

AND NOW FOR PERHAPS the most important point for young players learning to bat.

As I said in a previous chapter, "What to Expect at Each Level," learning the strike zone "is the single most important skill a player can develop" when he starts seeing pitches from a real pitcher in competitive play: meaning, the Minor division in Little League (or its counterparts). When the player is no longer batting off a tee or a pitching machine, the pitches will be all over the place. The player must learn to judge quickly, accurately and consistently the pitches that are over the plate (or close enough that they're hittable and also called as strikes by the umpire).

Rote repetition in practice will develop the needed concentration, discipline and confidence that will translate to success in games. (Even at the Farm level, I wanted the players I coached to have seen at least 500 pitches in practice before Opening Day.) The player will train over and over again to swing at pitches that are in the zone and take (not swing at) pitches outside the zone. Taking a ball is as important as hacking at a strike.

Mastering this skill will add up to many more swings at pitches in the strike zone, many more takes or checked swings at pitches out of the zone, more at-bats with contact made, more hits, and more (many more!) walks. Getting on base is always a thrill for the youth player, so any way he can do it is useful and fulfilling.

Most of all, it will develop the player's batting eye for the present and future seasons.

# Hitting Drills

A brief list of drills to correct common bad habits and develop good ones:

**1) Top hand through the ball.** This drill is a cure for the uppercut swing. By concentrating on having the top hand (the right hand for a righty, the left hand for a lefty) come through the ball, it forces the batter's shoulders and arms to swing down on the ball so it will be hit on the ground (and hit more often, too), instead of being popped up or fouled back (or missed completely).

Why is it good to hit the ball on the ground? Because it puts the ball in play and gives fielders the opportunity to commit three different mistakes while trying to record an out: missing or muffing the grounder; making a bad throw or throwing to the wrong base; not catching the throw at the base. Hitting the ball on the ground up the middle is the object of swinging down on the ball. In contrast, swinging up on the ball and hitting it in the air gives fielders a simple task for recording the out: catching the ball.

The other advantage to swinging down on the ball is that it results not only in grounders, but solid line drives. And if the batter gets the right pitch, he'll crank the ball on a rope all the way to the fence.

**2) Two strikes, look away.** This drill is to pretend the batter has two strikes on him. He prepares himself for the next pitch to be outside, since the pitcher will want to make the batter go for a difficult offering. With two strikes, the batter always wants to protect the plate and not watch a third strike sail by. If he's looking for the pitch away, then he'll be ready to get his bat on it — and drive it into the opposite field. He'll wait on the pitch ... watching, watching,

watching . . . then explode on it with a sharp cut.

(Another point: youth-league pitchers are usually afraid of hitting the batter, so they often shy away from pitching inside. With two strikes on a batter, the pitcher won't want to come inside and risk plunking the guy at the plate and giving him a free pass to first (plus risking retaliation away from the field, on the playground).

In this drill, obviously, the coach (or better yet, the pitching machine) pitches the ball outside. The batter is not to watch the pitch go by (unless it's way out of the strike zone). He is to get his bat on it. If he watches a third strike, or whiffs, he goes to the end of the line and it's the next batter's turn.

3) **Pull two, back off plate, look away, hit two away.** In this drill, the player pulls two pitches, backs off the plate, then hits the next two pitches to the opposite field. To pull the ball, the batter will try to swing a little earlier than normal. To hit it the other way, he'll swing a bit later. This drill is facilitated by throwing the "pull" pitches inside, and the "away" pitches outside. That way the batter will just "go with the pitch." This drill teaches bat control, and exploding on the ball.

4) **Hit and run.** In this strategic offensive drill, the batter pretends there is a runner on base, set to take off for the next base at the crack of the bat. The batter's job is to hit the ball and put it in play no matter where it's pitched (unless, of course, it is simply unhittable, being in the dirt or way too far over his head or wildly outside or inside). If contact is possible, then the batter must hit the ball and put it in fair territory.

This drill, of course, teaches a skill that is the only exception to the general rule that a batter should not swing at junk. Coaches must make sure their young players understand this.

# Simply Pitching: Speed, Spin, Spot

I never got to pitch when I was a kid. But I knew about pitching because I was a hitter. I learned plenty about pitching so I could improve my hitting. I also knew plenty about pitching because I was a catcher. A catcher has to know more about pitching than the pitcher to get batters out. You catch a lot of different hurlers, you come to know a lot about pitching. I finally came to know a lot about pitching from the pitcher's point of view when I was an old guy trying to teach my sons and other players how to hit.

There's nothing like pitching to a lot of different players day after day, trying to help them pick up their hitting game, to get a pitcher the experience he needs. As a pitcher (when I was an old guy), I learned control by pitching the ball to where the hitters could hit it. I learned the importance of speed, by trying to throw at the same speed all the time so the young hitters could tag me for a home run. I also learned about spin and angles, so as players improved their hitting, I could help them further improve. I challenged them by playing a game called Strikeout. They started with two strikes on them, and if they swung and missed before getting a hit or walking (or getting plunked) — they were out. After many years of improving my skills as an old guy, I can get most youth-league players out. Especially when I'm calling the balls and strikes from the mound as I pitch.

The most important thing for a pitcher to understand is that the idea is TO GET THE BATTER OUT. Not necessarily by striking him out, either. In fact, I would say that tossing the most perfect game of all would be a nine-inning affair in which just 27 pitches were thrown, each one resulting in a ground ball hit evenly at the shortstop or second baseman.

After all my years of pitching, and at my ancient age, I'd say that I still have the physical skills of an above-average 11-year-old, the pinnacle of my pitching expertise. But I can still pitch with confidence, because that's all it takes if all you're trying to do is GET PEOPLE OUT, not necessarily STRIKE THEM OUT.

Pitching is simple. And if you can do it, you'll always be in demand. There are never enough strike-throwing pitchers.

IN PITCHING, YOU WORRY about three things: Speed, Spin and Spot. How hard are you going to throw the pitch? What kind of pitch is it going to be? And where are you going to pitch it?

Speed, Spin and Spot. And most important of these is Spot.

• SPOT. If you can put the ball where you want to every time, you don't have to worry about how hard you're throwing or how much the ball is breaking. Moving the ball in and out, up and down on the hitters is enough to get most hitters out. You must be able to consistently hit spots if you want to be good.

Now, in youth-league baseball there are really just two pitches. Some coaches will agree with me on the number, but they'll say that these two pitches are, "Fast ball and changeup." I maintain it's more basic than that, and that the two pitches are: over the plate, and not over the plate. That's where it starts, and it goes up from there.

It is not easy getting the ball over the plate. Take a piece of string that is 60 feet, 6 inches long and stretch it out on the ground. Now take a second piece of string of the same length. Start it just a half-inch away from the first string, then stretch this second string down at a slight angle and see how many feet apart it is from the first string by the time you reach the end. Imagine how releasing the baseball just a half-inch too soon or too late when pitching can dramatically alter the results. That is why some people can be very successful baseball players, but are not able to pitch, no matter how hard they try. It is also why some people whom you wouldn't even figure to be able to gracefully walk across the street can make it to the majors as pitchers. They just have that delicate touch that it takes to let the ball go at just the right instant so that it winds up at the spot they planned for it to hit.

One coach I knew used to take all the players on his team and line them up on the pitcher's mound facing home plate. They would throw to the catcher and then move back 20 feet. Then they'd throw again, then move back another 20 feet. They continued until only three players were left. By this time they'd be out in center field somewhere. These were the only three left who could throw the ball that far to the catcher on the fly. The coach would make those three players his pitchers. He'd found the strongest arms. However, things never went all that well for him because the strongest arms were not necessarily the ones able to throw strikes, or hit the spot where a pitch could do some good.

Again, Spot is more important than Speed or Spin. The players who can throw strikes most consistently are the ones you want on the mound.

• **SPIN.** This will do you plenty of good if you can make it work for you. Here is a basic explanation of the physics. The ball moves because it is spinning. The raised seams — the stitches — cut into the air as the ball rotates, causing pressure differential on the sides of the ball and making it move up or down or to either side. (In the case of a knuckleball, where there is no spin, the air flows across the seams and makes it move in one direction or another.)

Here's a demonstration of how spin works. Drive down the road in your car at 55 mph. Make a fist with your left hand and stick it out the window. Twist your wrist this way and that. You'll feel just how strong the forces of the atmosphere are at that speed, and how raising a knuckle here or there can make your hand move a lot. Here's another demonstration. Throw a rock into a swimming pool and watch how it moves. Rarely does it ever go straight to the bottom. Its shape alters its trajectory. That's the same effect you have with a ball moving through the atmosphere.

• **SPEED.** This is the quality that everyone in youth-league baseball is most interested in. HOW FAST AM I THROWING? Players on my Little League and Babe Ruth teams have thrown the ball between 36 and 75 mph. If you're a coach, rent or borrow a radar gun (try the local high school coach or a batting-cage business) and see how fast you're throwing and how fast your players are throwing. (If you spring to buy a radar gun, it could cost more than $1,000, so you may want to consider how many seasons you'll be using it; perhaps you can talk the league board into making the purchase for all its teams to use.) It is worth checking pitching speed every so often. You'll be surprised at how slowly people throw. I know I was. (More on this at the end of the chapter.)

In Little League, a pitcher who can throw strikes in the 55 to 60 mph range will be effective. (Remember, the pitching machines in the Farm division are typically set at 40 mph.) As you move into the summer all-star competitions, 60 mph-plus is necessary to get the job done. And by the time the Little League players are on television in the World Series in Williamsport, Pa., you can see that they've gotten there because they've got a pitcher who can throw 70 mph-plus from the 45-foot distance. Hot stuff, and impossible for most players of that age to hit. If you're up against a guy like that, just start to swing when he goes into his windup and hope you connect. Or try to bunt. Good luck!

BUT ... 70 mph won't even get a Major League Baseball scout out to look at you. As players get older, speed picks up. Pitchers ages 13 to 15 are tossing from the full 60 feet, 6 inches, and those who typically hit the high 50s to high 60s and are throwing strikes are effective at winning. High school pitchers are all over the map because they start to get some real muscle power by age 16, but you'll commonly see velocities in the high 60s to low 80s. (The prospects may hit in the high 80s and 90s.) In college, it gets a little better speed-wise, but the pitching gets smarter there, too. More breaking stuff and off-speed stuff. Pitchers develop arsenals. (The hardest college-age throwers, incidentally, have probably been drafted to the pros.)

In the minors, it is the toughest pitching of all to face. This is because you get guys throwing 90 mph-plus AND THEY CAN'T THROW A STRIKE. Wear tap-dancing shoes if you're batting against them!

NOW, A FEW MORE words about the radar gun.

I always put the gun on the coaches who were helping me. The parents were dying to see how the coaches did. Radar guns hadn't been invented when most of them were playing, so it was great to see how anxious the coaching dads were to give it a try. On a Babe Ruth League team I was coaching, it turned out the dads were in the high 50s to low 60s when they threw it as hard as they could. My best dad thrower was a lefty, a former star on his high school varsity. He hit the mid-70s consistently. After experiencing the exhilaration of being back on the mound and firing off against the radar gun, he couldn't lift his arm above his shoulder for three weeks.

As for myself, I threw the ball 37-38 mph when just tossing it, and then in the high 50s when I threw hard. (I probably could have pumped it up to the mid-80s, but I didn't want to hurt the catcher's hand.)

I recommend that you as a manager should always put your coaches on the radar gun and be sure to let ALL the players take a shot at it, too. Everyone wants to know where he stacks up. And be sure the players understand that not every successful major leaguer throws 100 mph. There are some who get the job done with pitches in the 80s and even 70s. In the case of knuckleballers, they can get it done in the high 50s. Once, while watching a game on TV, I wrote down the speed of a series of pitches of a major league knuckleballer, which the commentator announced: 57, 56, 76, 54, 68, 56.

My best pitch as a coach was a 39 mph fastball, low and outside. I'd pull the outfield in and put the infield out. A pitch thrown that slowly and in that spot usually cannot be hit very hard, and would inevitably result in a groundout of some sort. (Rarely would it be a strikeout.) It takes a powerful human being to hit a 39 mph pitch out of a baseball park. Slow speeds can be effective, if you can hit the spots.

# Pitching Drills

........................................................................................................

T he essential point of the drills in this chapter is to teach developing pitchers the motion that takes the ball to the plate, instead of being all over the place.

I've found that just about every player in youth leagues can learn an effective pitching motion and throw strikes, at least from the stretch (if not the windup). Many coaches would be surprised that even the ninth- or tenth-best player on the roster can find the plate from the mound. But I know from experience that it's true, and as a manager I gave the opportunity to pitch (to at least a few batters) to any player who expressed the desire and could prove to me in practice to not to be a safety hazard.

Pitching is lots of fun for youth players, but one of the first things they need to learn how to do is throw the ball with some authority and grace when they are simply playing catch. Often, young players will "shot put" the ball as they start learning to throw, and that can be detrimental as they move up the ladder of youth baseball. Here's a good throwing drill (described here for right-handers; reverse for left-handers):

Try having each player stand with left shoulder pointing in the direction he wishes to throw. He holds the ball in his right hand with the two-finger grip, if his hand is big enough, or three fingers if not. Then he lifts both arms so that they are parallel to the ground. The ball should be facing the ground and the back of the hand pointing toward the sky. The glove hand should be pointing in the direction the ball will be thrown. Then he bends the elbow of his right arm to a 90-degree angle, with the hand up. At this point the ball will be pointing directly backward from the player's head and the back of the player's right hand will be pointing toward the back of his head. The player is looking in the direction he will be throwing. The player steps forward and throws the ball.

Practicing this drill will help a player develop a fluid motion that becomes natural for him over time. As he throws the ball, his wrist and arm will turn in the direction of the throw and his elbow will stay up. Remind the player to keep the elbow up.

As I start players out on this drill, I usually tell them to imagine there is a wall behind their right shoulders; or, if an actual wall is available, I have them line up with that wall behind their right shoulders. Then I tell them to put the "ball to the wall" and then throw. From then on, when you mention that they should put the "ball to the wall," they can remember how to get started with an effective throwing motion. And then, on to pitching!

Coaches will find it useful to practice this drill themselves using their left hands (or right hands if they're left-handed) so that they can find out how it feels for young players just starting out and trying to learn something new. After a time, a coach will be able to throw left-handed batting practice, and have learned something new himself, as well as having found a way to build some strength in the weak side of his body. (If the coach is naturally left-handed, though, forget about the benefit of picking up this new skill of throwing with the opposite hand. After all, there are plenty of righties around.)

PITCHING MECHANICS SHOULD BE broken down into parts. It's all about repetition, developing muscle memory. And the drills should be practiced on a pitching mound.

First step: Stand sideways to the mound so that the pitching arm will go in the right direction.

Second step: Stand and balance. Lift the front leg up, knee bent at a 90-degree angle, and hold it there for a count of five. The pitcher should pause in this pose, finding his balance point. He can bend the knee of his standing leg and dip down a few times, finding that point of equilibrium. It's a good drill. Repeat as often as necessary. (Beginning pitchers can even employ a brief pause (not for 5 seconds), knee raised, during the pitching motion of an actual game.)

Third step: Drive to the catcher's mitt. Drive off the back foot toward the plate.

Fourth step: Develop a fluid motion, including a follow-through. (It may be helpful to some players to tuck the elbow of their glove arm in toward their side, to increase control.) Again: repetition is the key.

Fifth step: Work on pitching from the stretch and then the full windup. It will all slowly come together. Amazingly.

In the last analysis, if a player can throw the ball normally, then the player should be able to pitch strikes.

# Notes:

# Simply Fielding

D on't roll your glove. That's the best advice going when it comes to fielding, and if you — a player — follow it, you'll be a really good fielder.

So, what is "rolling your glove"? Simple. Stand and face north (don't have your glove on). Let your arms hang down and your hands relax. You'll notice that the backs of your hands naturally face in the same direction. If you were going to catch a groundball with your hands in that position, you'd catch it with the backs of your hands. Not an effective way to get the job done!

Now, turn your hands so that your palms are facing due north. THAT IS THE WAY YOUR HANDS SHOULD BE WHEN YOU ARE GETTING READY TO FIELD A BALL!

OK, put your glove on your fielding hand. Now stand the same way as before, hands hanging naturally at your sides. The back of the glove will face north. Now, TURN THE GLOVE OVER. The pocket should be facing north.

You're ready! Just don't "roll the glove" so that its back is facing north.

Now, bend your knees. Crouch down. Open your glove and your throwing hand. Stand on the balls of your feet. You're in the "ready position." This is the position you get into every time the pitcher goes into his windup. Only in this position will you be ready. By being in the ready position, you will be able to handle a ball that is hit to you on the ground, or lined in the air at you, or popped up. You will also have your best chance of handling a bad-hop grounder.

Now, I don't care if a fielder is standing with legs crossed, and looking like he has to go to the bathroom, or with the glove on his head and one finger picking his nose. It doesn't make any difference, just so long as he is ready when the pitcher goes into his windup. (As a matter of fact, it is sometimes useful for a coach to give the signal for all the fielders to put their gloves on their heads or pick their noses. It is disconcerting to the hitter, and he gets overconfident if he thinks none of the fielders is ready. If you're a coach, try it. You'll be surprised. But when the pitcher goes into the windup, each fielder must be in the ready position with the glove poised to shovel the PALM OUT, ready for the ball.

Again: Don't roll your glove!

Rolling your glove happens when you get in the ready position but do not turn your glove over prior to the pitch. The back of your glove, not the pocket, will be facing the batter. If the ball comes your way now, you will roll your wrist to move the glove into position to field the ball. This split-second delay will doom you to failure. Time and again, the fielder who isn't ready with his glove rolls his glove and fails to catch the ball.

Watch an infield practice some time and you'll see what happens. Have all the players take a half-dozen grounders by rolling their gloves, and then another half-dozen the proper way. You'll be amazed at the difference it makes in clean catches. Plus, when your glove is at the ready, you'll have a better chance of getting a jump on a tough hit.

Don't roll your glove. Always get in the ready position when the pitcher goes into his windup. This goes for all infielders and all outfielders, too. Drill on this religiously. Get in the habit.

IT IS THE IMPORTANT FACTOR FOR YOUR SUCCESS IN THE FIELD.

HERE'S ANOTHER TIP: The fielder should always be focused on the pitch going into the catcher's glove or the bat hitting the ball. Watch where the pitch is going. Outside pitches aren't going to be pulled down the line (into left field by a right-handed hitter, or right field by a left-handed hitter). Inside pitches will be pulled. Low pitches will be hit on the ground. High pitches will be popped up or flied into the outfield.

Fielders should also pay attention to what kind of pitcher is up there on the hill. Is he a hard thrower? If so, the batter will probably be swinging late and hitting to the opposite field. Is the pitcher slow? The batter may be swinging early — or clobbering the ball. Is the pitcher a junk-ball hurler? The hitters will be hitting cheap chip shots. Know what kind of pitcher is throwing for you.

Here's another important tip: As a fielder, always know what you are going to do with the ball if it comes to you, and know what you are going to do if the ball is hit to the other places in the field. If you're in left field and the ball is hit toward third, you'll be backing up the bag. Likewise, if a runner is on first and the ball is hit into right field, you'll be backing up third in case of an errant throw. Or if it's hit to center, you'll be backing up the center fielder. And so on. If you're playing second base and there's a runner on third with less than two outs, you may be going home with a grounder. And so on.

If you don't know what you are going to do, then ask. There should be plenty of talking to one another when players are in the field. Communicate. Talk it up. Tell your teammates where the play is going to be. "I've got the bag." "You've got the bag." "I'm throwing to third if the fly is to me." TALK! These are your teammates. Don't be embarrassed to ask. It is much more embarrassing to blow the play because you don't have a clue, than it is to ask what to do before the action starts. There's not a clock running and ticking seconds off in your game. There will be time before the next pitch to ask what to do.

The hitter, of course, knows what he is going to do. He is going to run to first base. There is no doubt in his mind. Therefore, the hitter has an advantage.

So do the runners (unless their base coaches are neglecting them.) So as a fielder, you must know what to do with the ball.

SOME FINAL NOTES ON fielding:

• When your body pops into the ready position, your glove and throwing hand are facing palms out. You're on the balls of your feet. Your eyes are on the strike zone. You'll be a great fielder because you can anticipate.

• Don't be afraid to use your body to stop the ball. Your shins are there, so be prepared to use them. Same with your chest. If the ball gets past your glove, you've got another line of defense. It will only hurt for a little while, and you'll be happy that you stopped the ball. Each bruise is a badge of honor. And when you've been smacked enough times, you'll try harder to use your glove properly.

• If you're in the outfield, try to make the catch. Your teammates will be backing you up. Charge the ball with confidence. A shoestring catch on the dead run is a great feeling. Try to make the catch unless there is some reason you're willing to just keep the ball in front of you and from getting by you, such as to hold runners from advancing, or such.

• Small kids should use big gloves. Big kids should use small gloves. The entire beef industry — steaks, chops, burgers, meat loafs — is simply the byproduct of raising leather for making baseball gloves. At least, that's the way I see it. I mean, would you really eat roast beef if you didn't truly believe that a fine new baseball glove was the result of the meal?

I don't think I would. But here I digress. We're moving in the direction of the baseball economy, and that's another story.

# Simply Base-running

I n baseball, it's easy to coach players about base-running, since a team will have base coaches standing off third and first base, to tell the runner what to do next. (Sometimes in youth baseball the first-base coach is another player on the team, which isn't as valuable as having an adult there.)

The first essential skill to teach a player, after the youngster understands which direction to go (clockwise, not counter-clockwise as sometimes happens in Tee Ball), is to run through first base. First, after all, is the only bag you're allowed to overrun. The key here is to train the player to TURN TO THE RIGHT after beating out a hit. The player can then return at his leisure to the bag. But if he turns to the left, the umpire can take that as a move toward second, and the runner will be fair game to be tagged out.

Another early skill to teach is to hit the inside corner of the bag when rounding it. And a critical lesson is that the runner must remain within the basepaths. (For a humorous account of one young player's travails with the legal and illegal routes between bases, see the Part V chapter, "Overrun.")

Then there are the special rules youth leagues set to promote safety on the basepaths, which must be instilled in players. These rules typically include no head-first sliding except when returning to a base, no takeout slides on infielders to break up a double play (you have to try for the bag, not the leg) and no bowling over the catcher who's making a play (you have to try to slide into home). At the Little League level, there also is no leading off base. When the ball is in the pitcher's hand and the pitcher is on the mound, the runner must stay on the base until the pitch crosses the plate.

A good rule at the upper levels of youth baseball is to NEVER leave the base unless the pitcher is on the mound with his foot on the pitching rubber. Never. Following this rule can prevent many embarrassing moments for a base runner.

PERHAPS THE MOST DIFFICULT skill for young players to grasp is the need to tag up on a ball hit in the air, and thus avoid being doubled off the bag (typically, second base) by a throw after a catch. Tagging up means, in part, that the runner must freeze on the bag when a line drive is hit toward his side of the field, until the ball clears the fielders and lands fair, or is caught at a safe enough distance for the runner to advance. Tagging up also means the runner stays put on the bag during a popup. On a fly hit far into the outfield, the runner can advance up to halfway down the basepath — ready to race for the next base if the ball lands on the ground, or to return to the previous base to tag up if the ball is caught.

Every player should be taught that when on third base with less than two outs, and a ball is hit on the fly to the outfield, the move is fast back to third base. That way, if the ball is caught, the runner has a chance to score after tagging up. If the ball drops in, it will still be possible to score because the runner has only given up his leadoff, and can dig hard for home. It is unpleasant to miss scoring a run from third because the runner is not on the bag when a fly is caught, but dawdling somewhere down the baseline hoping the ball will drop in.

This skill should be taught beginning at the Farm level. Every player will be doubled off base at some point. "Burnt fingers are best teachers," so hopefully the lessons about tagging up will be learned from the experience and stay with the player throughout his career.

# Signs and Misdirections

I never was much for using signs in youth baseball. Why? Because there are no routine plays at the lower levels, since the young players are learning to play the game and developing their skills. What's more, the disparity in talent among the players on the field at any one time is so great that it seemed to me, as a manager, to be impossible to control the action with signs the way it is done at the upper levels.

I preferred to just let my players play, and to see each game take shape, instead of getting too excited about influencing the contest with strategic moves via hand signals.

Of course, there is a place for strategy in the heat of battle, even when the soldiers are grade-school aged. But if a situation was so critical that it required communication from the sideline general, I found it effective to either call time or wait for a pause in the play to verbally tell a player or several players what was up. On occasion I'd activate a predetermined play by shouting out, "Play No. 1!" or whatever its designated numeral was.

This worked for me. And it kept things simple. However, there were a number of occasions when coaches on my teams were enthused about using signs. I supported my coaches, so I permitted them to employ signs. Also, I knew that players sometimes wanted to have signs because they'd seen the big leaguers on television using signs and found them to be impressive! The deft and mysterious swipes of shoulders, chests and thighs; the touches to ears, noses and elbows; the taps on hats and rubs of bellies. Mysterious combinations of silent communication. In these cases when proponents of the secret codes were especially eager — and after discussing my views on the subject — I'd embrace the use of signs and appoint a coach to get the players to learn and use the signs.

I knew what was in store, though. Frustration. Games usually were played twice a week, and it was tough for youngsters to remember signs between the games. During the games they'd become confused — and the results often turned out worse than if signs had never been used at all. Still, I went along with the program, and made sure that my own sons learned the signs to set a good example for their teammates. I instructed all the players to learn the signs and to always look to the designated coach (usually the one at third base) when batting to pick up the signals.

Sometimes it worked. Sometimes it didn't.

IN ONE GAME, MY son Charlie got up to bat. It was an important game against a good team and we could not afford to make mistakes. Charlie dutifully gazed down to the coach at third before the first pitch. What would the sign be? Take? Swing away? The coach delivered his set of quick gestures. The pitch turned out to be a ball and Charlie took it. He looked down again at the coach. Another series of hand swipes and flicks on various bodily parts. Charlie watched another ball go by. The count was now 2-0. He stepped out of the box, looked briefly to third, nodded, then stepped back to the plate and dug in.

He laid down a nice bunt and got safely to first. He went on to score. It all looked good to me. But after our at-bats, the third base coach came into the dugout looking upset.

"Didn't you see the sign I gave?" he asked Charlie.

"I saw it," Charlie answered.

"Why didn't you follow the sign?" the coach continued. "We've been working on the signs. Did you forget what the sign was?"

"No."

"Well, what was it, then?"

"The take sign," Charlie replied.

"The take sign! Right! But you bunted!"

"Yes."

"Why?"

"'Take,'" Charlie explained, "means 'don't swing.' I didn't swing. I bunted it!"

Hmmmm.

Signs. Always complications.


ON ANOTHER OCCASION OUR team's sign usage was working very well. It happened to be quite a hot day — perfect baseball weather, if a tad uncomfortable because of the soaring mercury. Our steal sign would be flashed from our third-base coach to the runner on first or second. Touching the bill of the cap was the "indicator" — meaning the sign given after the indicator would be the real sign. The sign for steal was a brush of the elbow.

We manager and coaches had told our players to "know your signs" and that they were an important part of baseball. If it turned out we decided to use signs during a game, then the players had better well be alert for them. And, indeed, during this particular game our runners were very watchful for the signs.

But then it all backfired. We had a runner on first with two outs. Unexpectedly, with no rhyme or reason, he took off running to steal second and got thrown out by a mile by the catcher. On our team's return to the dugout, our third-base coach asked why he'd gone.

"You gave me the sign," the player said.

"I did?" the coach asked, surprised. "What was it?"

"Touch the bill of your cap and brush your elbow means steal," the player replied, confidently.

"Right," the coach said. "That would be the sign. But I didn't give it."

The three of us were eventually able to puzzle out the source of the miscommunication: The coach had wiped his brow to clear the perspiration, and then had scratched a mosquito bite on his elbow.

Close enough to be mistaken for the indicator and the steal sign, and understandable why our very alert player had taken off on his ill-fated attempt.

COACHES MANNING THIRD BASE who are fairly new to coaching The Game and just learning the ropes sometimes have difficulty judging distances and get caught up in the heat of the action. This is normal, but can produce some sad results for players who have been properly instructed to follow the third-base coach's directions even if it doesn't seem right at the time. The dictum is: Coach knows.

One of our players blasted the ball to the fence in right field, which was guarded by a player who was not really game-savvy and also had a weak throwing arm. Our player rounded second and looked toward the third-base coach, who was windmilling his arm. Our player just reached third and headed for home. At this point, the coach had noticed that the outfielder had picked up the ball, although he was on the warning track.

"Stop, stop!" our coach instructed our runner. Then he quickly changed his mind: "No, go, go, go!"

Then: "NO, STOP!"

Then: "Go!"

"STOP!"

"GO! GO!"

Can you guess the rest?

Our player tried to follow these directions, as he knew that "Coach knows." But putting on the brakes, then starting again, then stopping, and so on, allowed the poor outfielder to relay the ball to the strong-armed second baseman — who then fired the ball to the catcher, who tagged out our sliding slugger at the plate.

He was disappointed, to say the least!

From that time on we labeled this sad bit of coaching, which recurred from time to time, as "COACHING THEM INTO THE JAWS OF DEATH."

And whenever that happened to one of our players, I made certain that the player knew he had done the right thing in following the coach's instructions, and I always apologized for creating the situation that made him get thrown out. For it is oh so disappointing to get out.

That's baseball.

# Notes:

# Avoiding Chaos:
# Bunt Defense and Pickoff Moves Kept Simple

A TOO-ELABORATE BUNT DEFENSE CAN LEAVE A TEAM VULNERABLE TO THE INSIDE-THE-INFIELD HOME RUN.

P layers in youth baseball, especially Little League, are often overcoached. When it comes to bunt defense, you'll find the first baseman charging toward the plate when the batter squares for a bunt, the second baseman racing to cover first, the third baseman moving in from his position, and the catcher ready to bound out from his crouch behind the plate.

The trouble is, this defense almost never works! Either the ball isn't fielded cleanly, or — if it is — the hurried throw isn't on the mark, or — if it is — the overeager second baseman trying to cover the bag doesn't get to first on time, or doesn't get the ball in his glove.

That's why the more sophisticated coaches at the Little League and Babe Ruth League levels employ bunting, especially with runners on base. It's a great way to wreak havoc on the team in the field, getting them to commit errors.

Here's what I recommend, based on my experience watching bunt defense backfire . . . all too often creating overthrows that land the batter-runner on second base.

Take the conservative approach. Leave the first baseman to cover his bag.

If a batter squares to bunt, then the pitcher has the assignment of charging in and covering the right side of the infield between the mound and first base. The catcher is assigned the area between the mound and third base. Either of these players (or the third baseman, if the ball dribbles far enough down the line toward him) will get the ball and fire to first. If it's the pitcher, great. He's usually one of the best players on your team, and capable of throwing accurately. He'll have a better chance of making a clean play in the pandemonium ensuing after a bunt.

And if the batter does beat out the bunt, that's OK. At least you haven't given him the present of second base due to a throwing error. And you haven't let any other runners advance farther than they deserve. Your second baseman will be there to cover second, instead of having the shortstop race over.

You're simply better off.


SECOND TO THE CHAOS of trying to implement a major league-quality bunt defense with youth players is the disaster of the pickoff play.

In Little League, there are no leadoffs, so pitchers' pickoff moves are a moot point. But once the transition to the big diamond is made at the next age level up, the pickoff move is part of the game and EVERY pitcher wants to give it a try . . . or two or three or four — slowing the game down and putting everyone into a comatose state. The end result is usually a bullet throw into the dirt and a runner advancing on the mishandled throw.

My advice to youth pitchers is this: Learn how to make pickoff moves to all the bags. Practice pickoff moves to all the bags. (In fact, all the players on the team should know and practice these moves.) Then never use them in a game, as the ball will just be thrown away!

However, use a slow pickoff toss, just to let the runners know that you know they are there. A good coach I know called this the "Howdy Doody move." A pitcher is only going to pick off a runner if the runner is asleep at the switch, and this is going to happen during a "Howdy Doody" throw to the base just as often as during a bullet throw, and the chances of throwing the ball away with the Howdy Doody throw are much, much less.

Probably the best thing you can do is tell your first basemen to ALWAYS be alert to taking a snap throw from the pitcher as he is walking off the mound. Time and time again, you will see a base runner strolling back to the bag (usually first base), looking at the ground and not paying attention to where the ball is. An alert first baseman can take a snap throw from the pitcher and get this inattentive runner out. But please know, as a coach, that having both your pitcher and first baseman alert to the pickoff opportunity at the same time is a rarity, and it is worth reviewing every game with your team. You will get some outs by being alert, and your runners also will be more careful if you talk about this. It is a worthy coaching discussion point.

IN SUM, LET THE traditionalists try the fancy bunt defense and the pickoff moves. If you're facing a team managed by such a purist, go ahead and bunt on him, and then be prepared to advance when your opponent throws the ball away trying to pick your players off the bases they were given by the poorly executed bunt defense.

# Baseball on
# Bended Knees

You can have great success in baseball, and great improvement in your baseball activities if you remember one simple thing, and practice that thing:

BEND YOUR KNEES.

Hitting, fielding, running, throwing, pitching and even sitting on the bench (or in the bleachers as a fan) will be improved if you bend your knees. The No. 1 thing for players to do is bend their knees. You can work and work and work, and do this and do that, but if you don't start with bending your knees, IT IS ALL FOR NAUGHT.

YA GOTTA BEND YOUR KNEES!

Why???

If your knees are bent, you will be able to use your legs to generate power. Your legs, after all, have the largest, strongest muscles in your body. USE THEM. Second, if your legs are bent, your eyes are ready to focus in on what you are doing, and they won't be moving up and down . . . they will be zeroed in on the target. Third, if your knees are bent, you are READY FOR ACTION. When the body goes into action, it automatically bends the knees. Bodies are smart that way. If your knees are already bent, YOU ARE ALREADY READY. You are then prepared for accomplishing your goal.

Why don't all players bend their knees? Because it takes effort, and many players are tired or lazy. Bend your knees when you are in your batting stance, and you will have success. Bend your knees when you're preparing for the pitch as a fielder, and you'll have success. Bend your knees when you are getting ready to run, and you'll get a quicker jump. Bend your knees as you're throwing the ball, and it will go farther. Bend your knees when you are pitching, and you'll throw harder and more accurately. Bend your knees when you're sitting on the bench, and you'll be more comfortable. Bend your knees when you're sitting in the bleachers, and you'll be ready to cheer and stand when your favorite player does well.

BEND YOUR KNEES!


ONE OF MY SONS was having some trouble at the plate. He was struggling. Matter of fact, each of my sons struggled from time to time. The first thing I did was check whether the knees were bent when he was in his batter stance. No? Then bend them! Well, when this particular son was struggling, I told him he'd do better if he bent his knees more.

"I am bending my knees," he replied. It was the natural answer.

"Yeah, you are, but not enough," I said. "Bend them more and you'll do better. Do you know why you're not bending your knees?"

"No."

"Because it's hard work!" I said.

To demonstrate how much hard work it is, I told him to just stand there with his knees bent for five minutes and see how he felt. I made it even harder by telling him to come up on his toes. Very quickly, after less than 30 seconds, his legs grew painful and it got pretty darn hard to hold his position.

"See, it ain't easy," I said. "That's why you don't bend them enough. But . . . this is baseball we're concerned with here. Not knee-bending contests! So, in a game or practice you'll never have to bend your knees for a minute at a time. Maybe six seconds — 15, tops — waiting for a pitch when you're in the batter's box, or getting ready to field, or preparing in your runner's stance from base. Bend your knees and you'll be a much better player with more success and better results."

My little experiment showed my son how much work it was to bend his knees for an extended period, but he listened to my advice about the importance of bending them for the required time periods during a baseball game. The next game, he bent his knees at the plate and got right back on track.

So, probably the No. 1 lesson for success in youth baseball is to ALWAYS REMEMBER TO BEND YOUR KNEES!

# Notes:

# Seeking Professional Help

The first professional help you'll need when you really get into youth baseball is a psychiatrist. Just kidding!

Many people offer help on improving your game. You can take pitching lessons, hitting lessons, seminars on all aspects of The Game, clinics and baseball camps. (The places offering these lessons aren't hard to find when you join a youth baseball league; fliers are mailed to players' addresses or posted or passed around at fields, and other parents start talking about their kids' instructors. If you're really stumped, just visit local sporting-goods stores or professional batting cages and ask, or check out their message boards.) I recommend trying out all of the avenues for lessons. It is time and money well spent.

Most dads have played The Game, but people offering help for a fee usually have more experience than the parents just starting out with children in leagues. Some of these professional tutors have played The Game professionally or in college. Buy some lessons. Your player will enjoy hearing someone else talking to him about what he needs to do and needs to stop doing, and you'll pick up valuable tips, as well as new ways of expressing the same old thing. Take the lessons!

But after you've paid your money, the next thing you'll hear from Junior is: "The hitting coach said to do it THIS way, the manager says to do it THAT way, you say to do it THIS way. Blah, blah, blah." Then you have a heated discussion with either your player or the manager or the coach, especially if the success in the field is not instantaneous. And of course, it is YOUR fault for starting the confusion in the first place.

So take this precaution: Tell your player, again and again, that as he goes through The Game he should listen to ALL the advice he gets and try to understand it. And he should try it out. It does not hurt to try something! But use the things that work for HIM. If it works — use it!

Maybe a player's team's coach will tell the player to bend his knees deeply at the plate to limit his strike zone. But the player's batting instructor teaches the player to stand straight up at the plate, relaxed, until the pitcher is in his windup, and then set up his stance. Different approaches work for different players — and at different levels. (Don't get sucked into the philosophy that, "If you don't do it this way now, you'll never make it at the next level.")

The bottom line for a player is: Use what works for you at this time. If you're standing on your head but still consistently hitting the ball hard, you're going to get the playing time. When you get to the next level and face new challenges (such as curveballs), then you can adapt and change.

If you are developing bad habits that are leading to failure at your present level, know what they are so that you can make the adjustment. Listen to everybody. Try everything. But again, I'll repeat: Use what works for you at the time. The "perfect" swing is no good if you're not getting any hits. Try another approach.

Look at the pros and you'll see huge variations among the players in the way they do things. Classic example: the contorted stance of Craig Counsell, who raises his bat straight up as high as he can and shifts back and forth awkwardly before the pitch comes in and he sets. He adopted the bizarre stance earlier in his career to get himself out of a slump. While his style is an affront to many fans, the slightly built infielder does possess two World Series rings. Or look at Rickey Henderson's exaggerated crouch. He's destined for the Hall of Fame. Be willing to experiment.

If you are confident in your command of The Game, you'll work your way out of any slump, be it in hitting, fielding, pitching or throwing. You'll get through it, and your confidence will be all the greater if you've heard a variety of approaches. Lessons can do that for you. I've never seen a kid who took professional lessons, and paid attention and tried hard, who didn't benefit from them. The list includes some hitting-challenged players on the teams I've coached who showed up to practice and all of a sudden were stroking the ball with finesse. When I'd quiz them about their surprising progress, they'd say, "Well, coach, I took a lesson."

I took a lot of piano lessons but never learned to play the piano. But I did learn how to sneak out of hearing distance when I saw the piano teacher drive down the driveway on lesson day! I wasn't interested in piano. But if you're interested in baseball, lessons can be extremely valuable.

Don't be shy about seeking out different instructors. There are plenty of them. Try new ones if you desire. Try a lesson or two with each. Hear what people have to say. Listen. You will benefit from it.

And when you digest everything everyone has to say, see how you are doing. Are you having success? Would you rather have two good seasons with bad mechanics or five bad seasons with good mechanics? You can make that call for yourself.

I SHOULD ADD THIS extra tip for coaches: When I was a youth-league manager, I had luck finding former pro players in my area who, for a very small fee, even as little as $20, would come out to our team's practice for a couple hours and give a clinic. These guys were eager to show up because they still loved baseball and wanted to do something to help The Game. They'd learned a lot from their years in youth baseball and the minors, and could ably show how to make a pickoff move, lead off base, turn a double play and other nuances that the typical dad youth-league coach doesn't know about and therefore can't demonstrate. Imagine young players running the bases with a former pro on the mound trying to catch them off; the youths get to experience what it's really like at a high level of play.

One more thing: practice. Taking a lesson once or twice a week will not get the job done for you unless you combine it with work on your own. YOU MUST PRACTICE! Baseball is an everyday game, and you can always benefit from working on something.

A final note: No one has enough time in a day to practice all the different parts of The Game. NO ONE. So try it all — then zero in on some things that you think you can do well and benefit from practicing.

# A Good Practice
# is a Busy Practice
# (and Here's an Example)

A typical practice should run about two hours. That's enough time in youth baseball to cover basic drills, and perhaps have some fun with a scrimmage — but not burn the players out. The objective is to keep everybody busy doing something productive and entertaining the entire time, minimizing talk time and standing around.

I used the following format for players from Farm (as young as 6) to Babe Ruth (as old as 15). This format worked because it kept everyone busy. Remember that the attention spans and maturity levels can vary greatly among players on a team, whether the players are first-graders or high school sophomores. You want to keep everyone as focused and involved as possible, so they can hone their skills and be confident and know what to do during an actual game.

The format:

• The manager calls everyone together on the grass or in the dugout and has a team talk, and makes sure it lasts no more than 30 seconds. The players don't want to listen to the manager yak; they want to be out there playing ball. But the manager has to take advantage of the rare opportunity to get the whole group together at one time, and to reinforce the concept of team unity. After all, in a group of a dozen or so players, there will be cliques and friendships that bond some players with others, and leave the remaining ones out. You want everyone to be pulling in the same direction during the season, and the pre-practice talk can help do that.

In the first few weeks of a season I'd pick out a different player at each practice and ask him to name all of his teammates. You may be surprised how long it takes young players to learn everyone's name. I'd tell the designated player not to be embarrassed if he forgot someone's name; that was the reason we were doing it. (This little exercise also helps the manager and coaches learn the players' names — critical to managing and coaching.)

The remainder of the brief team meeting can be used to remind players of upcoming games, take care of any other pressing team business (such as, has everyone's parents signed up for snack-bar duty?), and to review any special drills to be used during this practice.

• Next order of business, baseballs are passed out and players head out with partners to toss the ball around and warm up. They'll stand 15 feet apart, then eventually move back until they're doing long toss. They'll work on hitting each other in the chest.

• Next comes the "10, 10 and 10" drill. The throwing partners, standing about 45 feet apart (the distance from the mound to the plate in Little League; older players can stand 60 feet apart) will toss each other 10 grounders, then 10 pop-ups, then 10 pitches (going into the windup).

The "10, 10 and 10" drill can even be used the entire practice time, since it develops throwing and fielding. But I'd watch to see when the players were getting bored, and move on to the next drill. You don't want players getting bored. You want them staying engaged and busy. The point of a two-hour practice is to ensure the players have a good time, get a good workout, and work on a lot of different skills.

• Next, gather the troops again for a brief talk. Review the previous game: first and foremost, things that went right, then things that went wrong. Talk about the good plays that were made, and the mistakes (for example, not throwing the ball the right base). It's a time for education and instruction. But, as with the pre-practice team talk, you don't want to keep the players idle too long.

• Now it's time for hitting. Depending on how many coaches are available, set up different hitting stations. Have a tee set up at one station, and coaches at other stations pitching soft toss with tennis balls against a net, or pitching tennis balls, or pitching baseballs. (Manning a pitching machine can take up too much time, since the machine has to be pulled out of the storage area and set up with the long extension cords — if the power is working on that particular field — and then adjusted and readjusted to throw strikes, and finally packed up and put away at the end of practice.) Players divide up evenly for each station, and rotate to the other stations as their turns are completed. It's good to have no more than three players per station.

A good number of swings at each station is 25. After all, if the players are swinging hard, using good form, they'll get tired. Coaches need to watch for correct foot placement and shoulder, arm and hip movement, for keeping the head level (not pulling it), keeping the feet planted and not stepping out, and following through with the swing. Coaches also need to monitor signs of fatigue, such as dropped shoulders. These can contribute to bad habits, which can persist during games.

Here's another little note: You don't want players taking too many swings in practice. Why? Because during a game, a typical at-bat has five pitches. You want your players to train for a limited number of pitches, and to make the most of his at-bats, instead of making sloppy swings and expecting to get a lot more pitches. So, 25 swings at each station more or less translates to five at-bats at each station.

The coaches can alter these drills as they see fit, such as using the exercises described in the "Hitting Drills" chapter.

• Regular pitchers and catchers (or coaches filling in as catchers) can then go practice in the bullpens (I'd always have a few extra home plates fashioned from plywood, just in case). Instruct the pitchers to, say, throw 20 fastballs down the middle. Do not overwork them. Let all the players take a turn practicing pitching in the bullpens as part of the rotation.

• The rest of the players now practice fielding (with the pitchers and catchers joining in when their pitching practice is done). One of the most effective ways to rotate players through fielding drills is to set up two stations in the infield and one in the outfield. (I'd always have coaches hitting the grounders and flies, because the players themselves are just not effective enough. Besides, they need to practice their glove work.)

In the infield stations, pair up a coach with a bat plus a player to catch throws for him. One coach stands on the third-base line near home with his player. Put a player at the second-base spot with another player behind to back him up. The coach hits grounders across the diamond to the second baseman, who tosses the fielded ball back to the player standing by the coach. The second baseman then switches with the guy behind him. After a few rounds, one of the players in the field rotates in and the player catching balls for the coach goes to the infield. (The second coach in the infield stands on the first-base line and hits grounders to the shortstop area.)

This drill involves six players. The remaining six players (of a 12-player squad) shag flies in the outfield, with five standing in single file on the grass, each one taking his turn at catching when he reaches the front of the line. The sixth player stands next to the coach hitting the flies, to catch the tosses coming in. He'll rotate to the outfield after a few flies are hit. Ideally, there are two coaches dividing the six players between them so there is more action.

In this way — as with the warmup and batting drills — everyone stays busy. And when players have taken enough balls at one station, they'll switch with the players at the next station. Everyone will get a chance at second base and shortstop, and in the outfield.

• After the fielding drills, have the players run the bases a bit to get them familiar with the bases. I'd set up fielders in the infield and outfield, then have the remaining players put on batting helmets and take turns standing at home plate, ready to run when the coach at the plate hit the ball somewhere in the field. The runner would then try to make it home on one of the at-bats (the coach hitting the ball) and avoid getting tossed out. As with the other drills, players rotate in and out, so they'll be base runners and fielders.

• If there is time remaining in the practice, you can have a scrimmage. The players divide into two teams. Coaches take the outfield positions so the players not up to bat can have the infield. Either have a player pitch (a good chance to measure his ability to throw strikes) or have a coach with an accurate arm pitch. A side is retired after three outs (or sometimes, two, if time is short). Scores are kept to make it more interesting.

Sometimes setting up some bases in the outfield and playing pickle with tennis balls is a good way to end because it gets the players used to their capabilities in running the bases and is good exercise.

AT THE END OF practice, the whole squad gathers again. There may be a few more words from the manager — praise for good efforts, constructive criticism, details on the time and location of the next game, and so on.

Ideally, the two hours will have flown by, with everyone getting good work in, a chance to hit the ball, a chance to play an infield position, a chance to practice pitching, a chance to run the bases.

And everyone has had fun.

You'll be surprised at how many coaches show up from time to time and want to help with this approach. They want to participate, and doing things this way keeps them active with the players and The Game. They'll probably have some good ideas about fun drills from their days on the diamond, too.

Try everything, but keep everyone b-u-s-y!

# PART II

# PLAYING TIME

*There are two currencies in youth baseball. Two payouts, which are made according to skill, performance — or political clout.*

*For coaches, the currency is who gets to manage and coach, and which team they get to manage or coach. The political skullduggery involved is a whole game unto itself.*

*For players, the currency is playing time: "PT." This can depend not only on batting averages and golden-glove wizardry, but attitude — and blood relationship to the team's coaches.*

*For youth-league players, their primary goal is to get as much time in the lineup as possible. When their playing days are done, they'll migrate to the ranks of the fans in the stands ... or, perhaps, become coaches themselves when they've reached the parental period.*

*For coaches and players, they should spend their currency wisely, realizing that at some point the "money" will run out, and they'll have to take their place in the bleachers. They should enjoy it while they can and migrate to where they have the greatest chance to actively participate in the action. It is nice to be on a winning team, but it is great to be on a team on which you get to play and try everything the game of baseball has to offer.*

# Notes:

# The Four Truths
# About Managing
# (and You Still Want to Do It?)

H ere are the Four Truths of Managing:

1) The manager is a bum.

2) The manager can't win.

3) Every parent wants the best for his child. (Even if the child is a knucklehead.)

4) It's the manager's fault if the child doesn't get a college scholarship or professional contract.

Let's briefly examine each truth.

• No. 1:The manager is a total bum.This is because he is fully responsible for anything that goes wrong with a team, or any decision that isn't popular with every single family involved with the team.These issues can include whether practices shouldn't be on Sundays because of churchgoers, or should remain on Sundays despite complaints from the churchgoers. Or the fact the team lost because the coach gave the bunt signal to the batter with two strikes on the count. Or the fact the team "got lucky" and won after the coach foolishly risked the batter bunting the ball with two strikes, and the bunt turned into a hit that led to the go-ahead run.

Of course, the manager doesn't give adequate playing time to any of the players except his own son, but then refuses to put his own son in the outfield, claiming his son is too slow to chase down flies. But then he finally puts his son in the outfield, so that a parent who's whined a lot can have his boy play infield, and the infielder boots the ball and the manager's son has a should-be-routine fly drop in front of him, because he really isn't suited to be in the outfield.

The manager is a bum, bum, bum!

• No. 2: The manager can't win. This is true, even if he wins games. Sure, he has a winning record, but that's only because he puts the oldest and most experienced players in the key positions and batting high in the lineup. He doesn't give the other players a chance to develop and have fun.

But then, the parents say, "We absolutely shouldn't have lost the game last Friday night! All the manager had to do was keep the starting pitcher in, instead of giving the other team a chance to come back and score off one of our green 11-year-olds. It wasn't fair to our team, the 11-year-old, the 11-year-old's family, and us parents in the stands!"

The manager can't win for winning or losing.

• No. 3: Every parent wants what's best for his/her child — no matter what the kid is like. Sure, Junior misses lots of practices, but he has lots of homework, plus Scouts, and then he had the flu those three times. He still deserves a shot at pitching, even if he can't find the plate if he were standing over it. Also, his lack of a batting average (0 for 22) is due more to his lack of confidence from having to bat at the bottom of the order in every game, or only getting to the plate as a substitute in a later inning. A bit of support from the coach and, hey, Junior'll finally get that hit. Oh, and it's not his fault he doesn't pay attention when sitting in the dugout or out on the field. He's always been a daydreamer, even in school. Check his report card!

The manager just isn't looking out for Junior. Fortunately we, his parents, are.

• No. 4: Junior has many athletic gifts (albeit, some are rather hidden to the untrained observer) and — were he properly nurtured by a caring and astute manager — has the tools for making it to The Show one day. You did, after all, see him foul off a pitch before striking out against the league's premier fire-baller, didn't you?

But the manager just won't give Junior his due! He's killed off the child's enthusiasm for baseball, trampled his dreams of Major League Baseball stardom, nicked a budding talent in the, well, bud. At 12, Junior is ready to hang up his cleats after this season, because he can't seem to get in the groove. The manager just isn't working with him enough, and giving him enough second chances. Hey, Junior wasn't the first player to plunk the first two batters he faced on the mound. Nor was he the first outfielder to drop a fly ball, then throw behind the runner to the wrong base — committing two errors in a single play. All Junior needs is more opportunity. Why can't coach see the damage he's causing our child?

IF YOU DOUBT ANY of the above, or believe it to be exaggerated, go ahead and talk with managers and coaches in your league about the pressure parents and players put on them. Even ask some parents, if you dare.

So! Have the Fourth Truths about Managing killed off your desire to take on a team of your own?

Well, fortunately there are ways to minimize the grief you'll face.

My favorite strategy was to lay down the law at the team's first parents' meeting. After I introduced myself as the team's manager, here's approximately how my speech continued:

"We have a baseball team here. On this baseball team, which your children are going to be on for the next 90 days, there are eight playing positions available."

At this point, someone would raise a hand and say, "Coach, coach, there're nine positions on a baseball team."

"No," I'd respond. "This is youth baseball. And you've got to worry about the manager's son. That's my son, and a big reason why I'm here."

I'd then go into what I expected from my son: 100 percent effort in practices and games, attending every practice and game unless he had a good reason to be missing (such as illness or school function), playing for the team, backing up his teammates, being a good teammate, following the coaches' instructions, no whining, tantrums or use of profanity, and practicing good sportsmanship on and off the field.

The same was expected of every player on the team, I'd say. "Players who buy into the program will avoid being benched, and will likely get a chance to try different positions — even pitcher — during the course of the season. All will not be fair, but it will be reasonable.

"Every player on the roster will get at least one complete game — playing every inning — during the course of the season, and maybe more. I won't do what traditionalist coaches do: base the playing time solely on players' statistics. However, I am not to be approached by a parent or player the day of the game with a request to play a whole game or a certain position. At that point, I'll have already prepared my lineup and playing chart. I must be informed at least a full day beforehand about preferences — such as a request to play infield since relatives from out of town will be at the game."

(Parents, please note: The considerate, diplomatic, respectful approach is always the best tack to take with coaches; impulsive or aggressive demands are almost certain to backfire and cause ill will.)

"If a player must miss a practice or game, I must be called as soon as possible beforehand. While traditionalist coaches typically bench a player who's missed a practice or game, I'll not penalize players as long as I have advance warning of their absence."

I'd go on to explain that it is every family's responsibility to transport their player to and from the game. The managers and coaches are not chauffeurs. A list of parents' names, addresses and phone numbers would have been printed and will be passed around at this meeting in case parents needed to carpool.

"Please be prompt and on time, because I, the manager, will not leave the field until every player has a ride home."

I'd explain about the "Dream Sheets" passed around to the players at the first practice, on which they wrote down their goals for the season and the positions they were experienced playing and wanted to play. (More on the Dream Sheets in the chapter, "The Magic of the Dream Sheets," further on in this part of the book.)

"If we're contending for a championship later in the season, I'll be fielding our best lineup no matter what. A championship is special and all players on the team will share in it. Similarly, if we're not contending, but facing a top team toward the end, I'll still put our best lineup out there so we can be the spoiler. We owe that to the integrity of the game of baseball and to the players on the other teams who have battled their way into contention."

I'd explain that we had a long season — 20 games — so I'd plot it out and plan ahead and try to accommodate everybody.

"If your player is all-world and used to playing every inning of every game, on this team he will get the opportunity to sit on the bench, too, and be a motivator for his teammates in the field. After all, at some point of his career, as he moves up the pyramid of baseball — whether high school, college or perhaps the pros — he'll have to sit the bench. This is his opportunity to learn how to do so. And an opportunity to learn how to stay prepared for success on the diamond when only a brief chance to play is afforded.

"Any questions."

The reaction among parents to my little speech was always the same: a collective sigh of relief. At least the truth was being told! The manager's son would play where the manager wanted to put him: pitcher, shortstop, second base, or wherever. The manager's son would be expected to hustle and not conduct himself as a prima donna. And all the kids would have their chances at the choice positions, as well.

Laying the cards on the table right at the start preempts complaints later in the season.

I'd remind parents that each family had signed the league's code of conduct, agreeing to abide by rules such as no profanity at the fields, no jeering at opposing players or umpires. I'd remind them that they and the players must respect the umpires. The umpire is always right, even when he is wrong, and no matter how frustrating that may be, avoid backtalk, dirty looks or fits of anger such as stomping feet or throwing helmets or bats. And, again, everyone must respect the manager and coaches. Any subject may be broached, but all discussion takes place in conversational tones.

Then I'd close by establishing the open-door policy. "Anyone with a question or comment during the season is free to call me at home. However, no one is to approach me immediately before or during a baseball game, because I'm trying to manage the team. This is a firm rule. After the game I'm available, but only after the players have had their snacks, the team talk is finished and the players have dispersed."

Thus, the lines of communication were opened. The parents had been told what to expect. All was in place to start the season.

After this speech, the only other thing the manager will need is to keep his layer of thick skin intact until the season ends.

The Four Truths about Managing are immutable and eternal. The manager must be prepared to take the hits while remaining diplomatic — doing his best to create a joyous atmosphere for everyone involved, and the best baseball experience possible. Certainly not fair, but most certainly reasonable.

# Notes:

# Managing the Demands of Managing and Coaching

When you're a team manager in the Minor or Main divisions of Little League or in a higher-age league, and have made it through the tryouts and the draft, you've got your team for the season. This involves a lot of responsibility. A lot of people's expectations, dreams and demands are resting on your shoulders.

The first thing you've got to do is call the players and tell them what team they're on. DO NOT WAIT TO DO THIS! Do it immediately. Players are anxious to know where they are going to be, and you owe it to them to help them raise their enthusiasm level by telling them what team they are on. Call them and welcome them to the team. If the players are young, talk to their parents first, then the players. If the players are older, just talk to them. If you don't know the players from previous experience, ask what positions they have played in the past.

After you've made the calls, set up the first practice and get the players together. I'd begin by introducing myself: "I'm Jeff Kirst, and I'm the manager of the Reds this season. You can call me Jeff, you can call me Coach. You just can't call me bad names."

Then I'd give a bit of the history of the major league team that our team was named after. (If the team's named after a sponsor, such as a service club, then the manger can say just a few words about that organization. But it's much more exciting when your team has a major league name. More about this in the chapter later on in this part, "Bonding the Team with Its Big League Namesake.")

Next, I'd talk a bit about my history in The Game, including how I got started as a player their age back in Cincinnati. And I'd talk about my getting involved with their youth league, and how I was the board member who'd led the campaign to get Fall Ball started in the league. The bottom line was: We were all in the same boat — they, the players; and I, the manager. We were out there on the field because we all loved baseball. "So let's try to have fun this season and let's make everyone better players."

Now it was time for the team rules:

• No. 1 rule: safety. That's the primary focus so that no one gets injured. Bats are to be treated as weapons (which they are), and are more dangerous than loaded guns because they don't need a trigger to be pulled to become deadly. They already are deadly. Bats are never carried over shoulders, but instead with the barrels down.

Bats are never swung outside of the places they're supposed to be swung: at a plate while batting, at a batting station set up at practice, or in the on-deck circle. Players should stand a minimum of 10 feet away from a batter, because bats can fly out of a hitter's hands.

As for baseballs, they are never to be thrown unless the person who is being thrown to has acknowledged that he wants the ball thrown to him.

• No. 2 rule: Always try your hardest to do your best. A player may not always do his best; that's part of The Game. But he must try his hardest, all the time.

• No. 3 rule: Be a good teammate, absolutely all the time. This means being friendly to your teammates, learning their names, helping them through their rough times. It's not being a braggart when you have a good game and someone else hasn't. It's making everyone feel part of the team.

• No. 4 rule: When a coach asks you to do something, do it fast and do it with a smile. The manager can pick up all the baseballs and equipment himself after a practice, or clean out the dugout after a game, but he shouldn't have to. Those are housekeeping duties, and players are required to pitch in, and with no backtalk, and always with a smile.

• No. 5 rule: You can yell as loud and often as you want, but not out of anger or frustration. The yelling must be all positive — cheering teammates on, sharing in excitement.

Then the Dream Sheets were passed out. They were to be filled out at home with the parents, and needed to be returned.

Then the practice and game schedules were passed out.

Finally, players were encouraged to ask questions that were on their minds throughout the season. This was emphasized. "Don't be afraid to ask me questions. I'm not here to be your disciplinarian. I'm here to answer your questions as fast as I can, or get the answer if I don't have it. I don't know everything there is to know about playing baseball. You might ask me a question I don't know the answer to, but I do know where to go to get the answers. I know people who've been around The Game a long time, or I'll even contact a major league baseball team and ask. I'll get the answers for you, but you've got to have the questions."

NOW WE WERE FINALLY ready to hit the field. I'd have the players toss the ball around a little, then sit them all down in the dugout or on the outfield grass and make sure every player knew the names of all the other players. Learning names is important. If a player can't learn his teammates' names, he'll be hard-pressed to learn the coach's signs and other elements of the game that require memory. For example, suppose a pitcher is on the mound and the catcher flashes one finger. The pitcher forgets that one finger means fast ball, and throws a curve instead. The ball gets away. Runners advance. Frustration builds. The players must learn each other's names. That's the very first step toward getting their minds into the game for the season. Baseball is, after all, a thinking person's game.

As the manager, you should repeat your players' names often. "Jack, go to left field. George, go to center. James, go to . . ." and so on. (If you have a team with several players with the same first name, as I have had, it's great because you don't have to remember so much. "Pete," you say, and seven heads snap in your direction.)

After you've got the names down, talk about the fact that everyone is going to have to live with one another for the next 90 days or so, and you must all get together and stick together. This is the beginning of building a team. All for one and one for all. At this point, tell them that if they don't have something nice to say about a teammate, say nothing at all.

As soon as possible after this first team practice, have a parents' meeting. At this meeting, I always invited the parents to help coach if they wanted. You can always use another pair of hands, and many parents, you will find, will be anxious to help and get in the game.

PARENTS DON'T NEED TO know too much about the season ahead as long as you tell them to call you any time they have a question or comment. An open-door policy is the best policy, and occasionally someone will have a good idea or observations. You don't get too many "when is my kid gonna pitch?" calls if you're diligent about holding the preseason parent meeting and also give players chances to try new things in practice. Let all the players go to the bullpen during practice to work on pitching, often with a coach overseeing the efforts. This way, everyone knows the pitching capabilities of all the players on the team.

Always remember this, though: You're the manager, and you're in charge of the team. You will set the tone for the team; and the team's performance and attitude will, to some extent, reflect you. Try to do a good, honest job. You'll feel good about it.

Your assistant coaches are there to help you. Give them directions and tasks to accomplish with the players. These include pitching drills, hitting drills, base-running drills, fielding drills. Use your coaches. Tell them what you want them to do. Put some thought into it. There is nothing so depressing for a team as to have the manager and coaches standing around talking to one another while the players stand around twiddling their thumbs. Give everybody something to do. And be sure they do it. And follow up.

Sometimes you'll have coaches on your team who know much more about baseball than you do. Utilizing their knowledge and strengths to the fullest can make for a really great season for your players, parents, fans and the other coaches on your team, as well as enhance your own grasp of The Game.

Don't leave any coach on the same task too long. Monitor this. Your most diligent coaches will complain the least, so don't forget what you've asked them to do. Spread out the work and keep the people busy, then consult with your coaches and ask them how so-and-so did on such-and-such. You'll gain valuable insights about your players that way, and the coaches will put more effort into working with the players if you take a sincere interest. "How is Johnny, the slugger, hitting the ball?" By the way, don't save all the fun tasks for yourself. Everybody likes to pitch batting practice, so give everybody a chance.

There are two other volunteer duties for parents. One is the team mom — in charge of scheduling parents to bring snacks during the season, putting together the list of player names, addresses and phone numbers, helping hand out uniforms at the beginning of the season and retrieving them at the end, and perhaps arranging the end-of-season team party. As manager, a good team mom is a godsend; but be prepared to handle this duty yourself (or have your spouse do it), because it does take time and there aren't always volunteers. The other volunteer position is scorekeeper. This is the parent who keeps the inning-by-inning statistics during a game. In some leagues, the home team has the official scorebook, so this is an important role. Sometimes the scorekeeper also tabulates the player's statistics after every game as the season progresses, which can be very useful for the manager in forming his lineups.

The nice thing about finding a team mom and a scorekeeper is that parents are often willing to help, not only to contribute to the team, but because they know their kids may benefit politically in the currency of youth-league: playing time.

IF YOUR TEAM PRACTICES hard, you will be ready for the games. No youth-league team has enough practice time. Let the players and parents know that "baseball is an everyday game." Your chances for success go up with the time spent practicing. Remind parents that 20 minutes a day playing catch with Junior is time well spent, will help develop him and keep him sharp, and is fun. Explain to the players and parents that they shouldn't come to the games expecting to have a workout. Workouts are conducted during practice.

Go to your game prepared. Have the lineup done. Have a batting order done and ready for posting in the dugout. And have a chart of what positions the players will take inning by inning for the entire game. The most important piece of paper of all is this chart. It is your game plan. BUT DO NOT POST THIS CHART. The game, of course, has an ebb and flow to it, and the best-laid plans, blah, blah, blah. It is B-A-D to post the chart showing that Johnny Rag

Arm is going to take the hill in the fourth inning — only to have to disappoint him and not give him the call if the game is not going your way, or the starting pitcher is throwing a no-hitter, or whatever. Keep the chart in your pocket and call out the positions each inning. The only exception may be if you're sure you will be able to deliver the goods, then you can tip off a player privately. For example, it would be nice to tell your substitute right fielder that in the third inning he is going to be the third baseman. That way he can think about it and enjoy it more when the opportunity presents itself.

NOTE: SAMPLES OF CHARTS ARE AT THE END OF THIS CHAPTER.

Here's another preparation tip: Carry two pencils so you can mark down your changes as the game progresses. Different-colored pencils help a lot. That way you can see what you're doing even when dust and dirt, sweat and grime are marring the paper.

Oh — almost forgot. What about the league rulebook? As manager, you need to know the basics of the rules, and you will absorb them increasingly as the season goes on. There are all kinds of quirks and subsections, though — anything from how many innings a pitcher can pitch in a week, or on consecutive days, to when a starting player who is substituted for is allowed to return. The manager, especially a new one, should not be afraid to ask questions of his coaches or the umpire. Carrying a copy of the rulebook in your equipment bag can be invaluable. If you have time, leaf through it before the season starts and as the opportunity arises during the season.

Maintain a positive attitude during games. You almost always have a chance to win if you stay positive. Look for the bright side. And keep order in the dugout. Players should pay attention to the game. If they don't want to do that, they shouldn't be at the ballpark. A bit of dugout horseplay is fine, but it should be kept to a minimum, and let them know that.

Give every player a "good luck" when he goes to bat, and tell your players to do their best when they head out to the field. Be upbeat and positive, even if you're not feeling that way inside. You owe it to the youngsters.

If you win . . . enjoy the moment and tell your players to be good sports about it. If you lose, keep the after-game team talk to a minimum. Dwell on the good things that happened and look toward the next game. Enjoy your victories. Put the losses in the past as quickly as possible and move on to the next challenge.

AS THE MANAGER, YOU will on occasion be challenged by the coaches, parents and players. Get the season off to a good start by explaining at the initial parents' meeting to everyone that YOU are in charge. (Nicely, of course!) If decisions must be made, you'll make them in the way you feel they should be made, and you expect them to be followed. Requests for a child to play a certain position will be carefully considered, but will not be met right away. A request will try to be worked out at some point in the season. (See the previous chapter, "The Four Truths about Managing," for my preseason parents' speech.)

But the manager's door must always be open for discussion. It is best that way. Don't live in a vacuum. People like to express their opinions and give their input. The only time I haven't been open to a parent's words is when one has walked up to me on the field under the influence of alcohol or drugs. In such rare instances, I'd say politely, but firmly, that we could talk about it later over the phone or at the next practice, in private.

Any other time, I would carefully consider a parent's input or ideas. Usually, they were well-meaning. Sometimes they'd be a bit out of the norm. One time, a dad complained to me that I wasn't being tough enough on his kid. The dad, himself, was really tough on his kid. He was often criticizing the boy's efforts. He thought being harsh would make the child better. The young fellow cringed at the parental criticism. I felt sorry for both the son and the dad.

"Well, what would you like your player to do?" I asked the dad. I personally thought his son was trying hard to do his best, and having good results given his talent and maturity level.

The dad's response: "He needs to hustle more out there. He needs to toughen up and start going after the balls. He should be benched if he doesn't hustle."

"So," I said to the dad, "why don't we work out what you think might be good for him and what he wants to do as far as where he plays in the field and where he bats in the lineup? Maybe we can make him happy rather than having him go around with a long face and be unhappy.

"You're his dad," I continued. "Here's your chance to give your kid a break. If a kid can't get a break from his dad, he can't get a break from anybody. I'll let your son know that his new opportunities came from your efforts on his behalf."

Soon after, the son started coming to the diamond with a smile, and the dad was happy, too. A little communication between the father and son, with implementation from me, the manager, made all the difference.

I tried to work the positive side of The Game, not the negative side.

Apart from the regular parents, a manager's coaches, especially, need to be consulted about their opinions. But remember: MAKE YOUR OWN DECISIONS. Explain to all the parents, including coaches, that the manager jobs in the league are open to those who want to apply and put in the time. And everyone should manage a season or two if at all possible. It is fun.

In the last analysis, if you do take on the responsibilities of the manager, one of your most important duties is to be certain that your own player — your son (or daughter) — is entertained and having a good time. This doesn't mean letting your child pitch every inning or play shortstop all the time. But it does mean that you can help him develop his game because YOU are the manager. You signed up for it and are putting in the time. So have fun with it.

As you work to have your child have a good time, also look out for the other children and parents and try to show them a good time, too. And when you aren't the manager, be accepting of your team's manager and his efforts with his own child.

Sometimes a season will be great, sometimes not. But that's baseball.

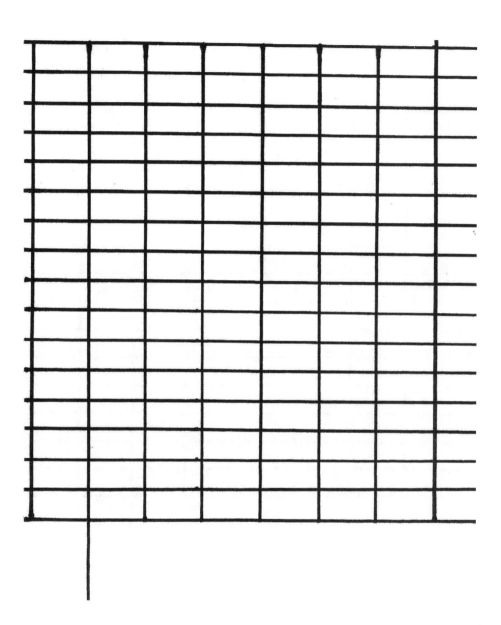

Feel free to photocopy this page. The players' names will go into the slots at left. The inning numbers will go above the columns starting with the second one from the left. Fill in the players' expected positions for each inning. (DO NOT LET YOUR PLAYERS SEE THIS GRID! KEEP IT TO YOURSELF!)

GIANTS (V) vs REDS (H)                    5/27/05
                                          GAME #12
                                          FRIDAY 8:00 PM

| REDS | 1 | 2 | 3 | 4 | 5 | 6 | 7 |
|---|---|---|---|---|---|---|---|
| DAN | 2ND | 2ND | 2ND | 2ND | C | 2ND | 2ND |
| TIM | LF | LF | 3RD | 3RD | 2ND | 3RD | 3RD |
| FRANKY | 3RD | 3RD | C | C | P | P | RF |
| ED | P | P | P | P | 3RD | 1ST | 1ST |
| BART (JIM) | SS | SS | SS | SS (JIM) | SS (JIM) | SS (JIM) | SS (JIM) |
| SAM | CF | CF | CF | CF | LF | LF | LF |
| MIKE A. | C | C | LF | LF | 1ST | C | C |
| SCOTT (ROSS) | RF | RF | RF | RF | CF (ROSS) | CF (ROSS) | CF (ROSS) |
| MIKE C. | 1ST | 1ST | 1ST | 1ST | RF | RF | P |
|  |  |  |  |  |  |  |  |
|  |  |  |  |  |  |  |  |
| ROSS |  |  |  |  |  |  |  |
| JIM | LATE |  |  |  |  |  |  |
| JACK | OUT-INJURY |  |  |  |  |  |  |

Here is a sample of a pre-game chart, filled out and kept secret by the manager.

GIANTS (V) vs REDS (H)    J/29/05
GAME #12
FRIDAY 8:00 PM

| REDS | 1 | 2 | 3 | 4 | 5 | 6 | 7 |
|---|---|---|---|---|---|---|---|
| DAN | 2ND | 2ND | 2ND | 2ND | ~~C~~ (2ND) | 2ND | 2ND |
| TIM | ~~LF~~ (3RD) | ~~LF~~ (3RD) | 3RD | 3RD | ~~2ND~~ (P) | ~~3RD~~ (P) | 3RD |
| FRANKY | ~~3RD~~ (C) | ~~3RD~~ (C) | C | C | P ~~C~~ | P ~~C~~ | RF |
| ED | P | P | P | ~~P~~ LF | ~~3RD~~ (1ST) 3RD | 1ST 3RD | 1ST 3RD |
| BART (JIM) | SS | SS | SS | SS (JIM) | SS (JIM) | SS (JIM) | SS (JIM) |
| SAM | ~~CF~~ (LF) | ~~CF~~ (LF) | CF | CF | LF | LF | LF |
| MIKE A. | ~~C~~ (CF) | ~~C~~ (CF) | LF | ~~LF~~ P | ~~1ST~~ (RF) | ~~C~~ RF | ~~C~~ P |
| SCOTT (ROSS) | RF | RF | RF | RF (ROSS) | CF (ROSS) | CF (ROSS) | ~~CF~~ (ROSS) (SCOTT) |
| MIKE G. | 1ST | 1ST | 1ST | 1ST | ~~RF~~ ~~LF~~ (1ST) | RF | ~~P~~ C |
|  |  |  |  |  |  |  |  |
|  |  |  |  |  |  |  |  |
| ROSS |  |  |  |  |  |  |  |
| JIM | LATE |  |  |  |  |  |  |
| JACK | OUT - INJURY |  |  |  |  |  |  |
|  |  |  |  |  |  |  |  |
|  |  |  |  |  |  |  |  |
| THEM | 0 | 0 | 1 | IIII | 0 | II | 0 |
| VS | I | I | ℍℍ | 0 | 0 | 0 | I |

Here is a sample of how a game might actually have been played out. Note the crossed-out positions where some players have been inserted elsewhere.

GIANTS(V) US REDS(H)

VICTORY FIELD

5/27/05

BATTING ORDER

GAME #12
FRIDAY
8:00 PM

DAN
TIM
FRANKY
ED
BART
SAM
MIKE A.
SCOTT
MIKE C.

ROSS
JIM — LATE — TUXEDO FITTING
JACK — OUT - INJURY
ARM HURT PYTHON WRESTLING

Here is a sample of a pre-game batting order to be posted in the dugout.

# Lifelong Lessons from Youth Baseball

Here's a partial list of the beneficial lessons a player can get from the experience of youth baseball:

1) Turning on the aggression switch. Meaning: How to dial up the physical and mental intensity within himself. There will be pregame butterflies, but the player will head out on the field focused and at his highest level of alertness, ready to be as competitive as possible. Once the player is "between the lines" — on the field of play — he becomes a different person. He will act with a sense of urgency, and be prepared to perform to his utmost abilities to make a fielding play, or hit the ball at the plate, or race down the basepath to first and — if the coach is wind-milling his arm — accelerate into his fastest running speed and slide as strongly as possible into the bag. The player can catch his breath and dust himself off afterward. After the game — no longer between the lines — he'll go back to his normal self.

This lesson translates into other facets of life, such as taking tests in school, or performing in the work environment as an adult. Youth baseball can set the standard for intensity that the player will be able to replicate when needed in other life situations.

The following lessons from the diamond also help prepare a young person for the challenges and pressures of the Real World:

2) Concentrating for extended periods. A baseball game averages a play in the field about every minute when a team is up to bat. Fielders pace themselves mentally, taking little breaks between pitches then setting into their positions as the pitcher winds up. The fielders have to know what to do if the ball

comes to them, where to throw it after fielding it, where to run to back up a base — all while keeping in mind how many outs have been recorded in the inning and what the count on the batter is. This takes discipline — especially for young minds — because much of the game is in "hurry-up-and-wait" mode. An outfielder, for example, can remain practically idle every time he's in the field. His mind can wander. The batter, meanwhile, has to read his coach's signals from third base, focus on the pitcher, zero in on the pitch and try to hit it. He has to keep the count in his head to know how to respond (such as protecting with two strikes, or taking on a 3-0 count, or swinging hard on a 2-0 or 3-1 count). Beyond that, the batter has to know where he is in the lineup and when he's due up, and has to keep his mind in the game as his teammates take turns at the plate.

Baseball helps develop strong attention spans, and teaches how to raise and lower levels of alertness between the down times and the pitcher's windup.

3) Acknowledging the benefit of hard work. Practice makes perfect — or at least makes marked improvement. Practice pays off big time. As I report several times in this book, baseball is an everyday game. It takes practicing various skills each day, particularly on one's own, to improve. The player with average ability who works hard at his craft will usually perform better in youth-league games than the player with talent who relies mostly on that talent, not practice. Major League Baseball provides many examples of players of average natural ability excelling, and players of prodigious natural talent faring only so-so. Who is the all-time career hits leader? Pete Rose: "Charlie Hustle."

4) Not fearing failure. Every player will find himself up at the plate at some point with runners on base and the game in the balance in the last inning. It's a lot of pressure, with the coaches and teammates and fans calling out the player's name and uniform number and shouting encouragement,

while the opposing team chatters, supporting the pitcher. But all the player can do is his best. If the player comes through at the plate — that's a lasting memory, a moment of glory. If the player strikes out or otherwise makes an out, well, life goes on after the game ends. Many, many more mini-dramas unfold for each player over the course of a season, and are multiplied over the course of a career. Each time the player steps into the batter's box, in fact, there's a chance for failure or success with an audience watching. Sometimes the player succeeds, sometimes not. But, always, life goes on. There's always another day, another play, another at-bat. That is a good thing to keep in mind in all aspects of life.

5) Winning — and being a good sport about it. You try your best to come out on top. It's the object of The Game. It feels great to win. But when you do win, don't rub it in on the opponents. Don't gloat. After all, no one wins all the time, and it's bad luck to get a big head. What goes around, comes around. If you taunt the losing team — or, during a game, deliberately run up the score — it will certainly come back to haunt you. The baseball gods are always watching.

6) Building a foundation of physical baseball skills. These are running, throwing, fielding and batting. If you try to pick The Game up later in life, such as in high school or with the company softball team, it will be very difficult. Muscle memory is instilled in young players. It's almost impossible to come into The Game late and be a success.

7) Developing a knowledge of baseball and an appreciation for what it means in our culture. The youth player is tied into the great national pastime, with its long, rich history, and its status in our society and communities. The player with youth-league experience can watch The Game on television, read the box scores in the newspaper or visit the ballpark and immediately be in a familiar world.

8) Developing lasting social bonds. The Game bonds the player, for life, with other players and fans. A youth baseball field is probably the only gathering place in our society where you will find a broad mix of people from all walks of life. In youth leagues, families form temporary little social communities for the duration of a season. For some families, this is their only social outlet for those three months. And friendships and acquaintanceships forged at the fields can remain beyond the leagues. Familiar faces encountered years later spark conversations about what former players are doing now — going to college, embarking on careers, married with children, and so on. It provides warm feelings.

9) Forming the foundation of a lifelong interest and activity. The player, grown up, will teach The Game to his children, and so on and so on. The player will always retain his moments of playing glory in his memory, which sustains his love of The Game. And the player can always go down to the fields and catch a youth-league game, which is one of the best free entertainment offerings anywhere. Games between evenly matched baseball teams — from the lowest to highest levels of play — are a joy to watch.

# The Magic of the Dream Sheet

I came up with the idea for a Dream Sheet out of an experience I had managing my first Little League team, a Minor division aggregation called the Pirates. I wanted to do my best to give every player a chance at a moment of glory, of playing a position he may not have ever played before, but craved to. That meant a lot of discussions with individual players. Finally, I hit on the idea of having them put down their wishes in writing. We were midway into the season when I had this brainstorm.

In subsequent seasons I passed out Dream Sheets at the first preseason practice. Here is a sample of a Dream Sheet:

---

**DREAM SHEET**

Please fill out this form and return as soon as possible.

Reds MAIN — South Reno Babe Ruth                Spring Season

Player Name:

Address (with ZIP Code):

Telephone number:

Team played on in prior season — Spring and Fall:

Other teams played on:

Positions played in the past on any team:

Positions you feel comfortable and confident playing:

Positions you want to try playing this season:

Any special baseball things you want to try and accomplish for yourself this season:

Comments:

Return this form to Coach Kirst . . . Thank you.

Call if you have questions: 555-HITS (4487)

Play hard. Try to do your best.

---

THE DREAM SHEETS ALWAYS were a big success. They gave players the opportunity to think about what they wanted to do during the season, and what they'd done in previous seasons. They gave parents reasonable expectations for the opportunities for glory their children could experience during that season. (And that's the most that should be expected in youth baseball. Nothing's "fair." But hopefully, it's "reasonable.") And the Dream Sheets gave the manager (me) a guideline for how to make all of my players happy by letting them experience their dreams during some point or other during the season. I had pieces of the puzzle before me, and therefore could attempt to make them all fit.

Of course, you'll wind up with, on a team of a dozen players, eight prospective shortstops, four second basemen and 12 pitchers. In their dreams! But you've got to give each player a chance. It is part of the integrity of The Game.

To be honest, I've never known of another manager picking up my idea of the Dream Sheets. I can understand why: it's just one more responsibility and headache added onto all the others. You have to create a master sheet, photocopy it, pass the sheets out, explain what they're all about, get the filled-out copies back from everybody, then lay out the dreams and work to implement them into the starting lineups and substitution moves as the season moves forward. It's a lot of work! (And if you don't implement players' goals, you've built up false hope in them — which is not a good thing.)

But it's worthwhile work, if you ask me. And here's one more aspect that bears stating, to put managers' minds at ease: No unreasonable dreams have ever been written down on the Dream Sheets that came back to me. No player ever scribbled: "I want to play first base every inning of every game."

Here is a list of typical requests that came back to me on the Dream Sheets:

• "I want to pitch."

- "I want to learn how to steal a base."

- "I want to play second base."

- "I want to be a better hitter."

- I want to try catching."

- I don't want to strike out so much."

- "I want to make all-stars."

So many players in youth leagues never get a chance to see what it's like to bat leadoff or cleanup, or play the infield, or pitch. These players typically aren't after a regular job at these spots in the lineup; they just want to experience them. So over the course of a season, consulting the Dream Sheets, I'd try to accommodate everyone, if possible. And there are clever ways for the manager to do this.

A perennial outfielder who has indicated he wants to try infield can be put at third base for a few innings with less potential to harm his team than at the other bases. There's usually not too much harm he can cause by missing balls or making bad throws. And getting a start at third will be a proud moment for him. And my experience has been that when a player gets his chance, he is usually so excited and attentive at what he is doing that he rises to the occasion and does a good job.

A good spot in the batting order is No. 4. The batter will be able to say, "I was the cleanup hitter." If two or three of your first batters — your best hitters — get on base, and the cleanup hitter makes an out, you still are alive in the inning. Even the leadoff is an OK place to put a non-regular starter, since if he makes an out he's back at the bottom of the order. (And since the opposing team won't know that you're putting a weaker player in leadoff, the pitcher may think your batter is a capable hitter and pitch carefully to him, perhaps giving up a walk. This is one of the reasons you want your players to really know their strike zone.)

IF YOU'RE A MANAGER, consider using the Dream Sheets. If you're a parent who's not on the coaching staff, consider trotting out the idea of Dream Sheets to the manager before the season gets started. Maybe show him this chapter of the book.

Nothing is "fair" in youth-league baseball. Some players will get a lot more playing time than others. But Dream Sheets at least will make the dispensation of playing time more reasonable. And that's the most a manager can deliver, and the most that parents and players can ask for.

# Bonding the Team with Its Big League Namesake

T eam names these days usually follow the names of the major league teams. Reds, Giants, A's, Pirates, and so on. That's fine. Back in my day, many of the teams were named after the sponsor, so you had a lot of fire-department, youth-organization or service-club names, which isn't quite as great as the other way.

The teams I've coached or managed have included the Reds, Giants, Dodgers, Pirates, A's, Rockies, Cubs, Tigers and White Sox, and a few others I can't recall. When managers vie for team names during the off-season maneuvering, the names of local favorite professional teams are in hot demand. In my part of the country, that meant the A's and Giants were always hard to come by in any of the youth-league divisions. Usually, the fix had to be in to get those names. Cash helped, but mainly politicking got the job done.

I always enjoyed being the Reds, because I grew up in Cincinnati. Also, the Reds — known when they started in 1869 as the Red Stockings — were the first all-professional baseball team. They competed in an early league known as the National Association, and became a charter member of the eight-team National League in 1876. I have followed the Reds from boyhood on. They've had many great teams and terrific players. I loved being the Reds, and this is what I've always told my players when that was our team name: "Once a Red, always a Red. Wherever you go on this great planet, if you've been with a Reds baseball team at any time, from Tee Ball to the pros, you're a Red and walking in the ranks of legends."

I'd go on to tell my players some Reds history, show them a picture of the stadium (the Reds play in Great American Ball Park, which in 2002 replaced Riverfront Stadium, which in 1970 replaced the park old-timers remember: Crosley Field), and let them know who some of the great Reds of the past were — Frank Robinson, Pete Rose, Johnny Bench, Joe Morgan, Tom Seaver .

. . Ted Kluszewski. Many players are forgotten as the decades pass, but I tried to bring a little life to the Reds. I'd talk about the glory days of "The Big Red Machine," which won the World Series in 1975 and '76. I'd even bring in some of my old baseball cards of Reds players.

It's easy for adults to forget, but players who were legendary two, three or four decades ago are probably utterly unknown to, or their names trigger only faint recognition from, a new generation of young baseball players. So if your team's the Giants, the players will all have heard of Barry Bonds, and probably seen him take his cuts on television; but they won't have a clue who Willie McCovey and Juan Marichal were, and may not have even heard of Willie Mays. And never mind Mel Ott. (Mel who? See! How quickly superstars of yesteryear are forgotten by the masses.) Anyway, if you're managing the Giants, you can talk about the major league club and its Hall of Famers, and also that the team once was the New York Giants and played at a place called the Polo Grounds. The New York Giants and Brooklyn Dodgers moved out West to California in the late 1950s, and when the New York Mets began play in 1962, their uniforms borrowed the color orange from the old Giants and blue from the old Dodgers.

NO MATTER WHAT TEAM you've got, try reading up on a little history about the club yourself so you can tell the players what's in a name. This is important: it instills a sense of tradition and helps make The Game what it is. And if you're wondering how to dig up information about a team, you can just go online and search for the team's home page. There are some good ones. Another avenue is to get hold of a good book resource, such as the Baseball America Directory, a paperback that's updated every year, and contact the team's front office via the email address or telephone number listed. Ask that information on the team be sent to you.

An interesting game to play is to quiz your players about what famous major leaguers wore the same uniform number each kid is wearing. Should be easy for whoever got No. 3 (Babe Ruth) or No. 25 (Barry Bonds).

One more good educational tool is the daily newspaper. Tell your players to open up the sports pages daily and check out the standings and box scores to see how their major league namesake is doing. It's a good mental exercise for the kids, and it's fun. (It may also lead them to branch out into different parts of the sports pages, and even the entire newspaper.)

You can also have fun with team names. Each of my boys, at one time or other, has been on the Pirates. It's great to go to the ballpark flying the skull-and-crossbones from the antenna of your car. You'll also have an excuse for a swashbuckling walk and irreverent manner.

"Hey you kids . . . keep it down!"

"Why? We're Pirates!"

I liked being associated with the Pirates. I remember my youngest son saying he liked being on the Pirates. Why? "Because Pirates, dad, don't have to brush their teeth, and they don't have to take baths!" Two good reasons.

A lecherous adult I know added this to the conversation: "Don't forget, kids, Pirates get all the pretty girls they want, too."

So, whatever your team name, as a manager — major league, minor league, college or youth organization — be sure to put some thought into it and build some pride and give the players some history. It isn't hard to do. And it is worthwhile.

# Know Your Strike Zone!

he biggest thrill in youth baseball — and of moments remembered pleasantly for life — is getting on base (especially with a hit). The player who is thoroughly familiar with the strike zone will experience many more thrills than the player who is unsure or tentative about the invisible boundaries.

The strike zone in youth baseball essentially runs vertically from the batter's armpits (or "letters" — meaning where the team name appears on the chest of the uniform) to the knees, and horizontally one ball width off the inside of the plate and one-and-a-half ball widths off the outside.

This is what must be taught, and taught, and reinforced, during batting practice. After all, young players don't know anything about a strike zone when they start. All they know is that a ball's coming in at them and they may be hit by it, but they're supposed to hit it. Thus the constant explanation and repetition by coaches of which pitches are strikes, and which ones should never be swung at (such as, "anything above your hands"). And thus the 500 or so practice pitches (50 pitches per practice) thrown to each player on my teams before the season even started.

Now, in a game situation, players can grow very anxious at the plate. Often what occurred in practice becomes practically irrelevant. The teams are in uniform, the scoreboard is lit up, there are parents in the stands, and the guy on the mound is trying to strike you out. Training can go out the window. So can the patience and better judgment of coaches feeling the pressure of competition.

Many youth-league coaches cannot tolerate watching their batters watch called third strikes. They drum into their players' brains that they must "protect the plate" and "swing at anything close" when there are two strikes in the count. And if a player freezes on a third strike — look out! His coach may erupt in disgust and level loud criticism ("Why dincha swing at that?!"), ridicule — or worse. At the least, a zealous anti-called-third-strike coach will probably file the at-bat away in memory as fodder for a team lecture.

As a manager, I did not chastise my players for taking called third strikes that weren't legitimate strikes. I'd even praise a batter who was called out on pitch that wasn't in the zone. (A secondary effect was that my praise also went into the umpire's ear as indirect criticism.) My teams were encouraged to not swing at pitches that weren't strikes. I didn't want my guys worrying about getting rung up by the pitcher on a bad call. I wanted them worrying about swinging only at strikes. This was a great relief to my players — to know that their coach wasn't going to be yelling at them for watching a third strike that was questionable. They'd relax more at the plate on two strikes, and be more effective.

On the teams I coached, we diligently worked on the strike zone in practice. Pitches outside the zone generally cannot be hit effectively. Therefore, my players trained to hit the pitches that were thrown where they could be hit hard. Meaning: strikes! (The only exception to this rule was the hit-and-run, as described in the Part I chapter, "Hitting Drills.")

I didn't change my philosophy when game time rolled around, either. In our practices I insisted on swinging only at strikes; and I stayed consistent during games, too. Youth-league players are still developing, learning the basic skills of The Game. And part of that process is learning the strike zone.

Naturally, players will watch a third strike go by from time to time. (With some players, it will happen time after time.) Some pitchers are very crafty and may master a breaking pitch or a tricky changeup that can fool even the best batters. It's also important to understand that umpires are human and don't always make the best calls. A tricky pitch can fool them as easily as a batter. Or maybe the catcher is deft enough to "frame" a pitch — subtly repositioning his glove after catching a ball that was outside the zone — so that it appears to have landed over the plate.

But the bottom line is: players must know the strike zone. When they do, the odds will swing in their favor, and they'll actually get more favorable calls from the guy hunched over behind the catcher. More on that in a moment.

UMPIRES, OF COURSE, VARY in their interpretation of the strike zone. Some are prone to call shoulder-high pitches as strikes, and some seem to confuse ankles with knees. ("Lowball Louie" was the nickname one veteran ump was known by in a particular Little League in Reno.) And so on, and so on. And don't be shocked if a strike is called a bit out of the zone on a 3-0 count . . . or if the strike zone expands for a team that's stomping its foe . . . or if the zone suddenly enlarges after the batting team's manager — or even a spectator in the bleachers on that team's side — has been jawing at the umpire.

To be fair, umpires are only human. If an umpire is calling 150 pitches a game, he's not going to get all 150 of them right. What's more, he has to bend his knees fairly deeply to crouch down behind child catchers and batters, so as the game wears on, his legs will get tired and he'll not crouch as low, or won't get down into his crouch as quickly as before, and therefore his strike zone will fluctuate from where it was in the first inning. That's life.

The best strategy is for coaches and their

players to keep a close eye on where the umpire is calling strikes, and share that information with each other in team spirit. That way, each player due up to bat will be primed and ready to know if the ump is calling 'em low, or high, or outside, or inside.

But, anyway, let's move on to the essential point of this chapter: There's a competitive edge to be gained from teaching your players to swing only at good pitches. And it has to do with the psychology of umpires.

If your team is known to possess that discipline, it can work in your favor with umpires. Youth-league umps are not big league quality. They're part-timers working for a small fee and because they love The Game. They were probably players when they were kids, and therefore they're initially on the side of the hitter. The ump remembers how it was to strike out himself and is sympathetic to the batter. And the ump is especially biased toward the batter who strides to the plate with confidence, ready and eager to take his hacks, expecting that something good is going to happen.

But the player who enters the box timidly will influence the ump the other way. The ump will recognize that this is a batter just trying to get through the at-bat, who will probably stare at good pitches, trying to beg a walk, or swing wildly just to get it over with. Therefore, the ump will help speed this fateful process along, giving any close calls to the pitcher.

Now, all this works on the subconscious level of the ump's mind. But, again, he is only human. And I've seen these scenarios play out over and over and over again, season after season, year after year. It's just the way The Game works.

If the ump knows that your team has the reputation of only swinging at good pitches, that the players really know the strike zone, then he'll respect your batters. If he gives a borderline pitch to the pitcher, or totally blows a call, he'll give the next close call to your side. And more often than not, he'll subconsciously slant his calls in your favor.

A final note:

Coaches, don't sabotage your efforts by questioning the umpire antagonistically. You can't win a confrontation with an umpire any more than you can fight City Hall. Umpires know when they've made a mistake. They're embarrassed about it. They'll be inclined to give the wronged team a break on a subsequent pitch to even matters out. A coach can call out something positive to his batter, such as, "Good take, Tony," on a ball that was called a strike. But a barked comment at the umpire such as, "Hey, you've got to call them both ways!" or even the milder, "Where did that miss, blue?" will usually backfire, and the borderline calls (and even not-so-borderline ones) will start going the other way.

You'll have unintentionally altered the strike zone for your players. And maybe for more than that game. In youth baseball, you get the same umpires over and over again during a season.

Best to just teach your players the strike zone, and praise them for swinging at good pitches and taking bad ones. It will pay off many more times than not. Your team will win more games. And your players will have a better time, because they'll be getting on base more.

# Notes:

# Extra Hats Are Essential

I nevitably, youth players will come to a practice or game hatless. They'll have lost it somewhere. Players like wearing their hats to school and seemingly everywhere else. No surprise that the hats get misplaced or forgotten; they can end up in a school's Lost and Found drawer, in a friend's back yard, in a creek.

At higher levels of play, umpires will not let a player take the field out of uniform, including without a hat. That loss of manpower can really hurt a team. So managers are advised to keep spare hats on hand. But they should make sure that players don't take the spares lightly. Otherwise they won't take care of their issued hats.

The spares should be used as loaners to be kept in and returned to the bat bag. If a player's hat is permanently lost, the manager can ask the parent to buy the kid a new hat.

OTHER EXTRA GEAR THAT'S good to have on hand to meet typical emergencies:

• A couple extra right-handed fielder's gloves.

• A good team bat for any player to use. (The bat should be light so that even the smaller players can use it.)

• A few extra cups. (I've never known anyone to want one, though. But if the catcher must be replaced during the game and the substitute doesn't have a cup, a clean borrowed one is better than nothing.)

These are the sort of items that an experienced manager learns to pack to every practice and game. Trust me, as a season unfolds, you'll be glad you did!

# Mandatory Play Rule, Anyone?

T he typical mandatory play rule in youth baseball at the Little League level is for every player to have a minimum of two innings in the field and one at-bat per game.

Many parents, at least in their first few seasons, don't understand that their child may get no more than that minimal playing time. But the manager is not obligated to give a player any more than that.

For a substitute player who never is given more than the minimum, the rule will provide him only 20 at-bats and 40 innings in the field (likely the outfield) during a 20-game season. Sounds kind of skimpy, doesn't it?

A good manager will try to give each player more than the minimum. It's not easy. If there's a 12-player team, it usually works out that six of the players will play every inning of each game, and the other six will alternate, with three at a time on the field, during each game. A good manager will end up giving starts to the subs against weaker teams, pull the starters when there's a big lead, and also take advantage of player absences to give the subs who show up more than the usual two or three innings and one or two at-bats.

I always tried to give every player on my teams some starts and some complete games during a season. Because players remember their moments of glory, these rare chances at ample playing time will be savored throughout the off-season and maybe even longer. A sub won't remember all the times he sat the bench, chewing sunflower seeds, feeling bored and impatient for his inning to arrive. But he will remember the time he was in the starting lineup. And you can bet he'll treasure the game when he was actually put in the leadoff slot.

A creative manager can actually turn the mandatory play rule into a competitive advantage.

In a six-inning Little League game, the typical pattern is for the nine top players to play the first three innings, then the three subs are brought in for the three marginal starters for innings four and five, and then the starting lineup returns for inning six. But consider if the manager gets all six of the bottom players into the lineup at the game's start, ensures every one of these players has gotten the minimum two innings plus one at-bat, then brings in his strongest lineup for the remainder of the game — when it matters most. The manager will likely have his best players facing some of the other team's worst players in innings 4 and 5 — which can lead to many offensive runs and defensive outs, and a cheap win.

And there's one more subtlety to consider: The baseball gods work in mysterious ways.

If Bobby No. 12 Hitter, with a batting average below .100, is put in the leadoff slot for the first time, he may very well reach base. The other team won't pick up on the fact that this is a sub in the No. 1 slot. The pitcher won't be entirely warmed up at game's start, and his fastballs may miss the mark. And there you have it — Bobby is standing on first base, grinning.

Or here's another thing that can happen: Bobby rises to the occasion. He steps to the plate feeling potent and capable, like the leadoff hitter he is in this situation, and raps a sharp grounder past short.

The baseball gods knew it was that player's chance to shine, and gave him a little boost. A moment of glory.

# Three Dingers – or, the Virtue of (Occasional) Selfishness

As a player, there are times when you play for your team, and times when you should play for yourself. A manager should recognize when opportunities for players to better themselves come up and encourage them to take a chance, even though that might not be the best way to approach a situation if you "went by the book."

One Fall Ball season in the Main division of Little League, one of my best players — we'll call him "Larue Stetson" — got up to bat and slammed a home run. It went more than 200 feet over the fence. Larue was very special. He was our first-string catcher, but also pitched and played any infield position. Yes, a very good player, and a team player, too. His next time at the plate, he did it again. BANG. Another homer out of the park. A solid clout. Nothing cheap about it. Two homers in one game! It's not done very often. Quite an achievement!

Later in the game, it was his turn at the plate again. The bases were loaded. We had one out, and a base hit would have really been nice. It was a tight game. A couple runs would have meant a lot. Larue knew he would get a pitch to hit because the bases were full.

I called him over before he was to go to the batter's box. He was an intelligent hitter and said he wanted to try to take the ball to the opposite field and drive in a run, even if it meant a possible groundout.

"Look," I said, "What have you done today? Hit two home runs, right? That's tough to do. Go for the fences and try to make it three. They're gonna give you a pitch to hit because they don't want to walk in a run, so forget about driving the ball the other way. Give it all you've got. Swing from your heels and see what happens."

"Are you sure, coach?" he asked.

"I'm sure," I said. "Go for the fences."

The count went to 2 balls and 1 strike. In came the pitch. WHACK!

A HUGE shot over the left-field fence for a grand slam. The third home run in the game for the player — and a grand slam at that! Everybody on our side was happy.

Sure, an opposite-field shot would have given us a couple runs, and swinging for the fences wasn't the best thing to do in that situation. But it was the RIGHT thing to do. Three real home runs in one game by the same player. The only time I've ever seen it done. And something I'll always remember.

When opportunity knocks, take the chance at cashing in on the opportunity. Moments of glory are great and not that easy to come by. Reach for them when you have the chance.


LARUE WENT ON TO have stellar Babe Ruth and high school careers, earned a college scholarship and had a good career at that level, and was drafted by the Mets, for whose organization he was able to play baseball professionally.

He got his moment of glory in his three-homer game because he was such a good team player, and it was all the more exciting for everyone on the team to see his feat because he always played for the team. When an individual effort like that happened, all the players and teammates were legitimately happy for him.

# Injuries, or – Why Do You Think It's Called 'Hardball'?

I njuries are part of The Game. I've seen plenty. None that were life-threatening, thank goodness and knock on wood!

With four boys, we had an assortment of injuries in our house, some of which put the children out of commission for a while. One boy broke his arm on the school playground. Of course, he was a pitcher, and that kept him out for a few weeks, but he came back strong. Another of the boys broke his hand when he was catching in practice. That put him out for several weeks and took time to get over.

And sick? We've been sick a bunch of times. My oldest son was trying to make an impression on his coach by showing up to practice even when he was very, very ill with the flu. When I picked him up after practice, the coaches informed me that Junior had barfed in the outfield and wasn't feeling too well. That wasn't the impression Junior had been trying to make.

The son of a friend of mine tried to play sick. He was normally a very good hitter and usually made contact and had a good eye for the strike zone. Well, I pitched batting practice to him the day of a game. He missed 25 straight pitches. And these were right down the middle. So we did another 25 . . . and he missed all of them. Another 25. Missed each and every one. Not much could be done about it. The game was ready to begin.

He struck out three times. Talk about a disappointed young man! He could not figure out what the problem was. His dad took him to the batting cages the next day to build up his son's confidence. He missed everything there, too.

A week later, his health was back. And he was back to hitting the ball as well as ever. But . . . we all learned a valuable lesson. If you're under the weather, don't expect much good to happen at the plate; and for sure don't get upset about it, because there will always be another day, and a better day, if you're sick on this one.

INJURIES ARE PART OF The Game. There is always some risk involved with baseball. It's to be accepted. It's why leagues carry insurance and also require participants to sign waivers when signing up, and why safety is a prime consideration and worth talking about.

While baseball is generally considered a safe activity, it is estimated there are more than 100,000 acute baseball injuries every year in the United States among players ages 5 to 14. Those statistics were reported in an article published in June 2000 in the medical journal Pediatric Emergency Care by two physicians: Dr. Karl Yen and Dr. Jordan Metzl. The authors wrote that typical acute injuries (injuries serious enough that they require treatment and can require visits to the hospital emergency room) "often involve ball impact to the face and hands," that "impact to the chest results in a small but steady number of fatalities each year" and that young players can suffer "chronic or acute conditions of the elbow." (The issue of young pitchers throwing out their arms through too much repetitive motion — often harming the growth plate in the elbow — is coming increasingly to light. Ex-major league pitcher and current youth-pitching trainer Tom House calls overuse of young arms from too much pitching "an epidemic.")

Some perspective is needed. John Doherty, a newspaper columnist specializing in sports medicine, noted that the U.S. Consumer Product Safety Commission recorded 88 baseball-related deaths between 1973 and 1995 (an average of four a year) and that this was more than in any other sport. However, Doherty pointed out that in America, only basketball has more participants than baseball among players ages 6 through 17, and with more than 8 million youths playing baseball and softball, there are bound to be a number of serious injuries and a few fatalities. Doherty also reported that baseball, according to research by the National Collegiate Athletic Association, is the safest sport played at the college level.

One year, a mother came to a board meeting of the Little League I was involved in and asked that mouth guards — the kind boxers or football players wear — be made a mandatory part of uniforms. The board members, to their credit, turned thumbs down. Buying that many mouth guards would be expensive. And it would be one more regulation to enforce. What's more, how many players lost front teeth each season? Not many.

When the mother grew agitated, a board member suggested that perhaps she would supply a mouth guard to her own son, and feel secure that he was adequately protected.

That suggestion did not make her happy, either. Were her son to be the only player with a mouth guard, he would be made fun of by the other players, she said. But her argument was to no avail.

I believe her son went without a mouth guard that season. Somehow, his dental state made it through intact, as well.

During another season, the board considered improving the safety aspects of batting helmets by adding mask-like screens in front, sort of like catchers and umpires wear. These Darth Vader-type helmets are sometimes used by players who've suffered injuries, such as broken noses or cheekbones that are healing. But making them standard for every player?

Some leagues around the country adopted helmet masks. But our board decided against it.

It is baseball, after all.


INJURIES ON THE DIAMOND can occur in an endless variety of ways, and every season seems to offer up a new variation. Some of the injuries I've witnessed are unforgettable:

• My youngest son, Paul, was learning to pitch. He was on the mound during a game in the Minor division, and noticed that his second baseman had crept in behind the runner and was standing on the bag. My son was off the mound — meaning, in Little League rules, that the ball was in play and the runner didn't have to be on the bag. Paul whirled around and threw the ball right on the mark to second. Unfortunately, the infielder misjudged the ball and it sailed over his glove by a fraction of an inch, right into his nose. CRACK! Blood all over the place. Another handkerchief down the drain. The runner scored.

• A young man I'd coached returned to play the next year and was assigned to another team. On Opening Day, I saw a crowd gathered on the field. This player had frozen at the plate as a pitch came toward his face. When he unfroze his attention, he turned into the pitch instead of away from it. Of course, it missed the hard plastic of the helmet and caught him on the cheek. By the time I got there, his face had swollen so much the helmet would barely come off. But he was A-OK in a couple weeks. Quit The Game the next year, though.

• One of my sons was in the on-deck circle waiting to bat. A teammate didn't notice my son there, or didn't watch where he was walking. As my son was taking warmup cuts, his teammate walked right into the path of the bat swing. Decked him. Lost a couple teeth. Could have been worse, though.

Thank heavens it was my son, and he didn't have that much muscle power at that age. Ya gotta watch where you're walking!

(A bat must be treated with respect. I always gave a talk to my teams about bat safety, and hoped it sank in, and repeated it often.)

• An umpire was calling the game from behind the mound instead of behind the plate. I was standing on a different field a couple hundred feet away. During the infield warmups, the first baseman threw routine grounders to the other infielders. It went in the usual rotation: to the second baseman, then the shortstop, then the third baseman. I noticed that each time the third baseman made his return throw to first, the ball came closer to the umpire's head. Just as I was on my way over to tell them to be careful, the third baseman took a grounder a bit off to his right. He threw a shot to first — and caught the umpire behind the right ear. The man went down like a ton of bricks, and lay there motionless. Very scary. Then he moved, and got up. He was OK, but had to go into the concession stand and sit with an ice bag on his head for a time.

• My second-oldest son, Charlie, went the furthest of all the brothers in baseball. He played all four years in high school, and had a chance to play in college. One time, playing catcher during a Babe Ruth League team practice, he caught a fastball foul tip on the back of his throwing hand.

"Shake it off," I said. "Keep going."

He did.

Some pitches later, he said, "Dad, this really hurts."

I took a good look at it, and noticed it was swollen on both sides.

"Better take a rest," I said.

We finished up practice. Charlie iced his hand overnight. The next day, it was still swollen on both sides. X-rays revealed that it was broken. Did I ever feel bad having him keep playing with a broken hand! But . . . I guess that toughens kids up. Couldn't have felt so good throwing the ball back, though.

• One time, Charlie was playing shortstop in a Little League game. The runner on second was the biggest kid in the league, by far. Huge, round, heavy, very substantial. The ball was hit to short. Charlie fielded it. The runner from second trudged toward third — and collided mightily with Charlie. Charlie ended up on the bottom, the big kid fallen over him. As if in slow motion, the big kid tried to get off, but bounced up and down on Charlie's back like it was a mattress, mashing him deep into the infield dirt. A cloud of dust rose. Charlie picked up the ball and crawled a few feet toward third and tagged out the big kid, who had rolled off but was still not on his feet. The wind had been knocked out of Charlie, and he had the look of a flattened cartoon character. He recovered and resumed his spot at short.

• I instructed my players in how to turn away from a ball that's coming too far inside. You don't step out with your feet, but instead twist around clockwise (or counter-clockwise if you're a lefty) to catch the ball on your shoulder or back. (Of course, you can duck if it's coming at your head.) I started training players at the Farm division level, throwing painless tennis balls at them so they could practice getting out of the way.

This is a difficult skill to master. Turning one's back to the ball is counterintuitive. One of my players, a kid we'll call "Frederick," suffered a brain freeze at the plate during a game. Instead of twisting away from an inside pitch, he more or less backed into it. The result was disastrous. The ball smacked him right on a rib, breaking it.

• The most dangerous place on a youth baseball field is right behind first base during infield warmups. The first baseman is tossing grounders in turn to the other infielders, and they're firing the ball back to him at the bag. If you should happen to stand anywhere behind him where an errant throw or missed grab could nail you somewhere on your body from the toes on up, you probably will suffer bruises. This will be your own fault for not paying attention and avoiding this hazardous area.

One of my coaches, we'll call him "George Dunham," was an experienced baseball guy. He had been drafted by the Braves and played outfield in that organization's farm system. But lo and behold, there he was, standing idly in foul territory behind first base during pre-inning warmups. As a former professional player, George took it for granted that throws would be good and caught. An off-line throw got by the first baseman, skipped in the dirt and struck poor Coach Dunham right where it counts. Put him on the ground. When he was able to rise, the words out of his mouth weren't found in most dictionaries. Then he composed himself and took a seat in the dugout, behind the cyclone fencing.

The area around first base should be respected. We had so many balls leave the field in this area — bounding into the parking lot, hitting fans, hitting little kids walking to the snack bar — that our league installed an 8-foot-tall fence. That did the trick.

• "Blaine," one of the players on my Farm team, wanted to be a catcher. His dad was one of my coaches. Blaine was a good little player, brimming with enthusiasm, and just learning how to catch. We put the gear on him for his first start in a game. The pitching machine fired the ball at about 50 mph. Blaine positioned his mitt to catch pitches on target. He settled into the position and was doing fine. Unfortunately, the machine isn't always accurate. A ball's seams can throw it off course, or the ball may be fed awkwardly into the feeder, or one of the tripods holding the machine could be bumped. The batter swung at a pitch and missed. The ball went straight into Blaine's mask and bounced off. He remained in his full crouch for a moment . . . then both arms dropped to the ground and his head slumped. He remained motionless in the crouch, head down, as if frozen in that position.

Time was called. We coaches gathered around. We asked Blaine if he was all right. No answer. Finally, the boy regained his senses. He said was OK. He got back into his position, and the inning continued. Yes, he was a tough young man. And he'd just had a new experience: what it's like for a baseball to strike your mask hard, and the sound of an invisible bell clanging in your ears. He had really had his bell rung.

• It was a latter inning in the last game of the Little League season, in Fall Ball. My youngest son, Paul, a left-handed batter, was up. On the mound was a fire-baller who could throw 64 mph. Like many serious, competitive youth pitchers, he had a private coach, and that coach happened to be at the game, watching. The coach had been teaching his student how to quick-pitch hitters to get a cheap strike before the hitter was set in the box. There happened to be only one umpire available for that game. The ump decided to position himself behind the mound to more easily make calls in the field.

Paul dug into the box, tapping his bat on the plate. He was accustomed to the ump behind the plate pointing toward the pitcher to indicate the ball was in play. But in this situation, there would be no such formality. As Paul looked out toward the mound for the delivery, the ball was already upon him. Literally. It hit him in the eye below the brim of the helmet.

Paul was wearing hard-plastic safety glasses — extra-thick prescription glasses designed for sports. The impact of the ball knocked the lens out of the glasses, and the lens dug a gash near his eye. A pinch runner was sent in for him, and Paul took a seat in the dugout, a towel stanching the blood. The game continued to its conclusion, and then it was off to the emergency room for him. Turned out his eye socket was fractured. The safety glasses were a lucky break; regular glass lenses could have shattered and made his injury much more serious. Consider wearing safety glasses or contact lenses when you play baseball.

• One of my Little League players, "Albert," was facing a lefty who could throw faster than 60 mph. Remember, this is from only 45 feet, so the ball gets there very quickly. One of the pitches clobbered Albert on his front thigh. It was like getting hit by a rubber bullet. He went down. In the dugout, he raised his pants leg. His badge of honor was black, blue and purple, punctuated by seam marks, and swollen bubble-like about 2 inches high. Just a reminder of how devastating a 60-mph pitch is.

• I was managing a 14-year-old all-star team in a Babe Ruth League tournament. I was pitching batting practice one morning before the team was going to drive up from Reno to Lake Tahoe for our game. I was in uniform, throwing off the mound, making sure they were strikes so the players could hit the ball. One of my pitches was right over the heart of the plate. The batter connected solidly. The ball came right back at my legs. I didn't get my glove down quickly enough. A stomach got in the way. Like a bullet, the ball hit my right ankle, then ricocheted and struck my other ankle. Pure symmetry. And pure pain.

I brought another coach in to finish pitching batting practice. I had to make the trip up to Tahoe to manage my team, so I deliberately avoided looking at my swollen ankles. After I got home that night, I still resisted examining my injuries, but finally pulled up the stirrups and peeled back the socks. The sight was disgusting: purple and red bruises, larger than silver dollars; worse on the side of the first impact. I had photographs taken. Later, I showed them to a friend who is an orthopedic surgeon, and asked if the bruises signified that bones had been fractured. "Absolutely, Jeff," he said.

I considered myself to be a man among men having managed my team through the whole game with broken legs.

• I have to conclude this list of memorable injuries with one that may be unique even in the age-old annals of baseball play:

A player of mine was sitting in the dugout for a couple innings, waiting for his turn in the game. He propped himself up on the bench. It was a cold night, and he wrapped his jacket around him. His feet also were up on the bench, and he was in kind of a crouch. Soon he worked his hands up the opposite sleeves of his jacket. In effect, he straitjacketed himself.

I was standing in foul territory in front of the dugout, trying to rally our defense and get a couple outs. From behind I heard a terrible sound: CLUNK, CLUNK. I turned around, and there was my player down on the floor, bound in his jacket. He'd lost his balance on the bench and fallen onto his head. He was conscious, but knocked silly and his face was white as a sheet. He also was covered in dirt from the cement floor.

Luckily, his mother was on hand, and off he went in her car to the emergency room. It turned out he was dazed, but OK. The lessons: Try not to get yourself into a pickle you can't get out of; life is a delicate balance; don't be afraid to ask for help when you need it.


MANAGERS AND COACHES SHOULD play key roles in preventing injuries among their players. After I became a manager, I thought back to an incident when I was 15, in my final season of organized play.

I used to hit a lot of doubles. I reached second base during one game, and took my usual lead off. The coach standing in the third-base box signaled me to advance to third when the ball was hit. At the sound of the bat, I took off charging.

I'd been reading a biography of Ty Cobb, and was influenced by the "Georgia Peach's" tactics. In fact, I brought a metal file to games so I could sit on the bench and sharpen my cleats, just as Cobb had. Cobb's style was to slide into a bag waist-high. I launched myself toward the third baseman, who was blocking the bag, waiting for the throw. I caught his uniform near the pocket with my metal cleats. His pant leg was torn all the way down to the ankle, and there was blood.

I was safe. He was knocked out of the play. I still remember the collision as if it had unfolded in slow motion. He remembered it, too, when I came upon him at a 20-year high school reunion. He wasn't mad at me; in fact, he hadn't been mad all those years before when it had happened, either. That's baseball. A rough game. But I did feel bad about it. I shouldn't have been filing my cleats. And when I became a coach, I taught my players to slide around the bags to avoid tags, rather than launch themselves into a fielder.

Up until the high school level, there's no reason for hard contact. There will be enough contact if a player reaches that advanced level (where the players are tough, mean and awful, some of them growing beards, and contact is expected to be dished out). But when I was a youth-league player, I hadn't had a coach telling me how to properly slide, so I'd gotten my information from an undesirable source.

An article by Jim Rogers, a trainer at Temple University Hospital's Sports Medicine Center, makes good basic points for youth-league coaches. "Children are not miniature adults and shouldn't be treated as such," Rogers wrote. "Children are still growing and therefore are more susceptible to injury."

Young players should stretch and warm up their bodies, as through light calisthenics or a short jog, before playing, Rogers said. He added that children should not be encouraged to "play through pain," and if a child suffers swelling or limitation of motion it can be a serious sign. Ice packs are a staple of the first-aid kit because ice controls pain and swelling from sprains, strains and contusions.

Besides coaching his players against unnecessary roughness, and ensuring his team warms up properly, the manager should keep an eye on several other potentially injury-causing situations:

• Soggy bags. Rain is an enemy of baseball because wet conditions can be treacherous. The outfield grass gets slick. The infield gets muddy. The manager should tell his players to make sure they bend their knees out in the field, for better balance, and to make sure their cleats are free of clods. But here's a hidden hazard on a damp field: slippery bases.

Runners can twist ankles or tear Achilles tendons sliding across the bag. I've seen wet bags take a number of players out of games. All the manager can do, though, is tell players to run carefully and watch it when they round a bag.

• Pitchers wearing out their arms by trying to throw too hard and too much. This is true at all youth levels, but especially true, I've found, of pitchers ages 15 and 16. They have newly developed muscles, but not brains (meaning: maturity). The manager should ask a pitcher before he starts the game, "How do you feel?" Pitchers will always tell you their arms feel good, because they want the chance to throw. But the manager should monitor the situation closely, and check back every inning or so. Even a pitcher who hasn't thrown in a game in several days may have a tired or sore arm. You can't know what he's been doing away from the field. Chucking rocks? Pumping iron? Besides not protecting their arms, and trying to throw too hard and too many pitches, younger pitchers have poor throwing motions and can damage their arms that way.

• Premeditated pickoff pegging. Getting plunked by a pitch isn't the only time players are reminded of how hard a hardball is. Runners sliding into bags or racing between them can get nailed by a throw. Where it seems to hurt worst is in the spine. Not a pleasant feeling. What bothers me is when the pegging is deliberate.

In Babe Ruth League, leading off base is allowed, and so are pickoff throws from the pitcher. I've seen a few nasty hurlers who deliberately threw at runners diving back to the bag to avoid the pickoff. The manager has to be aware of who the mean pitchers are, and warn his players. But umpires are hard-pressed to boot a pitcher for beaning a base-runner, since how can it be proved that the play was intentional? An even less desirable reality is when an unscrupulous coach will tell his pitcher to throw chin music at a batter.

If a manager suspects this is going on, it's imperative to call time and speak to the umpire and ask for a counsel with the opposing manager. Deliberately throwing at players has no place in youth baseball. Some players at that level are very strong and powerful and talented, while others can't even get out of the way of a slow-rolling grounder. The sport is dangerous enough without treating it as dodgeball.

# Notes:

# A Chance on the Mound, All Around

In my experience, every youth player would like to have a chance to pitch — or at least thinks he would. One year, when I had succeeded in becoming so active in my sons' Little League that I could wield a BIG influence on the rules, I decided to make pitching mandatory for every player who wanted a chance.

This happened to be for the Fall Ball season, when competition isn't as fierce as during the regular spring season. Fall Ball is generally geared to developing skills; in our league there was even a five-run limit per frame, so the team in the field would get its at-bats in before the two-hour time limit. I figured Fall Ball was the perfect time to try out my little experiment. My position was that any player who wanted to pitch in a game and could do so safely — not endangering the batters through gross lack of accuracy, or endangering himself by being unable to field the position — would have the opportunity to make an appearance. If a player could throw seven out of 10 pitches in the bullpen as strikes, and protect himself with his glove, he met my standard for getting an appearance in a game as a pitcher. My idea was that the player could have a shot on the mound, maybe start an inning, have the warmup pitches, get the thrill of the umpire saying, "Play ball!" and pointing at the player to begin, and face three hitters or so.

In my idealistic line of thinking, if the coaches worked with the players, they would be competent about knowing what to do on the mound, and therefore deserve an appearance. If the player walked three consecutive batters, then he got the hook and had had a day in the spotlight. So what if the bases now were loaded? This would give the defending team the greatest chance in baseball of getting an out, and also create the best odds of turning a triple play.

Not surprisingly, the traditionalists and zealots fiercely opposed my idea, as it made their lives more difficult as coaches because it required working a little differently with players whom the coaches might not normally want to spend a lot of time with. Plus, my rule opened the door to all the players asking their coaches, "When am I gonna get to pitch?" Nevertheless, I enjoyed enough political clout in the league that my piece of legislation prevailed, and all the coaches agreed to try the mandatory pitching rule on a trial basis.

I was elated! Many players and their families were thrilled with the opportunity. What's more, there also was a benefit for the coaches. Now, the players or parents who'd complained about never getting a chance on the mound would receive a reality check. They'd get to see what Junior could actually do on the mound during a game.

The Fall Ball season progressed. The players on my team were excited about the opportunity of getting on the mound. There were still rumbles from the traditionalists and zealots, though. Finally it came time for my team to face up against one of theirs.

My counterpart for this game was a fine manager and a great baseball person, with a terrific understanding of The Game. He also was vehemently opposed to my mandatory-pitching program. He opted to save his least-talented knucklehead for a pitching appearance in our faceoff — to embarrass me at the player's ineptness and demonstrate how my rule detracted from The Game by allowing such a soul to take the hill. To this manager's credit, however, he had prepared the young fellow as best he could.

The young fellow came in to pitch in a middle inning, slated to face the meat of our order: the Nos. 3, 4 and 5 hitters. He walked to the mound and tossed his warmups. There was great anticipation in the stands, for my opponent had made no secret of his disdain for my mandatory-pitching rule. Nevertheless, his sacrificial lamb on the hill was thrilled to be there. He was absolutely beaming. His warmups were over the plate, although the speed was, at most, probably only in the high 30s mph.

Batter up!

My No. 3 hitter was a star from another league who'd joined our league for Fall Ball. Before he stepped into the batter's box, I knew I had to have a word with him. I called him to the side and, as best I could, got across the dynamics of what was going on. He didn't really grasp the finer points of the politics, but certainly did agree to follow my instructions.

"No matter where the first pitch is, swing at it," I said.

"What if it's a ball?"

"No matter," I said. "Swing, and swing as hard as you can."

"What if I strike out?"

"Don't worry about it if you do," I said. "You're doing this for the good of baseball, and you'll be up plenty more times."

He said OK.

Everyone knew this was one of the best players in the league facing off against one of the worst. Tension hung in the air. The pitcher went into his windup and fired a 31 mph heater in toward the plate. It came in high. In fact, it was about a foot higher than the batter's head. However, fine man that my player was, he took a vicious tomahawk cut at it and missed by a mile, nearly flooring himself with the power of his swing.

As the ball sailed past the catcher and hit the backstop, the crowd roared with joy. The little guy on the mound had gotten a strike on a really tough hitter. He was a very, very happy fellow, after just one pitch.

My batter was flustered, but not upset. He dug in to bat the way he normally would. The next pitch was in the strike zone. The slugger fouled it off. Strike two. He was a little worried now about fanning, but the pitcher was delighted, as was the crowd.

My batter, in his nervousness, nearly went after the third pitch, but it was clearly a ball so he checked his swing. The fourth pitch came in. My batter swung . . . and topped the ball, sending a grounder to the shortstop, who was all-world, and made a smooth play to toss the runner out at first.

One out for the rookie pitcher! More smiles. Pats on the back from his teammates. Pleased fans. And I was happy.

"Job well done, thanks," I told my batter as he returned to the dugout.

The inning continued. Another groundout, a couple of walks, and the pitcher was pulled. But he was a very happy young player who'd had his day on the hill. I don't think he ever pitched again. But he'd had his chance that one time, and a moment of glory to savor for the rest of his life.

After that season, the traditionalists and zealots won out. My rule was discarded, sad to say. But I learned that with the right kind of coaching and the right format, just about any youth player can safely take his shot on the hill and have his memory-maker moment of glory.

I continued to let my lesser players have a chance to pitch from time to time as circumstances permitted, and I always led the league in pitching participation. I still won a significant number of games and had lots of fun.

So did the players and their families.

# The Longer You Play,
# the More Humble Your Stats

A s a player progresses up the baseball pyramid, through the Little League levels and into higher-age leagues, his skills will get better and better. But the other players will be getting better and better, too. And the pool of players will shrink at each level, with more concentrated talent as the not-so-talented wash out. Therefore, a player's statistics will get worse and worse.

The 10-year-old all-star in the Minor division of Little League who bats .600 will have an average of, perhaps, .500 in the Main division, and .400 in Babe Ruth, and .300 in high school. It's harsh to say this, but the batter with an on-base percentage of .500 before high school is probably facing the end of his career. In high school, the OBP will likely drop to .300 or .400, and that's not good enough to get drafted by the pros or even earn a ticket to a college team.

Consider fielding. A Little Leaguer who catches several fly balls in a season is considered a hero. In high school, a player who commits three errors in a season is considered a bum.

Yes, it's a paradox of The Game: The longer you play, the better you get, the worse you do. And sooner or later, if you play long enough, you wind up as the substitute right fielder.

BASEBALL IS A GREAT humbler of big egos. Consider the all-world player who dominates his Little League. He pitches in the low 60s. He bats .700. He hits home runs. He nails every runner who grounds to him at shortstop. He's the top choice for his league's all-star squad.

Let's say his team wins its district tournament. The all-world hero hit .500 in his No. 3 slot in the batting lineup. He was still striking batters out and giving up few hits, walks and runs. His ego is still inflated.

Then his team heads off to the state tournament. Here — he discovers, to his shock — there are more than a few players just like him. In this elite tournament, hitters connect solidly on his pitches — and not just the top batters in an opponent's lineup, either. What's more, our Little League hero is now struggling at the plate, seeing breaking pitches he never had before, and having to catch up to the type of fastballs he's used to throwing himself. He strikes out more than once. His team doesn't take the state title.

He assumes the state champion will easily capture the regional tournament and proceed to the Little League World Series. But — that doesn't happen! An even scarier squad of man-children prevails. As the now-humbled star watches on television, even that team doesn't make waves in Williamsport, against the world's finest.

Welcome to the big, wide world, son!

By high school, he has to play his heart out just to make varsity. The bench is hard beneath his backside. He's better than he's ever been, playing smarter, too, but so is everyone else.

The longer you play, the better you get, the worse you do.

# Smells Like Team Spirit

B eing a good teammate is one of the most important aspects of playing youth baseball, and one of the greatest lessons a player can learn.

Players and their coaches are forced together as a unit for 90 or so days, and it is important to the success and welfare of everyone during the season that each individual develop an all-for-one, one-for-all attitude. It's a life lesson that pays dividends down the road. It also enriches the baseball experience.

The essential bonding begins with the manager's opening, preseason team talk, and from then on, the "there is no 'I' in 'team'" point needs to be given as a reminder from time to time. Often an all-world talent will become frustrated with his teammates' playing ability. Quite often, the star is a pitcher.

When such a mini-tantrum happened on one of my teams — with the pitcher kicking dirt in disgust at a dropped pitch that might have been called a strike had the catcher held onto it and framed it in the strike zone; or reacting the same way after a fielder missed a grounder, dropped a fly ball or launched a throw into foul territory — it was time to walk out to the mound and replay the "good teammate talk" with the player and express the fact that it is his chance to make his teammates better by genuinely encouraging their efforts and trying harder himself.

Useful questions for the coach to ask his player at such a moment include, "Did it ever occur to you that your teammate might just miss a ball on purpose because he knows it upsets you, and that's his way to get even for the dirty looks and words you've given him?" And, "Do you really think the ump is going to give you the next call if you sulk around on the mound after a call that you thought went the wrong way?" You can add, "Your teammates and the umps are people with feelings, too, and they come to the baseball field to do their best and have a good time with The Game. Your sour approach can only make these people less than happy to do anything to help you out. Did you know that if you play long enough and stick with The Game, sooner or later you'll be on a team where everyone is so good that you're the knucklehead?"

That's true, by the way. Almost everyone who sticks with baseball long enough winds up as the substitute right fielder. (Even future Hall of Famers, in the twilight of their career, are reduced to designated hitters or pinch hitters, and see the bench a lot. Check out the final-season stats of the likes of Babe Ruth, Willie Mays and Hank Aaron.)

For the all-world player, it is frustrating to have others make mistakes. That's why you, as the coach, must lecture him: "If you want to play with major league-quality players and have major league-quality umpiring, YOU'VE GOT TO MAKE IT TO THE MAJOR LEAGUES, and you'll never get there with the kind of attitude you display."

On a well-coached team, every player is giving it his best, however limited his skills. And if your all-world player is pitching and struggling to get out of an inning because of the errors committed behind him, point out: "Yes, your teammates missed a few that might have been outs, but that just gives you more opportunity to pitch and improve your game."

If none of this sinks in, you can turn up the heat a little and say: "If you're that great at pitching, why didn't you let your teammates take it easy in the dugout while you struck out the side?"

The bottom line is it takes a t-e-a-m to play The Game. As a manager, you can help your players work well as a team, and in a positive fashion, by consistently instilling the team approach as the season progresses.

# Smaller, Weaker, Slower, Luckier: A Pep Talk!

A lot of strange things can occur during a course of a season. That's sports, especially youth sports. Expect the unexpected. David can slay Goliath. Not often, perhaps; but much of success lies in positive thinking.

When one of my teams was an underdog preparing to play a top team in the regular season, I'd give a certain pep talk. The opponent usually was coached by a traditionalist. I'd sit my team down. "They're bigger, stronger, faster and smarter than us," I'd begin. (By "smarter," I meant that their manager knew The Game inside-out, upside-down and sideways, and that gave his players an edge.) "But who is luckier?" I'd ask. "Could be us this time."

Nine times out of 10, talent beats hard work in baseball, and in life in general. But "timing is everything." That's an important slogan. The baseball gods will gaze down on the teams who are working hard, and for that one time out of 10, smile benevolently on them. Hopefully, this will happen during the big game when your group of underdogs is up against the league studs. (Remember, "timing is everything.")

There's a lot of luck in baseball. A team that strands three runners during an inning and doesn't move a run across remains tied with a team that strikes out three times. A shot caught on the warning track is an out as sure as a ball tapped back to the mound for a toss to first. A blooper that drops over the second baseman's head is a base hit as sure as a line drive drilled past the shortstop.

In my pep talk, I'd emphasize that though we were smaller, weaker and slower, with a manager who isn't that smart, we could still have the baseball gods on our side. This just might be the big day for us.

Timing is everything.

THAT WAS HOW I'D motivate my underdogs against the traditionalist coaches whose teams were perennially the tops, and who'd drafted the best players and otherwise finagled their way into having an intimidating roster.

My pep talk always worked to focus my teams better and motivate them to work harder in The Game. It also made them feel better if they lost, because they knew they were trying for an upset and that luck — or intervention by the baseball gods — would have to make an appearance. If that extra boost didn't come, well, that was life.

Over my managerial career, my teams did wind up several times knocking off a favorite. One of my favorite games involved my Reds in the Babe Ruth League Main division (for ages 14 and 15) against the Red Sox. The Red Sox were a top team, and their manager was a perennial coach, a tobacco-chewing traditionalist with no children on his team at that time. He knew his stuff. He loved to win. He really wanted to win this game, because both of our teams were in contention for first place.

I had some fun in the week leading up to the game. I sent some photocopies of old newspaper clippings and photographs to the Red Sox manager about the history of the Cincinnati Reds against the Boston Red Sox, how the Big Red Machine had bested the Sox in the 1975 World Series by 4 games to 3. This irritated the traditionalist coach, but he did have a sense of humor. We talked on the phone about the upcoming game. We agreed it would be a good one.

The game already had sub-textual rivalries, since each team had an influx of high school junior-varsity players whose prep seasons had ended. My team's players were from Wooster High School, while the Red Sox had players from cross-town Galena High. Also, I had been at odds at the board level with the Red Sox chief, since I had lobbied for allowing all players who wanted to pitch to pitch, while he, the strict traditionalist, reluctantly supported the mandatory-play rule requiring two innings in the field and one at-bat per game for every player.

So, Game Day arrived. The game would begin at 8 p.m., under the lights. We hit the field for pregame warmups. I gathered my players together and gave my pep talk about "Smaller, Weaker, Slower, Luckier."

The traditionalist started his strongest pitcher, a well-known player in local youth-league circles. He was a big strong kid, and he shut us down in the first few innings. Meanwhile, the Red Sox jumped out to a lead of three runs.

Before the fifth inning, the traditionalist pulled his starter to save his quota of innings for future games. He was taking a calculated risk relating to his season's strategy. His team was now ahead 3-2. His relief pitcher was excellent. It seemed like a good move. There were only three innings to go in the seven-inning game, but there was the two-hour time limit to consider, too. An inning can be completed but a new one can't start after a certain time. A manager with a lead can slow the pace of the game down and walk off with a cheap win. Sometimes you'll find yourself in a position of hoping your team will make an out to end an inning so that you can get started in the next inning and keep the game going.

Our team was the home team. Yes, we were trailing, but I considered that with the game clock ticking away, if we managed to have a huge inning at the plate, we not only could take a lead, we could use up the remaining time and win. It didn't happen. Our bats went cold. What's more, our ace pitcher had to come out and our replacements gave up four more runs. So I made what became my most satisfying speech as a manager:

"Reds, we're down, yes. You're disappointed, yes. We wanted this game. But all we have to do is bat through the batting order to win. It's just that simple. We bat through the batting order, and we can win this game.

"Remember this: Fourscore and seven days ago, I had a dream. I've come here not to praise Caesar, but to bury him. So ask not what your team can do for you, but what can you do for your team. Now, let's go out there and win one for the skipper!"

This wouldn't be easy to do at this level of play. It's never easy to do. It was the bottom of the seventh. But batting through our order — and scoring seven runs — was all we had to do to win. We were the home team. Time was gone. In the previous inning we'd struck out three times. In fact, 13 of our 18 outs going into the seventh had been strikeouts.

But my Reds rose to the occasion. We started the frame at the cleanup slot in our order. We were down 7-2 after our opponents had gotten three runs in the sixth and one more in the seventh. But we got cracking. A couple walks, then a couple hits, produced a couple runs. Then another walk and a hit, and we were right back in it at 7-6 with no outs and the tying and winning runs on base. Then there were two strikeouts in a row, putting us down to our last out. We had runners at second and third. Tension filled the air.

Our No. 3 hitter was at the plate. He was overanxious, a player who'd just joined our squad after his high school season had ended. He was a great player. He'd caught the entire game, keeping our opponents from stealing. He'd handled our pitchers well. He'd accumulated two hits and a walk himself. But I knew he was tight and nervous. He wanted so badly to prove himself. He was fully capable of hitting the ball out — a walk-off home run — and wanted to end it that way

Here came the pitch. He took a tremendous, Casey-at-the-bat swing. Yet he only barely connected. No fence-buster this time. The ball flailed over the pitcher's head and landed between the mound and second base. The defense converged on the ball to try and make the final out at first.

But what do you know? The placement was just right. Our runners scored, and our hitter sped safely to first. We won the game. Jubilation!

The baseball gods were grinning.

# Notes:

# PART III

# POLITICS

*There is a phrase sometimes used to describe faculty affairs at our nation's colleges and universities: "Never have the politics been so fierce... and the stakes so low!"*

*The same applies to youth baseball — except how can you say the stakes are "low" to parents whose happiness, personal validation and sense of fulfillment in the course of a three-month season can wax or wane depending on Junior's fortunes at the plate, or if he starts at shortstop, or if he makes all-stars?*

*Or what dad's winning percentage is as coach? Or which team dad gets to manage? And at what divisional level? And with which team name?*

*The bones of contention are many, indeed. Such as: Whose team gets first crack in the batting cages at the fields, anyway?*

*HEY! WHO SECRETLY CHANGED THE COMBINATION ON THE BATTING-CAGE LOCK?!*

*It's human nature to be competitive, to like engaging in the give-and-take. And mostly, the take.*

*Sports, even at the youth levels, are a form of ritual combat. Emotions run high, including among spectators. People on and off the field become hooked on the adrenaline rushes. They become addicted to the emotional roller coaster. But the drama isn't book-ended by the first pitch and the final out of a game. Emotions are brought to the field before a game begins. And they aren't always resolved on the field.*

*Youth baseball has so many dimensions that the possibilities for conflict are infinite. The game is played at several different dramatic levels. There are the players trying to learn The Game. There are teams trying to beat each other. There are managers trying to beat each other. There are managers and coaches trying to settle personal scores with their counterparts, whether it's to even out a playing record, or retaliate for a dispute relating to the draft or other league business, or even best the other because of a business hassle or off-field romantic triangle.*

*Intrigue is a beast that can take strange forms.*

*There was one season when I stood accused by rival managers of corralling the division's supply of "GLMs." This acronym stood for: "good-looking moms." I was surprised, but amused, when a manager came up to me before our game and leveled that accusation.*

*I looked in the stands on my team's side of the field. Sure enough, there a bevy of beauties sat. I turned back to my critic and said, "Y'know, you're right! But I didn't do it on purpose!"*

*The GLM allegation became an issue to contend with. This may seem ridiculous to any parent who's never been involved in the highly temperamental crucible of youth-league baseball politics. My official response to the other board members, at the powwow to discuss the issue, was three-fold: 1) I hadn't done it on purpose; 2) the GLM factor did me no good, since my back was always to the stands, focused on my players and the game; 3) for the season I was the president, player agent, chief organizer and commissioner of baseball, "So stop the complaining and play baseball. Do it anyway you want ... next season."*

*The complaint receded into the distance and my archives, and The*

*Game went on.*

*But the best way to approach league politics, should you get involved, is to understand that people will complain about ANYTHING.*

*Yes, the politics are sure to be fierce, the stakes extremely steep... in the minds of those involved.*

# Notes:

# Totalitarianism in the League

S o why are the politics of youth baseball so frustrating at times?

For the simple reason that youth baseball is the closest most Americans will ever get to existing in a totalitarian bureaucracy. The lay of the land of youth leagues makes it virtually impossible to obtain the type of satisfaction most Americans are used to getting in a capitalist/consumerist society.

To begin with, youth leagues are set up by their national organizations according to geography. Like nation-states, they have distinct borders. Within a specific geographic area there can be only one league affiliated with its national organization (such as Little League). Therefore, a family that wants to participate in a specific youth organization (such as Little League) really has no choice of which league it can choose. The family's residence dictates its league; a player is forbidden from signing up to play in an alternate league. "Emigration," if you will, can only be done at the great expense or inconvenience of moving elsewhere, which is beyond the reach of most families, as well as a great deal of trouble. Even the option of declaring "grandma's" house as one's legal residence is not always practical, because snitches in the league — or the league's secret baseball police — will see that you are hunted down and brought to justice, which often means being reassigned to one's geographic league gulag, and then missing the entire season because the Catch 22 in this instance is that one's child is late for sign-ups.

Here's a second totalitarian aspect of youth baseball: For all practical purposes, there is no accountability for those in charge, other than the workings of their own consciences. Organizational rules are made to be bent, broken, reinterpreted — or ignored. Cliques of vying power bases develop within leagues as parents vie for teams and playing time for their children. Influence is typically gained from volunteer work or contributions done for "the party" (league) — for instance, helping with the landscaping, running the annual golf tournament (or skeet shoot) fund-raiser, composing the league newsletter, serving as webmaster for the website. But there is no quid pro quo, no "if you do this, you will receive that." There is no sure pass into the inner circle, no point scale to rely upon to curry favor. Authority is diffused among many members, and particularly concentrated among the president and other key officers (vice president, secretary-treasurer, and so on).

If a parent cares to have a grievance addressed — for example, why one person was given a team to manage, while another with more coaching time in the league wasn't; or why Junior wasn't drafted to a Main team because his registration was "misplaced"; or why the traveling budget to reimburse parents for an all-star team's tournament is not even half of what the previous year's team's was — it's a matter of tediously climbing the bureaucratic ladder: the league board, then the district representative, then the area administrator, regional administrator, and finally national headquarters. "Slow" doesn't begin to characterize the complaint process. While a grievance crawls its way up the fog-shrouded rungs (with steps upward and downward as the matter is considered and reconsidered), the parent can be branded a troublemaker and the family subjected to ostracizing — or worse — from the rest of the league. And what if the family finally prevails in pushing through a change that impinges upon a league's status quo — including a change that may benefit all the members of the playing populace, making for a better baseball experience for all? By this time, the player may be too old to continue in the league and benefit from the change.

Thus, most people shrug their shoulders and accept their youth baseball fate as whipped dogs in a totalitarian bureaucratic system, pliant and pessimistic, worn down by the sands of time, eroded and exhausted. Resistance is futile; retribution, swift and cruel. And if a disgruntled member and a cadre of fellow baseball idealists decide to revolt and form a competitive league, the hurdles of finding fields, securing insurance and funding and recruiting players willing to join the new cause are so daunting and numerous that it is a practical impossibility.

Therefore, silence and silent bitterness are the words of the day.

That is the macro level of the frustration.


AT THE MICRO LEVEL, the totalitarian nature is palpable.

A player is assigned to a team with no input into the decision. The manager and coaching ranks are predetermined, so for a parental outsider there is little chance of gaining anything but a small edge by offering to assist with the team (hitting grounders in practice, grooming the field before games, keeping the scorebook, and so on). Although all the players on the team are "equal," some are more equal than others because of their special connections, such as their dads being coaches. And a player can't switch teams (unless the board or player agent can be convinced, in which case the family must be prepared to rebut the "if we allow you to do this, we'd have to allow everyone" argument). Therefore, a player is like an indentured servant to his team for the season, and possibly two or even three seasons (depending on the division and the league's rules about returning players).

Playing time is the coin of the realm, and meted out by the bosses sparingly and arbitrarily. Since there are only nine positions in the field, and there are generally 12 (in Little League) and a few more than a dozen (in upper-age leagues) positions, favoritism prevails. Who gets to start? Who gets the most innings in the field? Who gets which positions? Who gets the most at-bats? Who bats where in the batting order?

The competition for playing time causes deep-down rifts and resentments among families on a team. But there is only one czar making the decisions — the team manager. And the manager has much more than just the player statistics to review and consider when concocting a lineup. The manager has his coaches' needs to consider, and on down through the pecking order. So the team concept is, by nature, just a concept, not a reality. The overall frustrations of families on a "team" cannot be relieved. It is no "worker's paradise," no utopia. It is a dystopia.

This is why you find players who should be helping one another on the team instead hoping for teammates to fail because it will improve their chances of having a good baseball experience. The fix is in and the odds are stacked against the ordinary participants by the league's inner circle, the powers-that-be and the nature of the structure of the teams. Youth-league baseball is a mirror of life in a totalitarian bureaucracy.

Thank heaven it is only a game, and that here in America we do not have to live that way in real life.

God Bless America.

# Respecting Boundaries

**M**ost of the national youth baseball organizations — all I can think of, in fact — have boundary restrictions for their leagues. The set boundaries are included in the charter-granting process, and they are important. They are intended to prevent zealous or unscrupulous managers and league officials from stacking teams with star players from distant lands to produce sure winners. Boundaries play a worthy role in keeping the playing field level — both for individual teams during a league's regular season, and for the summer interleague all-star cycle.

Bribery, corruption and much ill will have resulted from these boundary limits. Real estate agents, too, have probably benefited, since families whose lives revolve around youth sports have been known to up and move to homes within the borders of a favored league (with Junior somehow ending up on the team of the favored coach).

Part of the problem with enforcing boundary rules is that leagues aren't equal. Some of have more sponsorship support or affluent families, and therefore better facilities. Some, due to parental support and the great good luck of deep player talent, more consistently produce all-star winners. Since all parents (Rule No. 1 of the "Four Truths about Managing") want the best for their children, they always seem to want to get Junior signed up in the "best" league. In this league, I suppose, he will have a better experience that will build the child's self-esteem . . . or better prepare him for the major leagues. Who knows what goes through people's minds?

One of the most interesting aspects of boundary discussions is that parents are just supposed to know in which league their children are supposed to be playing. Unfortunately, most parents, particularly when they are first starting in youth baseball, are in kind of a fog. They don't really know the lay of the land, and tend to think that youth baseball organizations are more organized than they really are. Often, these parents don't even realize that boundaries exist. Time and again, players are signed up in a league, get off and running on a good, grand career . . . and the shoulder-tappers come around and tell them they are playing in the WRONG LEAGUE. Tears, fights and bad feelings have been the fallout from such happenings. Too bad for the players! They're jerked away from friendly surroundings and a team they're comfortable with, and forced to go prove themselves all over again in a new environment with new faces.

I've seen this happen time and again. A family gets bad information and is penalized for it. The more devious parents in our midst have resorted to lying, cheating and subterfuge to have their children play where they want to play. Using business addresses. Fake addresses. Pretending the kids are living with the grandparents who just happen to live within the league's borders. The "we just moved into the area" excuse. Providing addresses of streets that don't even exist. All these ploys come into play.

One sage of The Game said, "If you don't like the league you're in, join the board and make it a league that operates the way you'd like it to operate." Good advice . . . but it takes some time to work your way into things so you can have your say and get it done.

Stacked teams are nice if you're on one and your kid is one of the good players. Stacked teams are not so good for the rest of the players in the league. So get to know your boundaries and be certain you are playing in the right area. It is indeed a wrenching experience for a player to be torn from the arms of his teammates. (And it's not too happy for the parents, either.)

The disputes over players being in the wrong league, by the way, never seem to erupt over the status of not-so-good players. Their cases seem to fly under the radar. A league president, though, may end up having to make a ruling on some pretty strange cases.

A reform school happened to be situated within a local league's borders. Now, a reform school is populated with youths who are tough and hardened, and usually physically strong. All good characteristics for being good ballplayers. The dilemma, however, was whether these young inmates truly were eligible to play in the league. Most really didn't live at the reform school as permanent residents; they were just there temporarily away from their families. The exceptions were the chronic offenders who lived a majority of their time at the school. The jailhouse was more or less their home. The decision of the league president was: Sign 'em up, let 'em play if they could make practices and games. But keep an eye on the equipment.

THE ISSUE OF BOUNDARIES extends to the international stage. Zamboanga City Little League, representing the Philippines in the 1992 Little League World Series, took the title . . . but was later stripped of it for using players outside the team's particular league back home. It seems players were imported from as far as 400 miles away to help the cause. The team's officials claimed they'd been doing the same thing for eight years and no grand official in Williamsport had ever made an issue of it until the Filipinos won the championship. Those Americans: sore losers! (Little League's governing body awarded the title to Long Beach, Calif., the team Zamboanga had defeated in the championship game.) There was also some question about some of the defrocked team's players appearing to be stuck in a stage of perpetual youth: 12 years old and growing beards. Had their birth certificates been falsified?

(One way to win, I guess.)

With the boundary issue suddenly a hot topic all over the empire of Little League baseball after the 1992 scandal, the secret baseball police made the rounds in my area and checked on players' addresses. It seemed some 120 players were outside the lines in my league alone. I considered that with 15,000 Little Leagues dotting the globe, there could be more than 1 million players competing in the wrong leagues. (Today, by the way, there are 2.8 million Little League participants on the planet.)

When you get right down to it, I say: "Who cares?" Maybe stringently protecting league borders from alien players makes a difference for the all-star teams; but for the regular season, it's much ado about nothing. But I bet that by-the-book officials got their jollies peeking in all those windows looking to see who was home.

THE BABE RUTH LEAGUE in my stomping grounds some years ago allowed sign-ups by a few players from outside its territory. Unfortunately, the secret baseball police didn't discover this until less than a week before Opening Day. Two of the players were summarily removed from their teams and placed in the correct league. One player was left. The league had signed him up, made his dad a manager and taken his sponsorship fee ... but when the word came down from on high about his ineligibility, the league officers (other than myself) were hesitant to back him up, saying it might have an impact on postseason playing eligibility for our league. RIDICULOUS. The officers were reluctant to admit that it was the league that had made the mistake.

I was a fan of the player and his dad. After lengthy discussions, I sent my opinion to the powers-that-be. No response other than HE CAN'T PLAY IN YOUR LEAGUE.

A fine kettle of fish! But tucked away in the corner of our nation's legal system is a small but growing area of the law: baseball law. The result of the higher-ups' decision was that the player's father (you guessed it) hired a lawyer and secured an injunction that lasted until the baseball season ended, so Junior could play the game with the team his dad managed and with which Junior had practiced since sign-ups in February.

I just ask: Where are the reasonable people when you need 'em?

WHEN I WAS PRESIDENT of my friendly local Little League, a boundary issue that had simmered for a year reared its ugly head. Seems the league next-door to ours figured its all-star team could have gone all the way to the state championship if it had only had a couple players from our league who just happened to be living within the other league's boundaries. The other league felt it just happened to own these players. Wrong plantation, I guess. Well, why had those two stars played in our league, instead? Seems they had just signed up at the most convenient spot. There were no maps of league boundaries available. They just were interested in playing baseball. How were they to know?

Well, the officials from the other league were HOT. I worked out a compromise. Players currently signed up in a league, and their siblings, could play out their careers in the league of their choice . . . but no new players would be permitted to sign up in the wrong league. Also, from now on, all sign-ups would be conducted with MAPS at the ready, so that addresses could be checked at the time of sign-up to ensure they fell within the proper geographical limits. Participants would be told at the sign-ups that if they wound up in the wrong league and made an all-star team, the league they were supposed to have played in could have the players removed from the all-star roster.

Sure enough, maps were posted at the next sign-ups. Everyone was dutifully told about the penalties. When I informed one baseball mom of the fact that Junior would be ineligible if he made an all-star team, since he lived outside the area, she got ver-rry huffy! Well, if he can't play on all-stars then I don't want to be here! He's an all-star and he's gonna be on the all-star team!

She hit the road with her check and the copy of her son's birth certificate. Junior did, indeed, make the all-star team in the other league, and played darn well. There was a dedicated mom! And she didn't even have to hire a lawyer to protect her progeny's inalienable rights.

The Great Compromise worked well for a couple years. We didn't protest the other league's players, and they wouldn't protest ours. Then all hell broke loose again, thanks to the fiasco at the 1992 Little League World Series. The folks from the national organization had players everywhere checked, and many in our league were still found to be out of place due to the compromise and directed to sign up in the different leagues.

By this time I, like Cincinnatus, the great Roman temporarily appointed dictator, had returned to my farm to raise cabbages. Therefore, I wasn't in the middle of the enormous mess. It seemed like everybody was mad. Our league lost its president, a slew of managers and several board members. What was to be done?

The solution was elegant: The powers-that-be readjusted the boundary. That was a subject that had been so verboten when I'd brought it up during my reign that it couldn't even be discussed then. It helped that several substantial contributors to the leagues were able to have their children stay put. The end result was that instead of 120 displaced players, only a dozen or so saw their careers wrecked. Such are the Boundary Wars.

The lesson from all this is: Parents, be sure you know that you have signed up in the right league. If not, your child's career — not to mention endless headaches — hangs in the balance.

# Notes:

# Coping with Lawyers in Your League

T he first thing we do, let's kill all the lawyers," says the character, "Dick," a butcher, in Shakespeare's Henry VI, Act IV, Scene II. And at the other end of the literary spectrum, Reader's Digest's compendium of the funniest jokes to appear within its pages includes: "What's wrong with lawyer jokes? Lawyers don't think they're funny, and nobody else seems to think that they're jokes." There's a reason these lines are written.

However, lawyers have children, too, and therefore you will have parents in your youth baseball league who are lawyers. The difficulty that arises with this reality is that lawyers are adept — make that very adept — at the use of language in verbal and written forms. Much more so than the general population. That is lawyers' stock in trade in this world, and they are used to achieving "success." So be aware that regular people will always come up short in confrontations with such professionals of the word. A non-lawyer cannot out argue a lawyer.

The second difficulty with the legal crowd lies in the nature of the profession, in that there is, for the most part, no "right" or "wrong" in the daily workings of the trade, only a defensible position. When all this flows over into your league's affairs, and it seems someone might be trying to unreasonably garner a special benefit, boil it all down to its essence and take the time to do so by asking that all be explained in simple, simple words. Then let decisions about league matters flow up from there.

Simplicity and common sense are great levelers. Let them be the guide.

If your league is blessed with good lawyers among the players' parents, as mine was, the lawyers will be invaluable in helping document, chronicle and organize the wishes of those administering the league for the benefit of the greater whole. Some of our lawyers spent hours and hours and great sums of money helping our leagues stay organized. Their service was largely unnoticed and unheralded because it took place behind closed doors and in smoke-filled rooms.

If you are confronted with bad lawyers in your league, they will find their way behind those same closed doors and into those smoke-filled rooms, which will provide the cover for machinations that may not be benefiting the greater good.

If you smell a rat in such situations, I recommend this: Suggest that a resource-raising committee called "Barristers for Baseball" be formed, and give it specific goals. Lawyers are often rich and certainly have many connections in the community. See if the "cloaked-and-wigged" crowd will deliver something tangible to your league's resource mix, rather than just seek self-gratification. If so, and if nothing else, the suggestion will remind all that someone is watching what is going on behind the scenes.

Then abide by the slogan, "Money talks, voluble verisimilitudes walk."

And then stick to your guns . . . literally, if necessary.

You'll have nipped some problems in the bud, and you'll have a much more sane and satisfying baseball experience provided to all those participating in your league, and your league may even have garnered some additional resources.

# Successful Fund-raising (Make an Accountant the Treasurer)

L awyers in the league may place stress on the administrative functions of the board, but a certified public accountant can be a real plus.

A successful CPA is a perfect fit for the position of league treasurer — and not only for his prowess with numbers. A good CPA knows where the money is in the community; he has clients of his own who can afford to donate to the league (tax-deductible, of course), and he knows who else is a good prospect to approach. A league needs sponsors for the multitudinous expenses in staging a season of 500-plus games. A CPA can use his connections to help find sponsors willing to pay the annual fee to have the business name on an outfield banner, or contribute to the campaign to build a new field or put up lights, and so on. The CPA benefits, as well, because his canvassing for sponsors gives him an opportunity to do something good for the community as well as renew contact with clients or would-be clients in a worthy cause.

Other good candidates for treasurer are stockbrokers and bankers. Professional money handlers can be a blessing for a league.

EVERY LEAGUE HAS ITS annual fund-raisers, to augment income brought in from players' fees, managers' fees and snack-bar profits. The board determines its target goal, based on its budgetary needs, and often forms a fund-raising committee. Forming a sponsorship committee to make the funding of the league's operations a team effort works well, too, and those in the public relations and advertising businesses are ideal candidates to lead such a committee.

The major fund-raiser could be a golf tournament scramble, with coaches and dads signing up as four-player teams, each participant forking over $100. Or it could be a skeet shoot, or a dinner with a celebrity speaker. Then there are the smaller fund-raisers to augment the big ones. Sales of sweatshirts, T-shirts and caps. Raffle drawings. Door-to-door sales of coupon books. Door-to-door sales of candy bars (which never seem to raise enough money to be worth the effort). Sales at the snack bar of league programs that feature team rosters, schedules, and blank score sheets in the back, and contain advertising space purchased by sponsors.

All these fund-raisers are crucial to a league's existence. An annual budget for operating expenses is in the tens of thousands of dollars.

The CPA who was treasurer of our Babe Ruth league when I was involved instituted a hit-a-thon fund-raiser, which the league still uses more than a decade later. He put a great deal of effort into it initially, then each year it became easier to run. The event is great fun, and raises the necessary funds. In the hit-a-thon, players raise money from their families, friends and neighbors (or by standing outside supermarkets) by getting donors to sponsor the players either for a flat fee or for a donation based on how far the player hits the ball during the hit-a-thon at the fields.

One year, I augmented the hit-a-thon with an auction of baseball mementos donated to the league. I got baseball cards, old Los Angeles Dodger programs and signed baseball bats by calling up the Reno Silver Sox, a minor league team that played in the city then, and whose owner also owned a farm club affiliated with the Dodgers. It only took a few calls to the right players to get some valuable assistance. People want to help, but you have to do the asking.

A community recognizes the importance of youth sports, including baseball. So, in general, an honest, earnest effort to raise funds will be rewarded.

The only challenge then is to put a pencil to it — make sure the money is collected and accounted for, and spent wisely.

A professional bean-counter in the treasurer's post can be invaluable.

# Notes:

# Identifying Zealots and Traditionalists

M ost coaches you find in youth baseball are average guys, dads with one or more kids playing The Game in the younger age divisions. These "average dad" coaches do the best they can. They're not great baseball minds, although they may have played in high school (and, on rare occasions, in college or the pros). They're typically not in the category of *Jeopardy!* contestants, either. These coaches will move up through the age divisions with their children, and finally muster out of the mentoring ranks when their kids drop out of baseball or hit a level of play where more experienced coaches are needed, or already exist (such as high school).

The "average dad" category includes enthusiasts, obsessives, involved, marginally involved, laidback, clueless, and nul.

I was an "average dad." I liked to think of myself as an enthused populist — looking for opportunities to give moments of glory to all my players, instead of catering only to the coaches' sons and all-world players.

Beyond the average dads, there are two other categories of youth-league coaches. One category is "the zealots," and a second (somewhat related category) is "the traditionalists." You'll find that both categories are essential to the youth baseball experience, and that the zealots mellow over the years and the traditionalists never change.

The zealots are dead serious about The Game. Or, more precisely, about winning at The Game. They want their teams to win — and win every season. Youth baseball to them is more than a game; it's a way of life. Zealots may be dads with kids in the league. If you notice there is a coach whose team seems to finish first year after year as he moves up in the age divisions, you may well have spotted a zealot. But the zealot also may not have any kids in the league; he may have at one time, but after his offspring outgrew the league, the zealot stayed behind, wielding political influence in the league, getting to be a manager year after year.

Zealots are perennial coaches. They didn't necessarily make it beyond Little League as players themselves, and they don't necessarily know The Game inside and out, with all its subtleties and richness; but they do know the league rules, they know how to play politics, and they know the commonsensical ways in which to assemble a potent squad and put the right players in the right positions so their team will win, win, win. They play the diamond like a chess expert, with the players as their pawns, bishops, etc., to maneuver around.

Zealots scout out the talent coming up in the league and plot their draft choices from season to season, always driven to put together a championship nine. They draw a great deal of fulfillment from winning in youth baseball. They would not be happy without this pastime, this passion, this outlet for their yearning for diamond glory. The exciting action of youth baseball is their addiction.

Whenever a dispute arises with a zealot, he'll generally maintain that he's there "for the kids." That's whom it's all about: "the kids." You'll find, if you spot a zealot, that his team seems to practice more often than any other team ("for the kids," of course; not for his need for success), has better equipment (perhaps team jackets), and always seems to land the big, tall kid who's just moved into the neighborhood.

I once had an argument with a zealot about the date of a makeup game from an earlier rainout. The date had been set. Then the zealot got the board to reschedule the game. The effect of the rescheduling would be to allow his ace pitcher to start against us, since the delay would allow the required number of rest days between the pitcher's appearances.

I insisted on playing the game on the originally scheduled day. "Jeff," the zealot countered, "why are we arguing about this? It's for the kids."

"Well," I said. "It's for the parents, too, and our coaches and fans. They'll have to fit a new game date into their calendars if we move the makeup game back. And our players wouldn't mind having our best shot at winning the game, especially since the rainout date was determined when the original game schedule was posted."

That's about the only way you can counter a zealot's "it's for the kids" argument. You can say that it's for all the families, coaches and fans.

The zealot, by the way, had enough political pull to reschedule the makeup day . . . and get his best hurler on the mound.


ZEALOTS ARE NOT BAD. They are a necessary part of the scene. They often offer great volunteer service to the league, and my experience has been that without their off-the-diamond help, the youth baseball experience would be greatly diminished, and leagues might just collapse.

The measure of a zealot is whether he does that necessary behind-the-scenes work to make the league function. If so, great. Enjoy matching your team up against his, and instruct your players to play with "zeal," for they will be shown no quarter.

Traditionalists are walking encyclopedias of baseball. They know the training drills, the homilies, the rules, the patterns. They may have played many years themselves. They know the "right" way to do things. They don't compromise. Baseball is their religion, and they don't abide heretics with strange ideas (such as using tennis balls for batting practice — one of my innovations). I'm not sure that some of these traditionalists have even come around to accepting that some girls can play The Game. Metal bats were probably a tough enough pill to swallow. Many traditionalists still argue about the transition to the "live ball" era and the designated hitter. Any change is an offense to the integrity of The Game.

Traditionalists are also fun and essential parts of the baseball scene. Just don't let their knowledge and reactionary views get under your skin.

So, if you have a kid moving up through youth baseball, recognize what category the manager of your player's team falls into.

• If the manager is an average dad, know that Coach's Son Syndrome will prevail, and your kid's best efforts and natural talent may or may not be enough to secure ample playing time and opportunity. Expect some baffling decisions concerning the lineup over the course of a season, and surprising moves made during games. It's all part of the comedy-tragedy of youth baseball.

• If the manager is a zealot, know that your kids' team will practice a lot, that the pressure will be on the players to perform well in every game, and that the other teams' parents and players may not be very fond of your group. During board meetings, the zealot will challenge scheduling decisions, player eligibility on opponents' teams, and the like. During games, he'll generally seek any competitive edge (within legal norms) he can. He may ask the umpire to call time, then whip out the rulebook to appeal some procedural matter or hair-splitting interpretation of the rules. If a runner on the zealot's team reaches second, he may be instructed to look down and try to steal the catcher's signs, then relay them by tapping fingers on his helmet so that the third-base coach can advise the batter what pitch is coming next. And so on.

If your player is on a zealot's team, expect that your player's and your own knowledge will be greatly expanded on how the game of baseball is supposed to be played. And don't expect to help with coaching the team.

The postseason team party — if the team took the division championship — will probably include lots of nice trophies for the players. A zealot experience can be a good experience.

• If the manager is a traditionalist, your child will learn philosophies and techniques of The Game that have existed since the turn of the 20th century — at least. The speedy kid who can consistently get hits or draw walks is the "table setter" leading off; the No. 2 hitter can bunt or hit to any field; the No. 3 batter has the best average; the cleanup hitter has the most power. The only players let anywhere near the mound are the hardest throwers, and two or three of them will pitch the entire season, because they "need the work." All the clichés will prevail. The first baseman will be a lanky string-bean, and so on. For Christmas, buy this coach a nice pack of chewing tobacco. And again — as with the zealot experience — you'll learn plenty about how to properly play baseball. And also, again, don't expect to help with coaching the team.


IF YOU'RE MANAGING A team yourself, know that board meetings can get very interesting. The zealots will have their agenda. The traditionalists will have theirs. Try not to take it personally. One year in one of my leagues, they banded together in one camp and I was in the other camp lobbying hard for a minimum-play rule so that no kids would sit out entire games. That ruffled their feathers. And there was a second battle pitting them against me: the issue of funds donated to the league being spread out among all the teams so that all the players had good uniforms, not just the teams who'd raised the most money from their sponsors.

Managers facing zealots and traditionalists should also try not to take matters personally when disputes occur during games. If you're managing against a zealot, expect that he will try to stick it to your side any way possible — including by throwing the rulebook at you.

A game I'll never quite forget was one in which the other team's manager was a young competitive guy; a real zealot. The team I was managing was the Reds; his team was the Pirates. It was a close game, and during the course of the innings there were a number of discussions (disputes) regarding close plays, substitutions, insertions into the batting order, and the like. The end result was that the Reds came up on the short side of the scoreboard at the end. I wasn't very happy about it. So I decided to turn the tables on the zealot — and practice a little zealotry myself.

One way or another, I was going to sink that pirate schooner!

I saw my chance: The Pirates had played the game out of the home dugout (the one along the third-base line), even though they were the visiting team, batting first. So I protested the game on that basis.

I wrote up my complaint and took it to the league board (satirically, of course; sitting in the wrong dugouts is no grounds for protesting a game that should have been won or lost on the field). I even invented my own rule about the improper use of dugouts, and gave it some sort of official-sounding name: "The Reversed Dugout Infraction," or some such nonsense. To my surprise (and perverse pleasure about the foibles of overly serious youth-sport officials), my complaint was pondered over and discussed for a good hour before finally being rejected, since my fabricated rule couldn't be found in the rulebook. Naturally.

My petty protest was worth the effort for its amusement factor. It made the Pirates manager sweat out the process. He got a taste of reverse zealotry, which I hoped raised his consciousness, if only slightly. I also found that it doesn't matter if a rule isn't in the rulebook; just make up your own rule and it will still get its due (or undue, depending on whose side you're on) consideration from a board.

Well, that's one way to exact a bit of revenge on a zealot!


I MUST ADD THAT one year, when I, as manager, took an all-star team to postseason play, where winning is very, very important, I read the fine print in the rulebook and noted that it was permissible to put coaches on the roster who had not necessarily coached in that division that season. I met the cutoff deadline, and "enthusiastically" recruited some zealots and traditionalists to help me.

They were thrilled to have the opportunity. I was happy. Our players got the best possible instruction for the tournament. We did well, thanks to their help, and had fun, too.

# Notes:

# Trafficking
# in Human Flesh

A fter I joined the board of my local Babe Ruth League, I took aim at a grossly unfair situation. Unlike in Little League, there was no national mandatory-play rule in Babe Ruth. Some of the lesser talents could sit the bench through entire games.

I decided that Little League's minimum of one at-bat and two innings in the field was warranted in Babe Ruth. Why treat players just as bodies, or numbers? Why not give them respect as players who signed up to actually play the game?

I managed to get enough board members to go along with me on this issue, despite the opposition from the two usual camps: the zealots and the traditionalists. The mandatory-play rule was instituted in our Babe Ruth League.

I'm proud to say that the mandatory-play rule stuck the next season, and the ones after that, even after I left the league. Seems the board members forgot that it wasn't a national rule. Such is the power of inertia!

The beneficiaries were players who now enjoyed the right to play. They were no longer slaves to the bench.

IN LITTLE LEAGUE, BABE Ruth League and other youth baseball organizations, off-season trading is usually permitted. If the managers agree, a player can jump from one team to another. Teams at the Main division level retain players from one season to the next until those players reach the age limit. But off-season trading means players can move around.

I thought it was a terrible policy. Off-season trading meant that a zealot could take a fancy to a player on another team and then work on that player's parents to get them to agree to send Junior to the zealot's team. All kinds of persuasion can be used, from promises of more playing time, to criticism of the player's current manager and chances for success on his current team. Then the family can pressure their player's manager to release Junior or swap him for a player on the zealot's squad (a player, of course, whom the zealot doesn't want.)

I saw how permitting trades can lead to teams unfairly stacked with talent. And I saw how the custom can cause all kinds of internal dissension among the league's managers and parents.

Off-season trading in the Babe Ruth League I was involved with was terrible. One team's manager would spend the winter months building and rebuilding his roster, making calls to other managers, until he'd have a lineup of all-stars. This squad would be the de facto, pre-designated all-star team for the year, and spend the season beating up on the other Babe Ruth teams as a preliminary to the summer tournament.

Restoring parity to the league meant getting rid of the off-season trade rule. I argued my point to other board members, saying we needed to put an end to "trafficking in human flesh."

This verbal spin did the trick: I got this rule change through the board.

THERE WAS ONE OTHER flesh traffic I set my sights on ending.

In Little League, managers at the Main division who'd ended up with an empty slot — due to a player getting injured, moving away or dropping out of the league — would scout the Minor teams and pick out a talented player to bring aboard.

But this policy was unfair to the player who'd already bonded with his

Minor team's players and coaches, and who was having a great time excelling in his division, but now would have to be a bench player on a Main team. It was unfair to the player's family who were enjoying Junior's success and who'd already gotten used to the Minor team and its families. And it was unfair to the Minor team whose season was now wrecked, having lost a star player.

As a member of the Little League board, at my prompting we devised a new policy: the Player Pool. At draft time, five players were designated in each of the Minor and Farm ranks as replacement players in case openings occurred in the division above them during the season. The players were ranked in order from one to five. Their parents were notified. In this way, players and families were pre-warned about a possible mid-season call-up. Also, managers knew whom they could call up if needed.

Now, everyone was happy. Except, perhaps, for the flesh merchants.

# Notes:

# Demands Never Cease

A league president receives requests of one form or another from just about every team manager. The president can't please everyone, but has to remain diplomatic and do his best. The pressure comes with the territory.

One season, when I was president of my Little League, I had a particularly demanding manager. The ones who want the most are the ones who pay you a visit before the season. It's a smart thing to do, since the president is the one who runs the board meetings. So if you want to put the fix in, you get to the ear of the president.

This particular manager was a good coach. But he was a zealot. (For a definition of "zealot," a term, such as "traditionalist," that I use frequently in this book, refer to the previous chapter in Part III, "Identifying Zealots and Traditionalists.") When I met with him, he had a long list of requests, indeed.

I thought to myself, "This is a very aggressive person." As a personal secret experiment, I decided to see how far someone would go if I didn't flat out deny any of his requests. Would he begin to ease off and show appreciation for my efforts to accommodate him? Or would he keep coming up with new demands?

His first request was for getting all of the players he wanted on his team. He had his eyes on certain players moving up into his division, as well as players whose families wanted to be with his team. His point was: during the draft, I, as president, could tell the other managers "hands off" this player or that player.

Instead of telling him that would be impossible, I said, "Well, OK, let's see."

His next request was for getting his team's name changed.

I said the board would to have to discuss that, so let's see what was possible.

He wanted new uniforms.

Let's see what our league budget can afford, I said.

He wanted the newest equipment.

Let's see what's available and what can be done, I said.

He wanted his own special choice of coaches, instead of selecting from a pool of parents who'd put in their time and built up league points.

I'd have to review the list and see if the board supports it, I said.

He wanted a preferred practice and game schedule to accommodate his and his coaches' business calendars.

We could look at the division and field schedules and see if the other managers can work with him, I said.

Anything else?

There was one more thing:

"I want respect from the league. I don't want anyone talking about me behind my back."

"I'll do what I can do," I said. "But you're the one with the history, not I. So we'll just do the best we can."

It was fascinating to see how far somebody would go in asking for things if you, as president, didn't cut him off at some point with a firm no.

Now I knew:

He wanted everyone to love him.

But, of course, the most demanding, egocentric and prickly tend to be the least loved.

A conundrum.

TEAM MANAGERS RECEIVE ENDLESS demands, too, during a season. That's one of the reasons I instituted the Dream Sheets (as discussed in Part II).

Sometimes a manager will run into the player who insists on starting every game, playing every inning, getting every at-bat, hitting where he wants in the order, playing the position he wants. He never wants a substitute going in for him. He sulks unless he gets his way.

When the ball comes to his part of the field, he wants to field it — not a player who may be better positioned. When he's up at bat, he wants to be swinging away, not taking a pitch or bunting. When he's on base, he wants the green light to steal, not stay put to be moved over by the next batter.

What I did as a manager was advise this sort of player, and his parents, that baseball isn't the game for him. He needs to take up a new sport, and it's called "tennis."

In tennis, every ball that comes to your side of the court, you hit it and it's your fault if you miss it and your glory if you hit back a winner.

Tennis is a much better sport for the super-egotistical type of person. It will better meet his needs.

Baseball's a team game. You can't catch every ball, bat every time. The action has to be parceled out among the other players.

I only made that suggestion a few times in my managerial days. The players got the message.

Some even took up tennis!

# Notes:

# The Smoke-filled Room

The smoke-filled room — the room where a league's officers and board members convene, sometimes out of sight and sound of the families and players — has its share of dramatic moments during the course of a season.

Principally, these moments occur during the meetings setting up the season and schedule, the assigning of managers and coaches, the parceling out of teams, the setting up of tryouts, the draft — and, at the conclusion of the season, the all-star selections. The meetings with the draft and the vote on all-stars are typically closed to the regular league membership, but the other board meetings are open to all, and I heartily recommend that parents interested in a league attend a few of these open meetings, just to get a look at the work it takes to put on a season, and get a feel for the politics of youth baseball. And there you'll meet new people. Many of whom are nice to know.

If you attend one of these meetings, observe and listen. You do not have to volunteer, so don't, unless you can fulfill your responsibilities. Some league officers prefer a small board. I prefer a large one, so that the duties and chances for administrative glory are parceled out among many people. The downside is that it is difficult to run meetings with 20 or 25 board members, as everyone often has something to say. But an organized agenda and a president's willingness to allow discussion while maintaining a firm hand on the gavel makes the meetings useful and a nice social experience for attendees.

Since the game of baseball draws people from all walks of life, I've enjoyed seeing how such a diverse group can come together to successfully put on a season. I've been on boards for which meetings were held weekly. But when

I became league president, I opted to do things my way, with three meetings and an open-door policy and telephone line sufficient to put on more than 500 baseball games for the season. If you end up as a league president, you will choose the approach you deem best; but do know that communication with the participants in the league is key. Most leagues now maintain websites by which to parcel out news updates, schedules and other information. This is a fantastic development.

Anything can happen at a board meeting, especially if the beer is flowing, and many baseball people do seem to enjoy a glass, pitcher or keg. This certainly heightens interest during the discussion periods!

IF YOU'RE A PARENT considering getting strongly involved with a league by managing or coaching a team, know that the job is always a challenge. Also know that you may need to start on the ground floor, when your child is in Tee Ball. It's fairly easy to get a team at that introductory level, but the higher up the age and ability ladder you go, the tougher it is to get a team, or even get a chance to set foot on the diamond as an official coach (typically there are two assistant coaches assigned to a manager, although there can be many unofficial coaches wearing team jackets and helping out during practice and pregame drills). In many leagues, coaches build up points based on their previous participation, and those with the most points get precedence. Politics, too, play a part; whom does the league president like best? Rationalizations for why one parent is passed over and another given a team to manage are as creative as the human mind is imaginative.

The jockeying for teams usually begins with schmoozing at the ballpark with the other adults, especially league officers, interested in coaching a team. There are generally two camps involved with this process: the zealots/

traditionalists, whose children may already have finished their youth-league play, but who stay with a league year after year; and the average dads/stepdads who are actually going through the baseball gauntlet with their sons or daughters. The zealots have the upper hand because they are ever-present, year after year, and do much to keep the league running. They also seem to be intent on victory on the diamond, and as such are eyeing the talent and recruiting the parents of promising players to put Junior on their team, either by having the parent be a coach and thus having the young star assigned to the team as a coach's option, or by prearranging with the parent to have Junior be a draft pick (the parent can flatly tell other managers that Junior will ONLY PLAY for the zealot's team).

The parents/stepparents who want to manage generally have enthusiasm for baseball and also want to help their children enjoy the experience. These new would-be managers typically team up with friends from their social life or professional life to be coaches. They should know that sometimes it takes several years of service to a league, in the form of volunteerism and board membership, to make it through the candidate process and be awarded a team. But openings do occur. A manager from the previous season can lose out on the chance to manage again if he had a bad season that included many complaints to the board from parents, umpires or other managers, or if league politics just happen to fall the wrong way for a season. (Selection of managers is an interesting process, and it can be worth it to throw your hat in the ring at one time or another, just to go through it and see how serious people become about these things.)

Now it is on to the smoke-filled boardroom. Managerial candidates are asked to submit their names and desire for a team in a certain division, along with their probable coaches. Much give-and-take ensues, and the board votes, parceling out the managerial spots for the upcoming season. Who gets which team? The managers with the most longevity or influence get the team names with the most local panache (for example, the A's or Giants, if the team is from northern California or northern Nevada). The lesser managers pick up the remaining names (the selection is usually limited to the uniforms the league has in stock, unless a manager has a wealthy sponsor who can pay for a batch of new uniforms, or a set of uniforms has outlived its three- to five-year lifespan and new ones must be ordered anyway).

In most leagues, a manager is responsible for finding a sponsor for his team, or paying the sum himself. So if you pass the candidate's process and are awarded a team, for $500 or so YOU CAN OWN YOUR OWN BASEBALL TEAM!

THE NEXT BIG STEP is the draft. Even though all players who sign up will be assigned to a team, at the upper levels they must pass tryouts and be drafted. Not every player is put in the draft, though. There are the coaches' options and returning players (typically the Main-division teams retain age-eligible players from the previous season) assigned to the designated teams. The rest of those eligible for Minor and Main teams because of age or experience are put in the draft. (Of course, some of those who are in the draft already are destined for certain teams, given the behind-the-scenes deal-making.) The draft by the Minor and Main coaches will be held in rounds, with the teams in each division rank-ordered, often according to their previous season's finish. (The team with the worst record goes first, and so on.)

The preliminary to the draft is the tryouts. These typically take place over a weekend day, with a makeup day if necessary. Players are organized according to ages and given numbers. Managers and coaches stand around with clipboards and printouts of the players' names and numbers, and rate the players on a scale of 1-5 (or whatever) as each takes a turn swinging at three or so pitches, fielding grounders and pop-ups, and running the bases. The rating sheets are HIGHLY CONFIDENTIAL. There is space to make additional comments and notes about the players and even their parents (some are potential troublemakers). Managers don't want these sheets falling into the wrong hands.

With the rating sheets in hand, the managers and official coaches enter the smoke-filled room. The only other people present are the president, who runs the league, and the player agent, who keeps track of returning players and the team rosters as they fill up with draftees.

The draft is actually a fun time, as the managers try to put together competitive teams as well as satisfy their friends and relatives who want to be on their teams. There are hoots and hollers and plenty of commentary as opinions on selections are verbalized. The beer flows.

As a manager, you will live with the team you put together for the next 90 days or so, so your judgments can land you in baseball hell or yield a very satisfying experience. As the draft progresses and nears its conclusion, some of the lesser talents find their way onto teams, and there inevitably will be an extra player or two or three who must be sent to a lower division, while designated as a substitute to replace a roster opening if an injury or no-show occurs at the upper division.

Then it's all wrapped up, and the season is ready to begin. The next time the smoke-filled room fills with drama will be when the season is in its final two weeks. This session will be very intense, because it is when all-star teams are selected for the postseason tournaments against the best players from other leagues. This is a very interesting process and can leave scars for years to come on managers and league officers, players and parents.

We'll leave that topic for another chapter, "The Anatomy of All-Stars."

# Notes:

# The Anatomy of All-Stars

The most serious and competitive youth-league families are always looking beyond the regular season toward the selection of all-stars. Sometimes it seems as if Junior is playing not for his regular-season team, but to rack up the stats to put himself in position to join the elite squad that will represent the league during the summer tournament.

For some players, and/or their parents, making all-stars is central to their sense of self-validation. In every league there are a few dads whose behind-the-scenes politicking to get their sons on all-stars is tenacious, unremitting, and even shameless. That's how important all-stars is to them.

Coaches' sons, naturally, have the inside track in the all-star voting among managers in the smoke-filled room as the regular season winds to a close. Typically, a league's all-star team will have the best eight or nine players in the league, with the remaining slots filled with lesser talents who have the political connections, or who are just good enough to get selected but aren't deemed as threats to claim starting positions, or as potential problems as whiners or sulkers for having to sit the bench. They're there just to round out the squad.

Anyway, the politicking for all-stars is fierce. The jockeying by candidates starts even before the season begins. Players with all-star visions want the chance to shine on their regular-season teams, and therefore need the playing time and the prestigious spots in the batting order and on the field. They need to be promoted as stars by their manager. Often, a player's dad will consult with the manager before the season to get this point across. (The proper, non-confrontational way to do this is to ask, "What chance does Junior have for making all-stars this year?") As for the coaches' sons, they're already assured of the necessary exposure. Perhaps the most unfair example of a manager unwilling to promote a good player is when the manager believes the player will compete too much with a coach's son for a precious slot on all-stars. This happens from time to time.

In most leagues, the managers nominate players from their teams as all-star candidates, submitting a list toward the end of the season after asking potential nominees whether they're interested in committing the time to all-stars. (Often, the players in the league are allowed to fill out advisory sheets of their top candidates; these sheets are collected and forwarded to the board, and can have a bearing on how managers vote.) But it's mostly up to the player to get himself nominated, by earning it. Earning it means having a good season. The numbers in the scorebook will be used in the smoke-filled room when the voting begins. In fact, managers typically tabulate their candidates' numbers — batting average, earned-run average, and the like — and bring them to the closed-door meeting. They'll also bring the season scorebook so they can refer to specific games. If one manager is arguing for a player on his team to make the all-star cut, another manager may leaf through his scorebook to see how that player did against his team. Ensuing debates can grow lively, indeed!

The politics can get quite fierce, and often the fix is already in on many if not most of the candidates. The board usually chooses the manager of the championship team to manage the all-stars, and he'll have tremendous influence on the voting. He and his clique of coaches (he gets to choose his assistants) will confer in private well before the voting meeting and decide on their choices. There will be few slots left unspoken for before the meeting. So any small advantage a player can gain should not be ignored. Hopefully, a worthy candidate doesn't have a parent whom the all-star manager and coaches consider a potential problem — a complainer, a meddler, or just an ill-tempered being. A parent problem can get a player blackballed in the smoke-filled room.

MY NO. 2 SON, Charlie, had the goods to make all-stars. But talent, of course, is not enough. As a manager, I knew the battle that lay ahead to get him on the squad. I inadvertently learned that it "paid to advertise." That is, make him stand out more in the minds of the other teams.

Charlie needed corrective lenses to have 20/20 vision. I took him to the optometrist and had special sports glasses made. Those heavy, hard-plastic, goggle-like glasses did the trick. Everyone in the league recognized Charlie. The other players didn't necessarily know him by name, but they knew he could play, and on their advisory ballots they wrote comments like, "The kid with the big glasses."

He made the team that year on the basis of the player vote. Another season, he had better stats, but wore contact lenses and subsequently got fewer player votes, although still making the team. It definitely had "paid to advertise" in that prior year. It works in reverse, too. If you play poorly, you can advertise yourself out of business!

So if a player really wants to be on an all-star team, he should consider wearing an armband, or pulling his socks up high — or something that makes him stand out. I remember a player in Babe Ruth League who wore red batting gloves. He was a good player, and deserved to make all-stars. But he also stood out. Everybody remembered the kid with the red batting gloves.

It pays to advertise. Keep it in mind.

IN THE SMOKE-FILLED room, all the players' names are written on a chalkboard or grease board. The moderator (the president, player agent or other designated league officer) passes out paper ballots. The managers all write down the names of their 12 choices. The ballots are collected. The moderator marks the number of each player's votes next to his name. Players with no votes have their names crossed off. Other players will make the team on the first ballot, garnering enough votes. In some systems, the first seven or eight players in player voting are automatically on the squad.

Then the fight is on over the remaining names, and it can get cutthroat. There will be much debate, discussion and disputes over certain players. There is an implied desire to include at least one player from each team; that means the best player on the worst team has a shot. And players who'd made all-stars in previous years may have some sentimental voices in their favor. Then there is the matter of the children of parents who've contributed strongly to the league.

The room can grow very tense, with emotions quite brittle. A manager may emphasize that his candidate has great versatility and can play a lot of positions. A manager may tout the player's batting average against the best pitchers in the league. A manager may praise the player's parents as nice people who haven't voiced any complaints at all during the season and always helped out at practices and in the snack bar.

Some managers will deliberately not vote for a good player out of spite or envy, or to manipulate the ballots by voting for a lesser player who will eventually wash out of the balloting, leaving more room for the player the manager favored.

Another set of ballots is passed out for voting on the remaining names. If needed, there will be a third and a fourth round.

During one all-star vote at the Babe Ruth level, a player had been nominated whose dad was a big, longtime sponsor of the local Little League and, now, the Babe Ruth League. But the player himself had gotten progressively worse over the years, although he had made all-stars every year in Little League. He'd fallen victim to the maturity trap. Others had gotten their adolescent growth spurts and increased muscular power, but he was still just a peach-fuzzed young fellow who knew how to play, but was frustrated in execution by those bigger, stronger, faster earlier maturers. Now, by comparison, he was really just an average player, and he had a mediocre season. Familiarity can breed contempt, and some of the managers in the room were nursing grudges of one kind or another against the player's dad. These managers now saw their chance to stick it to him by keeping his son off of all-stars. I could see it coming.

I thought to myself how sad it would be for this young player to end his playing career as not an all-star. He truly did love his baseball and baseball glory. So I voted carefully on the first two ballots, making sure to choose a few names of players who wouldn't end up making the cut — therefore leaving slots open toward the end, when I would vote for the player in question.

The strategy worked. He made the cut. I was happy for his family. His dad had been dedicated for so long to youth baseball. It was nice to see it end for them on a high note. (What's more, the player ended up having a decent all-star tournament.)

AFTER THE VOTING IN the smoke-filled room concludes, the roster will be filled. But the team isn't finalized just yet.

The manager will get on the phone afterward, call each player's family and ensure the player is still available for the intense commitment of time to the team, including a heavy practice schedule, travel to the district tournament and possible travel to the state tournament — or even the regional competition, if the squad makes it that far.

Some players may decline at this point, and the manager will begin calling players who'd received fewer votes and were designated as alternates. Finally, the all-star team is complete.

The happiest moment for most all-stars is when they get the call from the manager congratulating them and telling them they've made it. Then comes the hard work — long practices while other kids are enjoying their summers, relegation to certain positions (usually not the ones the player had on his regular team), a possible pigeonholing in a substitute role (the minimum-play rule is usually skimpier than in league play, meaning either one at-bat or one defensive inning in the field). And then there's the pressure of the games themselves, with the bleachers packed with supporters for both sides, the cars in the parking lots emblazoned with colorful painted messages across their windows, an announcer on a public-address system calling out the pregame lineups, the coaches nervous, strict and overbearing — not shy about haranguing a player who's not paying attention, or who makes a mental lapse or error in the game.

In all-stars, you gotta win.

Any excitement over a victory is short-lived, because there's the next game to think about. Even winning the district tournament is grounds for only a brief celebration. The state tournament looms.

Finally, all-stars ends, the bright uniforms are returned (but the nifty jacket and cap are kept as souvenirs). Hopefully, it was an interesting experience, and there were some great moments to retain in memory.


COACHING ALL-STAR TEAMS IS different from coaching teams during the regular season. Winning is much more top-line, and for good reason.

You're playing for the glory of your league against the best squads from rival leagues. The families involved with your team are sacrificing precious summer time for the sake of long daily practices and, then, the intense tournament play, usually at a field complex far from home. You're trying to make it to the state tournament — and beyond, if the baseball gods smile on you. And during the district tournament, the state tournament (if you make it that far) and the regional (ditto), if you lose two games, you're out. It's double-elimination. What's more, if you lose a game and end up in the loser's bracket, it's extremely difficult to make it all the way to the championship round.

As if this isn't enough stress for a manager to contend with, doling out the playing time is even more problematic than on a regular-season team. The all-star rosters at the Little League level contain 12 to 14 players, and each one is very good and was, no doubt, a full-game player on his regular-season team. The can't-win situation for the manager darkens the door often, but there is no choice but to grin and bear it and make the best calls he can to serve the players and coaches, parents and fans.

One year in an all-star tournament I managed what I thought was going to be a competitive team. It was. However, to have a chance at taking the title it was necessary for me to tighten things up on the playing-time front and field the best players we had for most of the innings. Frictions naturally occurred. One player sat in the dugout within my earshot, talking to himself incessantly: "I can do it. I know I can do it. I wish coach would put me in. I can do it. I know I can."

This monologue carried on deep into what was a very close game. It was going to be tough to get everyone in. Then we got ahead and the situation looked good. I felt some relief. Disregarding my normal rule of not promising players specific field assignments or batting opportunities in advance, I decided to give this poor fellow the nod and tell him that he could take my son's next at-bat. The player was extremely happy and began to prepare for his chance. His background chatter stopped.

Well, baseball being what it is, the other team came back, and sure enough

— when my son's turn came to bat, it was a critical point in the game. I would have much preferred to have my son face the hurler, a very tough one, as that was our best chance to do something positive. However, I'd made the promise to the player on the bench and he had his helmet and batting gloves on, his bat at the ready, and was warmed up.

What to do?

I harkened back to a game in the distant past when I was on the sidelines, just a spectator. The coaches had told a bench player to get ready because he was going to get a chance to bat. The player assembled the tools of the trade and prepared to face the pitcher. He walked toward the batter's box from the on-deck circle, swinging his bat and readying to get his cuts in. It had become a tense situation in a close game. The coaches huddled together and conferred, and then one shouted to the player, "We've got a chance to win this game. You need to come back here so we can have (So-and-So) bat."

The player was disappointed and embarrassed, to say the least! In those days there was no mandatory-play rule, and this player had sat on the bench for a couple games without seeing any action, and then the coaches had slammed him that way! A truly miserable thing to do, and a lesson for me as to how I would NOT treat my players on teams I might manage or coach.

With that sad baseball image in my mind, I spoke to my bench player and explained that this was a tough situation against a very tough pitcher, and did he want the at-bat — or did he prefer to wait until another time? I also told him that because this was a tight spot, it was his chance to be a hero, but it would be difficult. He said he wanted to bat. I told him to take his best shot and do his best. I had confidence he would give a 100 percent effort.

"Good luck," I said.

Well . . . of course it didn't turn out storybook style. The pitcher mowed him down, and all that could be done was to console him that he would have another day and life would go on. He did, and it did.

As for me — well, the manager can't win. That's a given. The bench player was upset about striking out, my son figured our team would have had a better chance with him at the plate, my coaches were mad because we hadn't put our best available batter at the plate at a critical time, and the player's parents were angry with me for putting their son in that position.

So all you can really do as a manager is try your best to hand the players a chance or two for some glory — and hope for the best.

We lost the game. It put us in the loser's bracket. But the bright side was that we got to play more games in that tournament (having to win a number in a row to try to make it to the championship bracket), and more of our players got to see action.

# Cap Night Banned

The Little League I was a part of had a tradition called Cap Night. A high school gymnasium would be rented for a night and all the players, from Tee Ball through Main, and their families would show up. Teams would be called to the floor, one by one, and players would receive their caps for the season.

I'd endured Cap Night for a few seasons with my sons. The event was noisy, chaotic, took up a lot of time and seemed to serve no useful purpose. Players could get their caps when their uniforms were issued at their team's parent meeting. I asked a league officer why Cap Night existed.

I was told it had been the league's biggest fund-raiser.

That surprised me. I asked how much money recent Cap Nights had raised.

Well, they hadn't raised anything recently, the officer said. But in the old days there used to be a carnival with ball-throwing games and the like, and Cap Night raised money by selling game tickets. However, it took a lot of effort to get the carnival going, so now they just used Cap Night to pass out the caps.

I suggested that Cap Night be banned from then on.

Blasphemy! My idea was quickly rejected.

But a few years later, I was president of the league, and took another shot at fooling with tradition.

"Let's just try banning Cap Night for this season, while I'm the president, and if it's a disaster, next year you'll have a new president and the new president can reinstall it," I said.

"We'll put a good effort, instead, into having a good Opening Day this year, and we'll let the managers pass out the uniforms and caps at the mandatory parent meetings."

The board went along with me, on an experimental basis.

Cap Night never was revived.

All league presidents should not be afraid of doing a little trimming during their turn in the top seat. Some things work and some things don't. Some traditions need to be preserved. Others deserve to die.

# Having a Field Day

F ield Day is indispensable to getting a youth baseball league ready for the season. The sprinkler systems must be reactivated, power turned on, snack bar swept and scrubbed, storage shed put in order, fields raked and trimmed with gopher holes and puddles filled in, pitching mounds built back up, bleachers painted, roofs refitted on the dugouts, scoreboards and lighting systems checked, restrooms and scorer's booths readied.

And the entire field complex must be arranged for the Opening Day festivities, during which league officers greet the 1,000 or so players and families who turn out, the previous year's all-star teams are congratulated, teams are introduced and their team photographs taken, games played, and sweatshirts, T-shirts and raffle tickets sold.

In my league, the most committed board members and parents were the only ones showing up for Field Day and doing serious work instead of just standing around talking for a couple hours. When I was president I required that all managers and coaches attend, and saw to it that reminder calls were made so no one "forgot." I also asked the old hands what specific tasks needed to be done. Therefore, I had my list ready ahead of time. Later, rules were added that each team had to be represented by at least one volunteer, and a failure to participate resulted in the loss of a top-round draft choice when players were selected. This worked wonders!

The people who show up to help out do want to contribute, but they need direction. So the administrator in charge of Field Day needs to be organized.

That's the recipe for a productive Field Day. Lots of bodies, and lots of organization. People can feel a great sense of community when they get together to get things done at the baseball field. I can still remember how good I felt in my early days in the league when we, together, rolled out the sod to cover the new T-ball field. It's still there. Snakes and all.

I MIGHT ADD THAT the right recipe for a productive board is in the numbers, too. When I was president we had 20 board members plus some advisory members. That meant there were more than two-dozen people among whom to delegate tasks.

We got an awful lot done that way!

Many leagues have smaller boards, because it's easier for officers to work with just a few personalities instead of a room full. But there is so much work involved in running a league of 500-plus players, putting on 500-plus games in the spring and fall seasons, that the more volunteers handling the many tasks, the smoother things go.

And the less exhausted the president will be when his or her term is up! And the easier it will be to recruit a new president. Finding a successor is one of the most important tasks of a league president.

# Fall Ball

Some of us coaches in Reno Continental Little League were sitting around late one spring talking about how sad it was to have the regular youth baseball season in Reno have such cold and miserable weather, with only about two weeks of good, warm baseball temperatures at the end of the season. (The joke was that spring doesn't officially begin in Reno until the day after Little League ends.) Then the lucky all-star players go off for a month or two of more baseball during summer, while all the other players have to go home with gloves under arms and wait until the next spring. Meanwhile, the late summer and early fall in Reno are glorious.

Wouldn't it be nice to have an extra baseball season in the fall?

It made perfect sense. I was heavily involved in the league by now, and had been voted into the president's chair for the next spring's season. I volunteered to get the paperwork together for what we decided to call "Fall Classic Baseball."

First order of business was getting the go-ahead from Little League, Inc. Our fall league would have to operate under our Little League's license, for insurance purposes. We got the OK. (Turned out that a few leagues around the country already were using a fall format.)

Next order of business was reserving a city-owned ballfield. The problem was that youth soccer and football leagues took over the fields that time of year. But I formulated a strategy. I applied to the city for eight lighted playing fields and 20 practice fields. As expected, that caused a conniption fit among parks-department officials. So I moved to the next step: compromising.

Our league was awarded one lighted playing field. And that was all we really needed for having a great baseball experience.

Now, what about a schedule? There would be only eight teams in the league, all in one division. Each team would play three games a week but have no practices. Players would just come to the field, have pregame fielding and batting practice in the cages, then the game would begin.

It was workable. It turned out to be great.

The plan was resisted by some on the board out of fears that the equipment would be worn out, and that the fall season would lose money. However, I sold soda pop for $1 a can out of an ice-filled garbage container, kept in the back of the converted Checker taxicab my wife drove as a passenger car, to pay for the umpires, and the fall league was a financial success, too.

It was obvious to me that fall baseball would have to accomplish several things to interest enough players and coaches and make it a meaningful experience. What appealed to me most was giving the 12-year-old players who'd finished their final spring in Little League one last chance for glory on the small ballfield before moving up to the Babe Ruth League with its larger diamond. The 12-year-olds (some who would reach age 13 over the summer) would not only be older, but bigger and stronger than they were when they played in spring. Therefore, some of them who hadn't been capable of hitting the ball over the fence in their official Little League careers could experience that excitement. And those who'd never gotten a chance to pitch in Little League, or play shortstop or catcher, now would get that opportunity.

Fall baseball, therefore, would provide these older players a final shot at Little League memories, and also develop their skills and let them try new things in advance of their next move up the youth baseball ladder.

But I had to consider the zealots' wishes, too. The zealots — the ultra-competitive coaches driven to win, win, win — would need something out of fall baseball, as well. They weren't necessarily motivated by just instructing players; they needed the thrill of victory, too. So I decided that even though our season would be shorter than in spring — five weeks instead of 12 — we'd keep standings and have a postseason, double-elimination tournament to produce a Fall Classic Baseball champion. (I enjoyed the thought of how inhospitable the weather would be then, in mid-to late October, while the zealots battled it out for bragging rights in the tournament, plotting and shouting encouragement to their players in the wind and rain while others would be home by the warm fire. Just the reverse of the spring season.)

FALL BASEBALL PROVED A rousing success. The weather was wonderful. Baseball fit in perfectly that time of year. Of course, September is when the major league pennant races are in full swing, and October is when the World Series runs. It is a great time to be playing baseball in youth leagues.

So Fall Ball took hold in our league, and the only big change in the ensuing years is that the players who'd graduated from Little League in spring were not allowed back for fall. That hurt me, since I'd invented Fall Ball in our league. My youngest son, in fact, was primed and ready to play during the fall when the rules changed, but I presented my case to the board, and finally the league's president issued a presidential decree to let Paul play. The only stipulation was that he not be allowed to pitch. But even that got overturned for one game, when the opposing team's coach (a zealot) said he wanted his hitters to face quality pitching. So Paul got to pitch, and was happy about it.

A lot of players have gotten a lot of satisfaction from getting to play baseball in the fall. It was a good move. And years later, they're still down at the diamonds playing in the fall program.

# Notes:

# Coach's Son Syndrome

C oach's Son Syndrome, mentioned in several previous chapters, is self-explanatory. Any parent with more than a season or two in youth-league baseball recognizes this condition.

The coach's son will get his fair share — or even more than his fair share — of playing time. Maybe he really is one of the best or among the best players on the team. Maybe he really is worthy of being a starting pitcher, and a No. 3 hitter, and a shortstop, second baseman and all-star candidate. Any questioning of his abilities, however, is moot, because his stature is a given. His status is protected.

If you're a manager, making the big commitment of time, effort (and, often, money), you should not feel apologetic about giving your son the opportunities to shine. The fair thing to do, however, is what I described in the Part II chapter, "Managing the Demands of Managing and Coaching": Let the parents know before season's start that your son is a permanent starter, period, and that there are eight other regular starting slots open on the team.

If you're a parent whose child is gunning for a spot already taken by a coach's son (whether the manager's son or one of the assistant coaches' sons), the most valuable thing you can really do is work off the field with your player and make him better, so that he performs well in games and earns an opportunity. And if that opportunity doesn't come, well, your player still has improved, and hopefully is having fun making the most of his season. Maybe next season he will have more opportunities. You should never give up after one bad season.

(In fact, you should always finish out every season. It's only 90 days. You've committed to the team and must honor that commitment. It's a good life lesson for your child. What's more, other players are probably disgruntled, too, and some may end up quitting — leaving more room for your own child. This is precisely what happened on one of my son's teams; he stuck it out, and ended up the starting third baseman, and had a solid season, one of his most rewarding.)

The other useful thing to do to try to work around Coach's Son Syndrome is to get involved with the team as a volunteer. There is a long list of duties with which you can help. You can assist regularly, and productively, at practices (refer to my mention of becoming an auxiliary coach in the Author's Note and in the Part I chapter, "Better Batting through Tennis Balls"). You can keep the scorebook. You can do the pregame work on the fields, chalking the foul lines, raking the basepaths and batting boxes, tamping down the mound, hosing down the infield dirt. All of these can score brownie points and translate into more PT for your player.

Apart from the team, you can do work for the league. Attend the board meetings. Get nominated to join the board. Help with fund-raisers. Donate labor to the upkeep of the park. Write the newsletter. Maintain the website. Volunteer your services to the league president. You'll be forming connections and building up at least a bit of political clout.

Maybe your child will end up getting that chance to pitch or play shortstop, after all. If not this season, then the next one.

And put in for your own team. You don't have to know that much about baseball to have some fun and help give a fun time to others. It's only 90 all-consuming, intense, baseball-filled days.

# The Bottom Five

Early on during my parental tour of duty with youth baseball, I could see that it would be a good idea to get more involved at the field level if my children were to get the sort of joy out of The Game that I had had as a young fellow. Practicing in the back yard and improving their skills wouldn't be enough to help them get PT — playing time — the currency of youth baseball, during their teams' games.

One of my sons was drafted to a team. At the parents' meeting, I volunteered my services. This offer was, not surprisingly, greeted with cold silence, save for a grunt, since the manager and coaching staff had already been formed and plotted out their season strategy and drafting plan during the off-season, long before I'd appeared on the scene.

My services were not needed or wanted. My son was just another body to fill out the mandatory player count on the roster. If he could play, fine; but if not, fine, too. Most of the key positions had already been spoken for by the coaches for their sons, with other favored players getting the rest, and that left mainly spots on the bench for the reserves.

But not being the sort of person to be negative or dwell on the dark side, I decided to interpret that solitary grunt as an indication of great enthusiasm. And so I began showing up at practices. However, the practice plans had been formed well in advance and there wasn't much for me to do. After a couple of these sessions, I took careful stock of which players were having fun and which weren't, and made my "pitch": How would it be if I took the bottom four or five players in the talent pool and worked with them on their hitting?

This idea was greeted with acceptance by the coaches, as it would keep me out of their way and allow them to spend even more time with the better players. So it was agreed. And after watching these players at a few practices, it was clear to me that they needed a great deal of help.

I swung into action with my tennis-ball system of hitting (see the chapter, "Better Batting through Tennis Balls"). This system is excellent, and had helped my sons in prior years. The lesser-talented players under my tutelage were happy with my involvement because an adult was paying some attention to them at the practice and they didn't have to stand around doing nothing. I was their batting coach. We worked and worked on stance, seeing the ball, swinging the bat properly, learning the strike zone, and all the other things you do to have some success at the plate. With this group, "success" meant hitting the ball instead of striking out, and trying to hit it hard.

These bottom-tier players saw lots of my pitches and had lots of fun slugging the tennis balls. And before long they were consistently hitting the ball. When they took regular batting practice with the rest of the team, they were doing OK. I could see success, and the players could, too, and so could the coaches. Most of all, the hard work these players were putting in was FUN. We would play different games: Strikeout, Hit and Run, Fence Buster, Bunt and Run, just to keep it all interesting. After we'd hit all the tennis balls, we'd head out together into the field and pick them up. I learned fast that the best retrieval method was for the players to carry bags out instead of throwing the balls back in to the mound, because with the balls thrown in you just had to pick them up all over again, and the exercise would usually erupt into a tennis-ball fight, anyway. (We did have a few sanctioned tennis-ball fights.) To speed up the retrieval, I'd put up a buck or two for the player who could pick up the most balls the fastest and bring them back to the mound. It was kind of like an Easter egg hunt.

The season progressed, and the bottom half of the lineup produced hits and runs, not just one strikeout after another. The tennis-ball training was good for everyone, and after a while all the players on the team were sent over for the batting drill with me. This team went on to be the division champs, which was gratifying, and I attribute some of the success to having worked with the lesser-talented players early in the season on their hitting, and keeping at it throughout the entire season.

The primary coaches of that team were very knowledgeable baseball people, so everyone on the team benefited by picking up valuable information on how to play The Game. And at the plate, ALL the players were able to have some fine moments of glory. They learned the value of practicing something diligently — that practice pays off. And to be able to top it off with a team championship was great.

From there I went on to getting more involved in the league at the coaching level, and eventually took my own teams as manager. Of course, I welcomed any parent who wanted to help with the team, and put many of them to work with our hitters and the tennis-ball system.

My teams could always hit from top to bottom in the lineup, and the players were happy about that.

# The 'I Told You So's'

I n the smoke-filled room, the draft was moving along. Round after round, my coaches and I were putting together what we thought would be a pretty good team. One player had been avoided so far by the other managers, but on our rating sheets from the tryout he looked good. He had been shunned because most of the coaches thought he would be a problem player.

Well! I drafted him anyway. When I called out his name, the room went silent, and then was filled with comments about how sorry I would be for making that choice, and on and on. But I had no second thoughts, because I knew I was up to handling any situation that might come up.

I telephoned the player later that day to let him know what team he was on. To my surprise, he handed the phone over to his mother, who informed me that he did not want to play on our team, and that he had other ideas about where his baseball future was going. He had hopes of being with friends on a different squad. So much for my astute innate ability for picking players.

A few conversations later with the player and his parents, and he was reluctantly brought into the fold. It helped that his alternative was not playing at all in our league that year.

The games began and the player did well and was an excellent teammate. Never a problem. I was relieved, and pleased. Yet from time to time, the coaches who had been in the smoke-filled room during the draft would approach me at the fields and ask how it was going with that player, expecting an answer that would lead to an "I told you so" comment. But no such comment was forthcoming from me. He hustled. He had a good attitude. His parents turned out to be fine people. I could not have been happier with the draft choice.

We made it to the championship game. We wouldn't have gotten there without the services of the "problem" player, I'm sure. He could hit, run, throw, catch — and do it all well. He was so good on the bases that we called him "Green Light" because he was the only player on the team given permission to steal without waiting for the steal sign from the third-base coach, and he was rarely caught stealing. He also never ignored the do-not-steal sign. Not once. Still, I fielded the occasional "How is it going with that player?" question from the other coaches. My answer: Fine as fine could be.

Now, for the championship game. It went down to the wire. The player was having his usual great game, and was key to us being in position to win. He came to the plate in a key situation with runners on, but two outs. He was called out on strikes on one of the worst calls on record. The pitch was WAY out of the strike zone. The umpire simply blew it big time. And this mild-mannered player, who'd been a keep-it-to-himself Silent Sam all season long, uttered his only profanity of the season and tossed his helmet down in disgust.

The umpire booted him from the championship game. The stands on our side, full of families and fans, erupted in outrage. The stands on the opponent's side, equally packed, were ecstatic. We took the field without our best outfielder covering his territory. Sure enough, we lost the game on a base hit that dropped in on what would have been an easy catch for our benched star. The savvy runner on first rounded the bases and made it home, not afraid to test the arm of our substitute outfielder. Such is baseball.

After the game, as we collected our gear and headed into the sunset of that season, believe it or not, several — not a few — people from the smoke-filled room came up to me and said, "See? I told you you'd have trouble with that kid." Such is baseball.

# Three Subs Sent
# by the Baseball Gods

O ur Babe Ruth League had a peculiarity in scheduling, because if a
player was on his high school varsity or junior-varsity team, he was
not permitted to join his team in our league until the high school season was
over. This was a high school rule. Our league's schedule started before the high
school season ended, which meant that the players on their high school teams
couldn't join their teams in our league until partway into our season.

This produced a few frictions and anomalies, but, overall, was not too
difficult a complication to overcome for the individual Babe Ruth teams. The
high school players would simply not be available to their Babe Ruth teams
until after the high school season ended; in the meantime, other players on
the teams would enjoy more playing time until the high schoolers arrived
and (typically) claimed the prime spots. In most cases where high schoolers
were arriving late to their Babe Ruth team, there would be just one or two of
them per squad. Since the squads each had 12 players on the roster, it was a
workable situation.

One season, however, the team I was managing had four high schoolers.
That meant I could not field a team until the quartet was eligible! Other teams
in the league that year were waiting for their high schoolers to join, but only
had one or two per roster. To resolve this issue, our league board allowed the
teams with the missing high schoolers to temporarily fill the missing roster
slots by bringing up the necessary number of players from the Prep Division
(for 13-year-olds). It seemed fair, since our division had 14- and 15-year-olds,
and the 13-year-olds could benefit from the experience of playing up while

the teams would have the necessary manpower until their high schoolers could play.

Of course, nothing is easy and simple in youth baseball. Or fair, when the league board is controlled by zealots. Which is often the case. The board did not determine which players could "play up"; that issue was left to be determined at a later date. Which left the new rules, as well as the scheduling, at the mercy of the zealots, who could manipulate the conditions to their advantage. . . .

As it happened, I was out of town on a business trip when the board determined the rules for sending Prep players to the upper division. After I returned, I learned that the other teams had picked the Prep players they wanted, and I could have what was left. This pool had been drained of the "big-name" players, of course, who had been tracked, probably from T-ball on, by the coaching staffs.

Quite logically, I suggested to the board members that maybe on days when some of these young stars were not occupied with their regular-season teams in Prep or playing up on the upper-division team that had picked them, they could fill in on my team.

Forbidden! I was told.

Why? I asked.

It was against the rules.

Where are those rules?

Ah, they aren't available yet. But we'll send them to you.

When will they be available and who is making them up?

Don't know and don't know. But the board decided all this and the request to borrow whatever star players were available was simply against the rules.

Well, there was nothing unusual in this youth baseball administrative reasoning, so it didn't bother me in the least. And it wasn't surprising to see that no one was looking out for Jeff Kirst's interests. What else was new?

OPENING DAY WAS COMING up. I needed to fill a couple spots. I picked up the phone and, since my team was the Reds, called the manager of the Reds in the Prep division to see if he had any players who would like to play up for a few games.

I didn't know this manager. He said he had coached in a Little League that was to the south of the Little League I'd participated in. Each of these leagues fed our Babe Ruth League. This coach said his son would like to play on my Reds, but would be out of town on a trip for the first of my team's games. However, the coach had another player on his Prep squad who was newly arrived from California and also would like to play. I said fine, and told the coach to send his son up for a chance after he got back from his trip.

When I mentioned that his two Prep players would be in the outfield on my squad, the coach said fine. I also happened to mention it would be nice if one of them could catch. My son, Charlie, had been pressed into service as a catcher, but we were weak at shortstop, and it presented a dilemma to me where to play him. The coach said his two players never had played behind the plate, but could try. Then I asked if his son and the other prospect really knew how to play The Game. He hemmed and hawed, and allowed that they were OK, but young, yet these two were about the best he had to offer to help us out. And they would really appreciate the chance to play up.

I DID NOT EXPECT much from these players, since the field of Prep replacement candidates had already been thoroughly picked over while I was out of town.

I was in for a surprise!

We were in a real jam that season, because the schedule mysteriously had my Reds playing seven games before our high school stars could join us. In contrast, a couple of other would-be contending teams had just a couple games on the docket before their high schoolers arrived to shine. I shrugged off the inequity and just figured, "That's baseball." What I didn't know was that the baseball gods had been working overtime for me.

The two Prep players turned out not to be just "OK" and lineup filler. Their manager's assessment had been modest to the point of ridiculous. These two guys were — and I'm not kidding — truly all-world. Young, yes; but definitely all-world.

Both could hit, throw, run and play any position with skill and zeal. When they donned the catcher's gear, you would have thought you had Johnny Bench behind the plate. These fellows helped mightily in our early-season games and made managing a dream. Imagine having two all-world players, happy to play anywhere, bat anywhere in the order, and even enthusiastic about just being on the team and sitting the bench. Incredible! (Incidentally, they went on to be big stars in high school baseball, and college players, as well.)

And this wasn't the end of the blessings from the baseball gods. In one game we were particularly shorthanded due to some school special events that cut our lineup to eight players, even with the two substitutes. Once more, I made a call to the lower-division Reds and requested a player. Request fulfilled — but with the manager's cautionary statements about the player's ability, experience and the like. I now took his words with a grain of salt.

The new player he sent me arrived, and I told him he'd be playing outfield. Fine, he said. That was the only place he'd ever played. OK! His last name had an unusual spelling, so just so I could get it right, I asked him how to pronounce it. He said, with a straight face and serious look, "Coach, my last name is pronounced 'WIN-ner.'"

You could have knocked me over with a feather. I had two all-worlds, plus a "winner," delivered by the baseball gods!

And a winner he was! Turned out he had only played outfield because he could cover ground like a cheetah at full throttle. In the game, he made two game-saving catches, got a hit, stole a base and scored the winning run. A "winner," for sure.

OF COURSE, WITH THIS kind of help from above, our team was off to a great start. And this was a shocker for some of the perennial coaches, fixers and dynasty-builders.

There was outrage. Protest. Bad blood. Confrontation. But what could I say? "You expect me to lose on purpose? You complainers made the rules. Remember: I was out of town. I'm just following them."

Case closed. Put another mark in the Reds' win column.

When our four high schoolers joined us, we continued our winning ways. The three Prep replacements returned to their division. But they were hardly forgotten.

The Reds finished with a strong record. It was a successful season, and when it was time to hand out the team trophies, three extra ones were ordered for the surprise Prep stars who had given us the early-season boost — and turned the tables on some of the league's fixers and zealots.

It was a happy ending for the good guys.

# Notes:

# My Only Recruit

..............................................................................................................................

**A**fter a little bit of exposure to youth baseball and the many frustrations it involves, I began to ruminate on ways by which it could be made fairer and less corrupt. Seeking a higher standard, much of my brainwork was directed at what appeared to be the excessive efforts of "involved" adults in manipulating the player-selection systems for building teams.

For a while I thought a lottery system might solve the inequities created by unscrupulous recruiters and under-the-table deal-cutters. Just pull the names of players and coaches out of a hat, I suggested, and pair them together for the season. I also proposed having the coaches draft entire teams, and then put the team names in a hat and have each coach draw blindly. While I thought these were good and reasonable ways to go, my ideas garnered little interest and no support from the other coaches. And on further reflection — and after more experience with youth baseball — I realized that all the adult machinations added to the fun and excitement of the baseball ritual, and that putting on a satisfying-for-all season required the involvement of so many people that it was absolutely necessary to do that which, while distasteful to me, kept people interested and active in our great baseball game.

The Game was, after all, played on several levels. There was the competition on the field itself, between the players. But then there were the battles for bragging rights among the coaches and parents . . . and the grudges settled among coaches and parents through the proxy war on the diamond . . . and the social and business networking conducted by the parents bonding with others on the same team . . . and, finally, the internal politics of administering the league, with all that involved, which, naturally, caused personality conflicts and other dynamic relationships that, too, were played out on the field.

Of course, I would never stoop so low as to engage in the pettiness that permeated youth baseball and caused a season to flow by like a stench-filled open sewer. Yet I came to accept the political and petty nature of the system in stride. After all, I wanted to be involved. To be a part of organized baseball was good. American. And I recognized that youth baseball was important to many, many people in many different ways. Most very, very good. So I followed the procedures, took part, had a good time. And I hoped I gave a good baseball experience to those with whom I was active: players, parents, fellow coaches and board members.

Nonetheless . . . team building irked me. The politics and skullduggery just seemed to be a little too much. As a manager, I always tried to draft a good team, and if some player wanted to be on my roster, I'd figure out a way to put him on it, whether the player could play well or not. And if a player didn't want to be on my roster — and that happened a couple times, at parents' request — I'd not draft the player and let a top talent go to a competitor. I was content to take my chances with what came my way in the normal course of events. Meaning: on the field of battle, er, play.

BUT ONE SEASON, WELL along in my managerial career — having long suffered the slings and arrows of outrageous team-building machinations by coaches and parents — I left my halo on the hat rack at home and pulled on my hip boots to wade into the muck.

The team I was managing was a good one. It had a core of returning players who were excellent. For most of the returnees it would be their final year in the league. They had been playing for 10 years, moving from Little League up to the big (regulation-size) diamond of Babe Ruth League, and some had made their high school varsity or junior-varsity teams. All these players and others in the league had played together or against one another in their leagues as they grew up and knew one another's ability from friendly competition and rivalries developed over the years.

In discussions with fellow coaches and parents about our team's prospects and those of our competitors, I discovered that one wonder player from the old days had never gone beyond his Little League career, but still had one year of eligibility left for playing in Babe Ruth. Perhaps he'd simply tired of baseball after age 12. Now in high school, he'd taken up basketball and hadn't touched a baseball or bat in three years.

I did my research. This player, we'll call him "Jim," was reputed to be all-world on the diamond. He'd been the starting shortstop on his championship Little League team, and a star pitcher, as well. He'd been the starting shortstop on his league's all-star team, and, yes, a star pitcher on that squad, too. In fact, he'd been a star all-star for several seasons. And he could hit. This player was beyond all-world. And he was available to be drafted! That is, if anyone thought of luring the now-15-year-old back to the diamond to resume where he'd left off at age 12.

I learned that Jim had blossomed into a 6-foot-4-inch young man who could run like a deer, as proved on the basketball court, yet also knew how to play baseball. He'd been coached in Little League by a master of The Game, so he really had the fundamentals down. His all-star playing experience had made him diamond-tough and savvy beyond his years. Still . . . could he be coaxed back to the ballfield?

Although I'd never recruited a baseball player for any team of mine, I'd done plenty of recruiting and persuading in other venues in my life, including the business world, and I decided then and there to try and bring this player aboard. His addition to my squad full of returnees could make for a magnificent baseball season.

But how do you recruit a 15-year-old star athlete?

Step One: Call his parents and get the facts.

I did. It turned out that Jim — after seven years of Little League — had burned out on baseball, listening to coaches and practicing and playing throughout the spring and (in all-stars) for most of summer. Enough was enough.

In addition, he'd become a very successful basketball player.

However, Jim's parents had lived and loved youth baseball, and were sorry to see their son hang up his cleats and glove. His mom was a great baseball mom and fan. (And a GLM, too.) His dad had been an all-world left-handed pitcher in his day and still ached for The Game. But as kind and thoughtful parents they'd elected to let their son make his own choices. As well as being an excellent athlete, Jim was a fine citizen.

From my phone call I learned that the other managers in our league were well aware of this diamond-in-the-rough, and had tried during the previous two years, during the winter before the spring draft for our Babe Ruth league, to bring him back out of the rough and onto the proper setting . . . the baseball field. But with no positive results. They'd failed.

This winter, too, Jim's family's phone had been ringing off the hook. They'd heard pitch after pitch to return their son to the field of battle. Well, I would make my pitch, too. And I wanted to throw a strike. When you've decided to wade out into the recruiting swamp, you want to give it your best shot to bring home the alligator.

In this case, I ended up bringing home not one, but two.

MY TIMING WAS RIGHT, my pitch was true, my shot was on the mark . . . and the baseball gods were looking down in favor on my efforts.

Jim realized that this — his last year of eligibility at the Babe Ruth level — was probably his last chance to test his skills on a major league-size diamond (which he'd never taken the opportunity to do). What's more, the memories of those moments of glory he'd experienced in Little League, slowly fading into the mists of time, probably tipped the scales in his decision to devote one more season to The Game.

Jim was the first prize I landed that evening. The second was Jim's father. Because I'd never before recruited a player, I had an assistant coach's spot open on my team. The vast majority of the time, a manager will recruit a player and work it so that the father is listed as a coach on the team, so that his son automatically is assigned to the team as a "coach's option," and thus protected from exposure in the draft. Anyway, I did as the other Romans did in the league, and brought in my trophy recruit as a coach's option, and his father as a coach. And the father was a good coach, having been a star in his high school days.

Yes, I'd scored a recruiting coup par excellence. My team had acquired an all-world player and an all-world coach in one beautiful package!

Of course, as soon as word got out about my dual prizes, great resentment festered in some quarters of the league. But our team notched win after win, registering itself as a bona fide contender for the league crown.

Jim's father coached third base for us all season long. He proved to be a great asset. He guided our runners to many stolen bases. He made our hitters better by properly implementing the take, bunt and hit-and-run signs in the right situations. He pitched great batting practice, which helped our hitters immensely. He gave wise advice to our pitching staff. He was astute in our discussions of positioning our players in the field to match up against particular opponents. He was cool-handed in motivating our players and in passing on useful tips and tidbits from his playing days in our one-on-one chats. And despite the "rare" mistakes I made from time to time as manager, never once did he step out of his role of coach or proffer a caustic comment.

And his son? Jim truly was all-world, despite having been out of The Game for three years. He carried our club in the early part of our schedule until our high school players could join the active roster after their scholastic seasons were finished. He pitched a couple of no-hitters and several one- or two-hitters. He played flawless shortstop. His bat initially was cold, but his mild demeanor in the face of difficulties at the plate encouraged our other players to step up and concentrate a little harder when a key hit was needed or a situation required some sacrifice.

His bat came alive after he successfully adjusted his stance from being a 4-foot-4-inch Little Leaguer to the 6-foot-4-inch player he'd grown into, and he racked up many hits and provided excitement running the bases with his great speed. And he was a selfless player, too. Which allowed me to learn and try a few things.

Often, a star shortstop-pitcher mopes when the manager — being a top-of-the-line skipper, of course — benches the star or plays him in a less glamorous position in order to give another player a chance at a moment of glory. But not this returned star. On the bench, Jim stayed involved in the game and urged on his teammates with genuine enthusiasm. I played him in the outfield, at first base, at second and at third. Having a great shortstop, with tremendous speed and range, playing at first base was not what a zealot or traditionalist would have done. But it was magic for our defense, as every would-be errant throw to first was reined in, and fouls and bloops to the right side of the diamond were caught on the fly. Jim didn't complain about playing first. And I remained neither a zealot nor traditionalist, just an average-dad enthusiast, even though I had — for this one season only — talked and cajoled a recruit into joining my lineup.

OUR TEAM HAD A satisfying season, and finished high in the standings. To my abiding disappointment, though, Jim was victimized by the machinations of the league's politicians when it came time to do the all-star balloting.

Apparently bearing a grudge against Jim, and against me as the successful courter, they passed him over when choosing the elite squad of 15-year-olds for tournament play. Instead of making room for him, they filled up space on the roster with a 14-year-old they said they needed on the mound. Their argument against Jim was that his season batting average wasn't spectacular (although it was solid). Of course, after his bat had heated up, it had been a potent weapon — along with his glove, throwing arm and fast-running legs. And then there was his mature, winning attitude. (More adult than many of the adults.)

So the all-star team competed without one of the league's premier players, and a deserving player. But Jim didn't mind not being included. He was happy just to have had his one season getting to play on the full-sized diamond.

He'd found out that he was still an all-world baseball talent and could outplay the best of 'em, and could go as far as he wanted to go in baseball anywhere. I think he had peace of mind about baseball.

He returned to the basketball court when that season started, and continued as a high school star.

In my book, he was a star at life.

# Notes:

# Cornering the Market on Catchers

A t the lower levels of youth baseball, the pre-draft tryouts are not very important to the players, because everybody gets on a team if he has signed up for that season. The biggest issue at those levels is whether a player "sandbags" — purposely does poorly so that unknowing coaches will pass him over and the team the player actually has designs on joining, and which has designs on him, gets first crack at him during the draft. By the time a player reaches the upper levels of youth baseball, however, looking good in tryouts is important. Also, coaches usually have a pretty good idea of who is who among the older players, anyway, so sandbagging doesn't work as well.

Tryouts at every level are always important for the coaches because who is picked in the draft generally determines a team's talent pool for the season, and possibly subsequent seasons. Coaches have different systems for rating players. Some have prejudices toward left-handed or right-handed players, or are partial to infielders or outfielders. The list of personal preferences is lengthy, with some reasonable, some ridiculous. But the idiosyncrasies help make youth baseball the challenge that it is. I've known of coaches who drafted on the basis of what we called in the 1990s "GLM." This stood for Good-Looking Moms. Such coaches didn't even pay attention to the tryouts; they spent their time matching up player numbers with the moms, whom they rated.

My own system of rating players was on a scale of 1 to 5, 1 being low. I'd score them in four areas: catching flies, fielding grounders, throwing and hitting. I'd average out my scores and refine my rating with nuances, considering the player's arm strength, speed running the bases and general field presence.

I also made special note of players who could not catch a fly and apparently would take an eternity to learn how to do so. Finally, I noted which players were to be avoided on the basis of general information and scuttlebutt — such as having a bad attitude, poor track record showing up to practices, or difficult parents who complained, or did not attend to responsibilities such as handling their snack bar shift.

At the conclusion of tryouts I'd get with my coaches, who'd have done their own ratings, and we'd make our list of players in the order of preference. Then it was on to the smoke-filled room.

As the draft proceeds, players are picked and their names crossed off candidates' lists. There are plenty of moans and groans as coaches react to losing one of their choices to another team. Tension mounts as the talent pool thins and names of lesser-known or unknown players come to the fore. In the backs of some coaches' minds are the conversations they'll be having with disappointed parents who wanted their child to be on a particular team, not the one he was drafted to. In underhanded pre-draft dealings, a manager might promise parents to draft their child, but in the actual heat of the moment during the draft the manager might pass up the chance and take another who might just be a little better.

Of course, the overall availability of the pool of talent already has been compromised before the draft as certain players are spoken for. They may be coaches' options (children of a team's coaches), sibling options (put on the same team to facilitate transportation), and — depending on the creative employment or blatant disregard of league rules — cousin options, neighbor options, sponsor options, dentist options, and on and on.

FOLLOWING ONE VERY SUCCESSFUL season, I was left the following spring with a roster decimated by departures of players moving up to the next age level. I had many holes to fill. It was going to be a tough season no matter what, and it would be my last season managing that team. I was hoping to finish out on a high note.

Now, during the draft, most managers look for pitchers or potential pitchers, because such strong-armed players who throw accurately can usually play any infield position effectively and probably catch, too. But I'd spent enough time in the league to know that few players want to play catcher. What's more, I'd learned the hard way that having effective catchers provides a great edge and can win many games for a team. Conversely, lacking a strong catcher can lose you many games. Without a catcher, or a good player who can be bludgeoned into serving as a reluctant catcher, a team is facing a tough row to hoe.

This insight formed the basis of my draft strategy. I decided I would try to corner the market on catchers. I'd attempt to draft every player who was cut out to stalwartly wear the catcher's gear — the "tools of ignorance," in the old baseball slang. I'd try to leave no backstops available for the other teams.

On Draft Day I made the rounds of the players while they warmed up, and found out who had been catchers, who had been good catchers, and who wanted to be catchers. I duly noted names and numbers and made out my draft list. I knew these players could have a good season even if they were on a team loaded with catchers. Even players who want to catch enjoy playing other positions. And I could rotate players in and out from behind the plate, since there is nothing like having fresh legs and a fresh, strong arm behind the plate midway through the game (which is only possible if you have an abundance of catchers).

During the draft I came so, so, so close to cornering the market on catchers! But for a couple of coaches' options, I would have had ALL the catchers in the league, and the season would have been a cakewalk for my team due to opponents suffering from passed balls, dropped third strikes, ineffective defense against the steal, and exhaustion behind the plate. But I didn't get them all. And while my draft strategy did produce some difficulties for some of the other teams, the advantage was not enough to help my team push over the top that year.

But it still is a great strategy worth considering by managers. One caveat, however, is that catchers often are not so fleet afoot. So if you try to corner the market on catchers, you better not count on stealing a lot of bases.

We had a few instances that season of people in the stands bleating the old line, "He ran like he had a piano on his back and stopped along the way to play it, too."

But we didn't have many passed balls!

# Traveling Teams

Youth sports in America are dialed up to such a high competitive level nowadays that the most serious players compete year-round. Not only are they involved in regular youth leagues, they join traveling teams playing tournaments in other cities, states and regions. A family's social life can revolve around out-of-town tourneys.

The managers of traveling teams are zealots who raise the money to carry around a talented group of players (usually handpicked from local leagues) to play against other talented players. Players on traveling teams continually hone their skills and therefore enjoy a competitive edge in regular league play. But I look at success a bit differently: how many moments of glory can you get? The sheer number of extra games a player can enjoy on a traveling team multiplies his chances for moments of glory.

Another facet of traveling teams is that the players play so many games that they can get tired of playing. They can burn out. That leaves space in the lineup for lesser talents to get in the game, and thus have more chances to shine. At this level of baseball, a player really learns to play The Game, and also learns just how committed he wants to be to it.

It's also fun for young players to see different parts of the country, to stay in hotel rooms, splash around the swimming pool, go out to eat and sightsee. It builds character, being among teammates and coaches in a strange city. If a player gets the chance, it's worth doing. But it does demand a lot of time and money. It's an arduous commitment.

The era of the sandlot, of kids just playing for fun, seems very remote indeed to American society in the 21st century.

# *Schadenfreude*

A s you go through your youth baseball experience, you will be torn by many powerful emotions. And I'm not kidding or exaggerating!

If you are a thinker, it will be all the more difficult. You may lie awake nights brooding about Junior's performance, or the coach's insensitivity, ineptitude or favoritism, or why So-and-So's son is excelling at the plate while Junior is always striking out by watching the third strike sail by, or whether Junior has an inside track or outside shot at making all-stars. You may mull over the injustices of the league, and the arrogance and cockiness of another team's coaches, players or parents, and how sweet it would be to exact revenge the next time your team plays them.

If you opt to ignore the varied feelings, you'll probably be unhappy in later years. Mental-health experts maintain that you should not suppress your emotions, lest they grow into demons.

What to do?

Why, adjust your attitude, of course!

Should be easy, huh?

Guess again.

You want Junior to excel. You want your team to win and you want everyone in the league, particularly those on your team, to have a good time. You are, after all, an adult. But here's a quirk of human nature:

You want the stars to be stars — but not too great of stars. You want the knuckleheads to provide some levity . . . but not so much as to injure themselves psychologically for life. (For a decade, perhaps, but not for life.)

SCHADENFREUDE IS A GERMAN term that essentially means delight from the misery of others. (Schaden means damage or harm; freude means joy.) Historically, and secretly, Germans liked their neighbors to fail and be miserable. An analogy of sorts is office politics. The office politicians secretly want their coworkers (and managers) to fail, so that they themselves can enjoy greater fortunes. Another analogy: beauty-pageant contestants.

Schadenfreude is alive and well on the baseball diamond. For some parents and players it is not enough that they and theirs do well; it is also essential that others are miserable.

My wife gave up sitting in the stands at our youth games after she heard one "happy" comment too many from the mouths of mothers on the team, giddy that one of our own team's players missed a ball in the field or struck out, because that would mean more chances at prime-time play for her own young major leaguer-to-be. It can be a cruel game. (Some leagues have parents sign code-of-conduct agreements, as part of the player-registration process, agreeing to abide by league rules, which include not making negative comments directed toward players during games. But try to enforce that! And what about negative thoughts? Thought police?)

My advice? Keep such beastly thoughts to yourself. Train yourself to be happy when others succeed and supportive when they fail, even if it's difficult for you. I've seen mothers howl with glee when an opposing batter strikes out, or a fielder boots the ball. Control your emotions. No amount of evil thoughts will change the outcomes of a game for the better . . . but may keep your team from doing better. (Superstition? Yes! Baseball lends itself to such.)

Voodoo . . . a powerful tool. I often let my opponents' coaching staff know that for the week prior to a game I had kept frozen voodoo dolls representing them in the freezer at home. As the game approached, the dolls came out and were allowed to thaw, then were filled with pins in appropriate places. I always asked the coaches how they felt and always watched for any unusual motions or contortions when they gave their signs. It always worked! I recommend it.

Seriously, though, try hard not to think ill of your opponents. The Game is a microcosm of life. And you don't want to incur the wrath of the baseball gods, bearing down on you in your everyday life.


NEVER HOLD A GRUDGE for more than a season. Sometimes this isn't easy to do — to let go of a slight, an insult or a jealous rage.

One year, I was a board member and board secretary for my Babe Ruth League. I'd raised money for our league, and been very involved. I'd done a lot of work, and managed a successful Prep team (that is, in the 13-year-old division). I wanted to manage the league's Prep all-star team. Another manager also tossed his hat into the ring, at the very last minute, with only moments to go before the cutoff deadline. The fix was in, and that board voted unanimously against me and for him. In fact, he and his camp of cronies took over all three of the league's all-star teams that summer. I thought it was terrible, but I was well aware of how the politics can work in youth baseball, diamond veteran that I had become.

I held a grudge against that board for approximately two weeks. But I got over it. Our league happened to be hosting the district all-star tournament and the board's organizing committee was desperate for help, so I agreed to put together the player program for the tournament. Someone else in my position, still tasting sour grapes, might have turned his back and said, "Forget it."

I followed through in getting the programs designed and printed up, although I let the board members know I was angry with them, and that they were doomed by the baseball gods. A couple members apologized for what they had done. Then locusts and grasshoppers ate the grain crops of others, and I heard something about a rash and an intestinal ailment making the rounds. OK.

So I savored my taste of *Schadenfreude* that season. And next season, what do you know? I was voted to be manager of the 14-year-old all-star team, and had a thrilling baseball run with the team. Well worth the wait.

Just remember, if things aren't going right for you during a particular season, there is always another pitch, another at-bat, another game, another season. And the season always does end. A blessing.

Why spoil the time you do have during a season by succumbing to *Schadenfreude*? Better to make an effort to be upbeat and positive. The baseball gods will take care of the rest.

# Banned from Baseball

Sooner or later you will be banned from baseball. It happened to me. My wife did it.

"Don't you think you've been spending enough time on this baseball stuff?" she asked. "There are important things to be done around here. The garage needs cleaning. The yard needs work. I'm sick of all this dust and dirt and baseball junk around the house. You're banned from baseball!"

It was a day of heartbreak for me. No longer would she tolerate me signing up again to coach. But it was inevitable. And it's likely that you will someday be banned from baseball, too. Maybe your spouse will demand it. But this book will at least help you have some pleasant memories to tide you over during the boredom of leading a fruitless, everyday existence.

Your children can ban you from baseball, too. At some point they just don't feel like playing any longer, and then it is time to let them go on to other things. When they are out of The Game, it is difficult for you to keep an interest. And worst of all, if they are still playing, they will probably reach a point at which they don't want you around any longer. You're too old. You're not contemporary. You're history. They don't need your advice. They don't need your help in practice. And they don't need your support or commiseration, either.

Consider that the further your kid goes in The Game, the worse his statistics will be. So why does he need to have Dad hanging around saying something like, "You're batting .300 in Babe Ruth, but when I was coaching you in Little League, you hit .650. Let me give you some tips . . ."

So, The Game is over for you. No more baseball. BUT . . . if you can hang on long enough, there will be the grandchildren. Enthusiasm again! New little guys to show all the tricks to, to help succeed and have some success. You can gain reinstatement to The Game.

But be careful. You're not the man you used to be.

I had a quite elderly fellow ask me (through an intermediary because he was embarrassed to ask, fearing rejection) if he could come out and help coach the team I was managing. His grandson was on our roster. Of course, I said fine, for there's always room for one more coach. He did well. Imparted some wisdom. Enjoyed it. The players enjoyed it.

Then one day, with a bad twist this way and a bad turn that way, he hit the turf and couldn't get back up. I drove my yellow truck, the "A's-mobile," out on to the diamond, loaded him up and took him to the hospital. He had injured his hip. He recovered to see another day.


THE WORST THING YOU can do in youth baseball is run a kid off a team. Coaches, however, do this every so often, and it is B-A-D.

Imagine that: Banning a kid from baseball!

You never see the best players run off a team. It is always one of the worst kids. It starts by the coach singling the player out for great fun stuff, such as picking up the batting helmets, gathering up the bats, carrying the gear, retrieving the ball that rolled into the sewer drain, cleaning the dugout, sweeping out the batting cages. Asking the kid to find "the keys to the batter's box" (an unkind joke — the baseball equivalent of, "Who's buried in Grant's Tomb?"). Tasks the kid does because he is eager to please the coach and have some good baseball fun.

Then, when it is practice time, he's always sent to deepest outfield, and just as it's his turn to take a fly ball, it's time to move on to the next drill. During infield practice, the shots to him are always a little out of reach, or take a bad hop off a rock, and he doesn't get a second shot, which the other players would. When it's hitting practice, he is called in to bat as the last guy, just as it is getting dark. And then you're out of time, you can't see the ball, so it's time to quit because, he's told, "YOU MIGHT GET HURT."

During throwing drills, the coach tells him he throws like a girl. "Get something on it!" When the team's running the bases, he comes in last and the coach ridicules him for being a slow-footed wimp. And when the team talk is given, the coach is sure to say, "Now, you hit the ball like this, not the way So-and-So does . . . And you catch the ball like this, not the way So-and-So does."

There are snide remarks about his playing ability spoken under the coach's breath when he's not really out of So-and-So's earshot. And then one day, So-and-So doesn't show up to practice. When he shows up the next time, because his mother made him, the coach applies the pressure a little more. Finally, he quits. HURRAY! The coach has run him off the team.

This is the worst thing a coach can do in youth baseball! But the coach announces So-and-So's departure to the team and encourages them to give a cheer at their good fortune.

The pits! But it happens more often than you may expect. It happens all the way down at the Farm division level of Little League, with 7-year-olds. And it often happens on good teams, which is all the more terrible, because if the team is good the coach has an even greater opportunity to help the lesser players have moments of glory and some success.

One season I was managing a Farm division team. The first-half champions would play the second-half champions for the season title. My team's goal and strategy was to tighten the screws and turn up the volume to win either half, just to get into the championship game.

My coaches and I decided to go for the first half and live with possible player and parent discontent and make it up to them in the second half. Our practices were tailored to give all the players vigorous action both in the infield and outfield, and lots of hitting. But in games, we fielded our best players in the key positions and our most potent batting order. We were winning, and everyone was content with that. We had a happy team. Everybody showed up for everything.

The first half came down to a final game. The winner would be in the season-ending championship game. Well, we brought our full roster to the big game, but our opponents were missing three players. Guess which three?

It's just not right to ban a kid from baseball.

We lost the game, and with it our hopes of making it into the championship game at the end of the season. For we stuck to our guns in the second half and divided up the infield action amongst some of our lesser talents, and modified the batting order to give some of the fellows some extra chances at moments of glory. Our win-loss record was mediocre. We were the spoiler a couple of times, which was nice. But all our players had a ball that season, and everybody was still showing up to all the practices and games as our season drew to a close.

That was the best part of all.

ANYWAY, YOUR CHILD WON'T be playing baseball forever, even if he's passionate about The Game. With slumped shoulders and baseball-capped head tilting toward the ground, tears in his eyes and a choked-up voice, your player will quietly make the announcement that he was cut from the baseball team.

It will probably happen in high school, and it is a sad time for all. The only consolation is that he will get over it. The scars will remain scars, but heal. And in retrospect, it should be a day of jubilation celebrated by uncorking magnums of champagne and festivaling long through the night. For you and your player will have an abundance of new, unfettered time, and be able to plan different and interesting things.

It is best to have set the stage for this day with your player over the years by going to baseball games being played by older players and pointing out their size, speed and ability. That way, he will know realistically how he stacks up as he goes through his own paces. Then, to console your player, look for and find a late spring or summer program in which he can play out his career if he cares to. Those opportunities are out there. Or consider a final baseball camp. That, too, is a nice way to go out.

Of course, he may just not want to play anymore, and that's fine and to be supported. In that case, seek out other venues of activity. The high school years are the time in baseball when players are being led into making the choice of whether they'll be trying to or even able to play The Game for money, either by getting a "free" college education or signing a professional contract.

If your player has been cut from his high school team, chances are those options are not in the cards for him in the near future, anyway. But assure your player that he has certainly played long and hard enough over his prior seasons to know The Game and how to play. And after that it is just a question of numbers and statistics, for the simple fact is that if he blossoms and grows to the point that he is 6-foot-3 and 220 pounds of solid muscle, and can throw the baseball in the low 90s, baseball will again be there for him, and someone will find him. Someone with a fat wallet and a checkbook, as well as the knowledge to move that fastball up near 100 mph and show him a variety of other ways to throw a baseball effectively.

And if the blossoming doesn't occur, he's gotten a nice jump on taking a base full of fun, new things for his life. At that stage of growing up, a rest from baseball only does the body good and enables it to come back with vigor and enthusiasm should the genes deliver the goods in making for a bigger, stronger, faster young person.

So let it go, and JUMP FOR JOY!!

MY PERSONAL OPINION IS that high school baseball should be there for every person who wants to be a part of it. If the teams have 100 players, so what? It is manageable. Most of the players just want to be a part of something they can take pride in, practice and train for, have a reason to stay in good shape, have something to do after school, wear a uniform representing their school, and win a letter for their dedication and participation.

It works for high school football programs. You'll find plenty of high school football players who suit up for four years and see only minutes out on the gridiron in actual school-to-school competition. Just practicing and being a part of the team is fulfilling and more than adequate.

The same would work just fine with baseball, but I've never seen or heard of a high school baseball coach who agrees with me. Why not? It would take a little extra effort and thought to offer it to the young folks, and that is just not in the cards with high school baseball today. And it is too bad. In my opinion, this is one of the few times when baseball, The Game, and those involved, let America down. It should change.

Maybe it will one of these days.

PART IV

# THE CHURCH OF BASEBALL

*To true aficionados, baseball is more than a game. It is The Game.*

*It is history, comedy, tragedy, drama, tradition.*

*It has superstitions, a vernacular, rituals rooted in murky origins but well-honored and faithfully perpetuated.*

*It has temples both glorious (major league ballparks) and humble (your neighborhood parks-department field).*

*It has its pantheon of Hall of Famers, its devoted practitioners, its hierarchy of priests (such as sports-talk television and radio hosts) and peons (the guys who call in to sports-talk TV and radio shows).*

*Baseball is a way of life.*

*Once a player, you will always remember what it was like when you played.*

*Once a fan, always a fan. A believer both in the written laws of physics, and the unwritten laws of diamond miracles.*

*You can leave The Game. But The Game will never leave you.*

# Notes:

# Moral Lessons
# of the Diamond

A t one stage of the Kirst Family's involvement in youth baseball, we had four sons on teams, plus the dad (I) coaching two teams, and the mom (Abby) pressed into service as a team mom, fan and taxi driver. (Ironically, Abby's vehicle was a real, bona fide, former Checker taxicab.)

Every day or evening of the week, except during late fall and winter, could be a baseball day or night for the Kirst household. Even Sundays were spent on the diamond.

I made the point to my wife that baseball teaches the same moral values as organized religion. We agreed that we'd try to get these values across to our kids via baseball. The values include being kind to your neighbor; being humble; knowing that things may not work out in the short run but will in the long run if you're a good person; working hard at what you're doing without expecting an immediate return, but trusting it will pay off in unexpected ways; forgiving people for their mistakes; turning the other cheek.

And so Sundays were permitted as baseball days. My boys and I practiced every day of the week during the 90-day season. As I've said several times in this book, baseball is an everyday game. You forget to bat one day, you're worse the next day.

Discipline is a moral value, too.

# Notes:

# Waffles Can Play, Too

A brief look at baseball history shows that the sport was played in biblical times by the Egyptians (note the arms twisted in a throwing motion in their artwork), and in merry olde England. However, The Game was popularized and taken to its heights of sophistication here in America. Foreigners don't quite grasp the fine nuances of The Game, but through continued exposure they come around to an appreciation of baseball . . . thank goodness.

Here in Reno, Nevada, we've got people in our youth leagues from many ethnic backgrounds. American Indians, African-Americans, Asians, Caucasians, Latinos . . . people from just about everywhere. Most players have been exposed to The Game at home and have some understanding of it even when they are just starting out in Tee Ball. However, when you have a transplant from a non-baseball-playing foreign country who joins the league to give it a go, it does get interesting.

When I was starting up the Fall Ball program in Reno Continental Little League, a married couple with whom I was friends took in a foreign-exchange student for the year. They didn't have children of their own, and wanted to be sure that this young guest from Belgium had an All-American experience. Naturally, they called on me when it came to baseball. Of course, since they were friends of mine, I told them I would accommodate them by putting Jean-Claude on a team. I was the league president and commissioner, as well as player agent for the fall league, so I could do anything I cared to (within reason and not risking assassination).

Jean-Claude had never held a baseball before, so to be fair, I put him on a team with my two sons and under the management of another friend of mine, a plumber. I figured Jean-Claude would be a liability to any other team and any other manager would cry "foul play." I also figured that Jean-Claude would benefit from his experience on this particular team. He'd be treated with patience.

When the young Belgian showed up for the first team meeting, he didn't have a glove. He barely spoke English. But he was full of enthusiasm to try The Game. It was the American thing to do. French was his native language, and he spoke broken English with a thick accent. His teammates were dumbfounded when the player introductions were made, and Jean-Claude spouted: "Baaassaboool . . . I vanant to play. Show me!"

He was kind of a pushy little kid, but that was worked out quickly.

My friend the plumber dubbed Jean-Claude "The Waffle" due to his heritage and accent. Well, anyway, he got a nice glove and was taught how to throw and catch, bat and run the bases (it took a while and a few game outs wasted on overrunning the bag, but he caught on). It was kind of fun to see him come along so quickly, since he had never even seen a baseball before coming to Reno.

After a few games, he was desperate to try pitching. Outfielding he could handle. Infielding, no way, because he didn't know the rules. Catching behind the plate? Forget it. But pitching . . . that was for him!

All the players on the team were going to be given the chance to take the hill and try their luck, it being Fall Ball. And before long, Jean-Claude's turn would come around. He practiced for a couple weeks. And then it was his day to make an appearance.

He was confident: "I veeelll ztrike zem all out!" Five walks later, he was relieved of his duties and sent to the outfield. He was disappointed and it was difficult consoling him since he didn't understand the translation. But he took it pretty well.

He tried again later in the season and had a better outing. He became a good teammate and had a good season. Got some hits, and learned the rudiments of The Game. It was a success, and everyone lived through The Waffle Experience and was better for it.

I WAS IN FLORIDA one spring vacation (kids hitting lobster floats for batting practice) and in the apartment building at which we were staying, one of our neighbors was a foreigner. We gave him his first taste of baseball.

The boys and I were out playing catch in the parking lot. We had our gloves and a new hardball. Reinhard, the neighbor, was just going out to do some work on his sailboard. He was a champion windsurfer as well as a body builder; very physically fit. He worked on the lines on his board while we were laughing it up, tossing the ball around. He would occasionally look over at us out of the corner of his eye. His glances became more frequent. He was an athlete, after all. Finally, I went over to him and asked if he would like to try playing catch. He said yes, he would.

I gave him my glove and told him he could toss the ball with Charlie. Reinhard took the glove and looked it all over: inside, outside, all around. Then he put it on his hand and worked his fingers and palm around. Then I handed him the ball.

He took the ball and hefted it a couple times, examined the leather, rubbed the seams. Then I showed him how to throw it. He tossed it to Charlie, then caught it. Tossed, caught, tossed, caught. And a slight smile appeared on his face.

Then he said he better go. He returned the glove and took one last look at the ball . . . and said he understood baseball better now. He had never played

The Game or even played catch before. He thanked me and left.

Later, he went back to West Germany. He had our address. He ended up sending me a piece of the Berlin Wall. He'd torn down that section with his own hands.

I keep it with my baseball stuff.

# Baseball Cards
# Are Forever

I recommend that coaches get their players to collect baseball cards and baseballs, bats and any other memorabilia the coaches can get their hands on. It is FUN. And it is educational for the players.

I collected cards for a couple years when I was a kid and really interested in The Game. I had a couple old cards my dad gave me when I was a kid, plus standard Topps® bubblegum cards, cereal-box cards, the Cincinnati Reds Sohio Gasoline collection book, and an assortment of Kahn's Wieners cards. We kids used to ride our bicycles to the local general store and buy baseball cards. It was a reason to take a trip. The kids in the neighborhood would flip cards, toss cards at walls and cracks in the driveway — gambling games to win each other's cards. It was fun.

During baseball season I'd get the Sunday paper and take out the sports section where batting averages were listed of all the players in the majors. Every Sunday I'd sit on the living-room floor and get out my cards and line them up in the order of the player's averages for the current season. You really got a feel for statistics that way. Yes, again: it was fun!

The Kahn's Wieners cards were something else. You'd get a pack of hot dogs and inside would be a baseball card. Unfortunately, the card would be dripping with hot-dog juice, so you'd have to wash it off and then set it out to dry … and when the card was still moist, flatten it out so it didn't curl up. Good cards! I still have them and they still smell like those good hot dogs. Powerful wieners! Kahn's slogan was, "The wiener the world awaited," and we awaited those wieners and the baseball cards with eager anticipation.

We'd also take the cards and hook them to our bike frames with clothespins so the cards would flap when we rode. The faster you went, the louder the noise, and the quicker the cards were torn to shreds. Sounded great, though. And you'd pedal like heck with a huge cheek full of bubblegum that you'd chew until it got hard as a rock and your jaws ached.

My mom, bless her heart, stowed away my baseball cards after I grew up and left home. Years later she brought them out to me in the shoebox I'd kept them in. I hadn't seen them in many, many years, and as I looked through them, memories flooded back. They were like old, forgotten friends. Quite a reunion! So when you get tired of your baseball cards, put them in a safe place, because many years on you'll enjoy the feeling you get looking at all those old familiar faces on the cards.


A FRIEND OF MINE came through town with his family for a visit. He had his 16-year-old son with him. The son and I got to talking, and he said that he was collecting baseball cards; it was the in thing to do again. I mentioned that I still had my cards from when I was a kid. His eyes bulged!

"Would you like to take a look at them?" I asked.

He said he sure would, so I got out the shoebox. As he picked through them, he looked like he was going to go through the ceiling. Mickey Mantle. Hank Aaron. Stan Musial. Yogi Berra. Duke Snider. Pee Wee Reese. Sandy Koufax. Don Drysdale. Warren Spahn. Whitey Ford. And on and on. I even had some old gum that had come with the cards!

After he found seven Mickey Mantles in the bunch, I told him, "Yeah, I used to have a lot more, but the Mantle cards made the best sound on our bikes, so that's what we did with most of them." We finished looking at the cards and put them back in the shoebox.

I ended up giving my collection to my sons, and they mixed them in with their more current card collections, and spread them out on the floor, kind of like I did, except they arranged them in order of their prices in card guides, not in order of their batting averages. Times change.

I also collected autographed baseballs and bats, and game programs. I still have the programs from the 1957 World Series (the Milwaukee Braves vs. the New York Yankees), and the 1961 World Series with my hometown Reds vs. the Yankees. It's great to look at all that stuff from time to time.

I also recommend buying autographs. Not so much because they are worth money, but because you get a close-up look at a baseball star. I liked Willie Mays for a time when he was a player. I got the wind knocked out of me plenty of times and suffered plenty of bruises trying to perfect Mays' famous "basket catch," but I got it down. I read Say Hey: The Autobiography of Willie Mays, and was inspired by his speed and ability.

One time when my sons and I were headed to the world's biggest baseball-card show in San Francisco, Willie Mays was a featured celebrity. I thought to myself that I'd like to see him up close, and I'd like my boys to see him, too. Mays was BIG TIME in my day. In fact, some think he may be the greatest player of all time. (The debate never ends.) I bought the $25 ticket to get an autograph from Mays and paid another $6 for a baseball. I took the boys and stood in line. Finally, we made it to the platform and I got a good look at Willie. My boys did, too.

Up close to him, and even though he was middle-aged now and two decades into retirement, you could see why he could swing a bat the way he had from the size of his hands and forearms. He didn't say a word to us, just nodded and signed the ball and we were on our way. But it was worth the fee just to see a boyhood hero up close.

We put the signed baseball in with the rest of our memorabilia, and you can bet the boys were feeling good when an authentic Willie Mays autographed ball went for $525 at a baseball fund-raiser I took the kids to the following year. They were happy . . . and I was, too.

MY DAD GAVE ME an autographed Cubs baseball when I was a kid, and I can't remember which Cubs signed it, but I can remember what happened to it. Today, having been a youth-league baseball coach, I could go in the garage and pull out 200 or 300 baseballs. But back then, baseballs were in short supply. We kids in the neighborhood would use them and use them until the covers came off, and then we'd cover the balls with electrical tape and use them some more. We got our money's worth from a baseball. I don't know why we didn't have more of them, but we didn't.

One day I was heading out to practice batting and couldn't find a ball. The Cubs ball on my shelf beckoned. I figured, well, one or two hacks at it couldn't hurt . . . and besides, I'd hit it on the side where there weren't so many autographs. I took the Cubs ball out and hit it a few times. It rolled around on the grass. Then I took it back in. A couple days later, still no new baseball, so out I went again with the Cubs ball. Hit it a few more times. No harm done. Well, maybe a few grass stains.

The long and short of it was that by the time I had "gently" hit it day after day, it had gotten grass stains and walnut-juice stains, and the dogs had grabbed it a couple times and chewed on it before I could get it away from them. Well, I didn't have a nice autographed Chicago Cubs baseball anymore. Live and learn.

I held off taking out my Cincinnati Reds autographed ball and subjecting it to the same treatment. I still have it today. But, alas, the signatures start fading as time goes by.

Anyway, collect baseball stuff. You'll like to look at it when you hit geezerville, and your kids will like having it, too. If you're a coach, then your players will get a nice — and fun — history lesson from examining the artifacts from a distant era.

So moms: Save them shoeboxes!

# Notes:

# Girls in Baseball

Everything in this book applies to girl players as well as boy players. Sometimes I have skipped the gender-neutral constructions — "he/she," "him/her" and "his/hers" pronouns — but that's just to avoid making sentences more awkward than they already are.

A few girls play youth-league baseball, but as they get older they generally gravitate to fast-pitch softball. There are more opportunities for girls there, but I recommend that young female athletes interested in the sport put in a season or two playing hardball. It's a good experience. And softball beckons to both males and females in their "maturing" years. When former baseball players and fast-pitch softball players slow down, but still want the action The Game can provide, they'll head for the slow-pitch softball leagues. There is a lot of commonality between baseball and softball.

Times have changed, and gender equality continues to inch ahead, but it wasn't that long ago when, as president of the youth league I was involved with, I caused a stir by letting a lady train to be an umpire and work for a season. Several women had said they wanted to try, but only one came forward when the opportunity opened up. I took heat all season from traditionalists for giving the woman a chance, but our league's chief umpire worked with her and soon she was ready for the diamond. She was bright and interested in doing a good job.

Indeed, she turned out to be excellent, but when her season was up she said enough was enough. She was tired of the headaches, and of listening to complaints from the stands. All umpires get razzed, but she was singled out by the less-progressive fans (including some women). And the managers were merciless in their comments. If a bad or questionable call was made, or a borderline pitch went against a manager's team and set him off, it had to be because the WOMAN was on the job. My experience is that if a person wants to do the umpiring job, and can do the job, let him or her do the job. A league needs all the good umpires it can get.

And then there are the female managers. As league president I opened the door to "lady managers," too. Big mistake? Not at all! Again, if an adult is sincere about doing a good job, he or she will do very well at it. But I took gas for letting females try.

During a game when I was coaching 14- and 15-year-olds, I was very surprised to see a woman coaching the boys on the other team. She walked the walk and talked the talk, and I was surprised when she coughed up a big loogie and spat it in the dirt when she was coaching third base. Hey, times change!

SO THE GIRLS WANT to play, too, and I've seen some pretty good girl players, especially at younger ages. There was even a professional league of women players — the All-American Girls Professional Baseball League — that was successful for a time, organized by Philip K. Wrigley. He was head of the chewing-gum empire, and his family owned Wrigley Field and the Chicago Cubs. The league of 14 teams in the Midwest began play in 1943, and was intended to fill ballparks and sustain fan interest in The Game at a time when the professional leagues were suffering a manpower shortage due to World War II. The AAGPBL, with teams such as the Rockford Peaches and Milwaukee Chicks, lasted until 1954, and was immortalized in the 1992 Hollywood comedy A League of Their Own, starring Geena Davis, Rosie O'Donnell and Madonna.

I guess the level of play in the AAGPBL was very good. Play every day, and you're going to get better.

So you'll find a few girls on the baseball diamond nowadays, sprinkled among the youth-league baseball ranks although thinning out at the upper-age levels. And you'll find a great many girls filling the rosters of youth-league, traveling-team and high school softball squads, playing in baggy shorts and high socks, hair often drawn back tightly in ponytails. They viciously swing bats, fire the ball around, dive for grounders and flies, chew gum, darken their faces with charcoal. Maybe even hock a loogie from time to time.

I WAS OUT ON the ballfield one day, pitching batting practice to one of my boys. He was hitting balls to the outfield, and there was no one there to catch the flies. The park started to fill up with other players. Two girls came up to me with their gloves and asked if they could shag the flies. They were maybe 13 years old. I looked at them. I couldn't resist. With a straight face, I said: "Wellll . . . I don't know, you're GIRLS."

They turned red and didn't know how to respond. I told them I was just kidding. They perked up and got a little feisty.

"Yeah, we're girls. We'll show ya, you old man."

Turned out they were good. They could run, catch and throw as well or better than most of the boys that age. They were obviously competitive softball players. And every ball they threw in toward the mound landed a foot away from my glove and kicked up dirt in my face. I knew they did it on purpose.

So I finished up with my son hitting. The girls had dutifully thrown in all the balls hit into the outfield. I asked if they would like to take some cuts themselves. Of course they would.

Well, I couldn't wait to strike 'em out a couple times each, and told 'em so.

"Yeah, like, sure," they said.

Both were fast-pitch softball players. The girls their age pitch the ball 60 mph from 45 feet. So I reminded them how little the size of a baseball is, compared to a softball. "Yeah, like, sure," they replied.

I pitched my best 38 mph, looping, off-speed pitch from 60 feet 6 inches. Struck 'em both out three or four times. They were SO sad. They had SOOOOO wanted to do well.

Then I relented. I watched their swings and picked up the speed a little on my pitches. I put the ball right where they could hit it. They pasted my pitches all over the field and went away happy.

It had been fun.

They were good sports, and could really play.

# Sounds of the Diamond

There are great sounds on the baseball diamond. The whoosh of heavy air on a swing and miss. The sound of a fastball whistling as it goes by the batter into the catcher's mitt. The churning of cleats in the dirt and the rush of a slide. The thwack of a well-hit line drive. The thunk of the ball bouncing off the sponsor boards on the outfield fence. The announcer calling the names of the batters as they come up to the plate.

The "HEYBATTAHEYBATTAHEYBATTAHEYBATTA" chant of the infielders and outfielders. The umpire's "Steeeeeerike one!" and, "Yer out!" and, "Foul ball!"

And all the exclamations and shouts of encouragement of the fans and parents. But my two favorite sounds in youth baseball are these:

1) The foul ball as it goes up over the fence (or backstop screen) and heads for the parking lot, where it lands with a WHOMP on the hood or roof of a vehicle (perhaps a heavily-fortified SUV). No matter how many times you tell people not to park in the area that's within harm's way of flying balls, they do it anyway. (In some ball-field complexes, home runs accomplish the same feat.) It is a unique sound, and a favorite.

2) An even more interesting sound is when a ball leaves the playing field and lands on a windshield. There's the SMASH — then the "what the . . .!" exclamation when the owner discovers what has happened. (I've lost one windshield — on my yellow truck, the "A's-mobile," which is fitting, I guess) and I've gotten lots of dimples on the family's cars, but so it goes.)

The finest windshield sound I've ever heard came on a warm night near the end of one particular season. Our team wasn't doing very well, and we had a pitcher of lesser talent on the mound, just to give him a chance. He walked a few batters, and the manager told him to just throw strikes and let the batter hit it. After all, the pitcher had some of the finest fielders in the league backing him up, the manager said encouragingly. (Ha!)

Well, a big slugger was up, and our pitcher put one right down the middle. A towering fly ball came off the bat and went out of the park, disappearing in the dark, far out in the weed patch near the Veterans of Foreign Wars hall. That's pitching. If you're going to give up a fence-buster home run, it might as well be a monster blast.

The next batter up was another slugger. Typically, by the time it's late in the season the fans who didn't know better at the start have wised up and park their cars a respectable distance from the fences and foul areas (especially if the cars are nice and expensive). But on this night, a married couple was watching the game from their car parked in straightaway center. It provided a good view of the field, and really, what are the chances of being hit by a home run? There are dozens of foul balls in a game, but few home runs!

Our pitcher wasn't too happy about giving up a home run. As he faced the new slugger, he wound up and fired a pitch down the middle again, hoping to blaze it by. Didn't work. The ball came off the bat as hard as I've ever seen one hit. It was a rope that started to rise, and it was in a HURRY to leave the park. Of course, it was hit to dead center. The center fielder ran over to position himself in its path, but the ball reached him so fast he had little time to react, and it just flew over his head. Then it dipped, but cleared the fence and with an awesome THUMP and SQUOOOSH embedded itself in the windshield of the couple's car.

The safety glass spider-webbed. The ball held fast for several moments, then rolled down and off the hood to the ground. The eyes of the fans were as big and round and white as the baseball. You could see them clearly all the way across the field and hear the hissing gasp of the air rushing from their lungs in their astonishment at what had happened.

Truly the greatest windshield smack I've ever heard. And the man in the driver's seat was HOT.

What can you do? When your windshield's number is up, it's UP.

A great sound.

# Take Yourselves out to the (MLB) Ballgame

As you make your way through the youth baseball experience, make it a point to see some Major League Baseball games. Besides the sheer entertainment value and chance to participate in an all-American ritual, taking in a major league game will put in perspective just how good a player must be to turn the fun of playing baseball into an occupation.

Get to the ballpark early so you can see the pregame batting practice, and the players swinging in non-game situations. You'll note these athletes are very, very big people. Watching major leaguers on television makes it difficult to appreciate how large they are. Of course, if you're watching a televised game, you can compare the players' sizes to those of the umpires. The men in blue also happen to be big fellows, and many were excellent players themselves at some time in their lives; but they look like tiny people among the giants who are players in the majors. Just comparing their arm sizes is sufficient to give you an idea. Quite a difference!

To plan your visit to a major league park or a tour of several (or even many!) you can obtain a copy of the Baseball America Directory, which — as noted in the Part II chapter, "Bonding the Team with Its Big League Namesake" — is updated annually and contains teams' contact information. You also can use your favorite Internet search engine to find teams' websites, schedules and ticket information, or simply — if your local newspaper publishes a complete major league schedule for the upcoming season (which good papers do close to Opening Day) — save the season schedule to help you plan your trip.

Seeing major league games with your player(s) is a thrill. The Kirst family ended up visiting about half of the big league parks as our four boys were growing up. Whether making it to a game when visiting relatives in a different city, or just undertaking a family excursion, we would make a point to fit a game or two into our vacation schedule. We found that each city has a flavor of its own, and each stadium is different. A visit to a ballpark in a different city ends up being a cultural and learning experience — along with great entertainment. Therefore, using the goal of attending a game at a distant ballpark as a rationale for visiting relatives or friends or taking a family trip to a far-off city is certainly an acceptable itinerary-maker. Young players will accumulate moments to savor later in their lives. And if the park has a "fan day" when fans are permitted on the field before the game, by all means try to fit that day into your schedule.

THE SAN FRANCISCO GIANTS, at their old Candlestick Park, held a special day when fans were even allowed, before the pregame warmups, to take a turn on the bases. Youth players will really get a thrill from this sort of treat. Our sons did. It mostly was children who ran the bases in that promotion, but adults should also take advantage of the chance to get down to field level when possible. Being on an actual major league playing field gives the average fan an unforgettable angle on The Game.

When viewed from the playing field, a big league ballpark is a very imposing and forbidding place to try and play baseball. This is true even hours before a game, when the crowd has yet to arrive. The seats rise so high, to the dizzying top rows of the third deck, and it is readily apparent how easy it would be for a fielder to lose the ball against such a background. There's not a lot of blue sky against which players can measure the ball's flight path. This reality alone helps put big leaguers' skills into perspective.

Yes, an up-close look at the size and scope of major league playing conditions, and at the players themselves, can aid the parent in counseling a child about making the right life choices as the child's career progresses. Because someday it will be time for the child to put away the baseball glove. A friendly reminder of just how good one has to be to be a professional ballplayer — and a "remember when we saw ... at such and such ballpark ... and how big, strong, fast he was" — can sometimes tip the scales in a positive direction for the player and spare time and disappointment from unreasonably prolonging a career or having it abruptly end.

But let's not ignore the main purpose for going to a big league game: the fun. It instills a lifetime joy for The Game that can be duplicated every time a person passes through the gates and finds a seat, to watch the spectacle unfold on the emerald expanse in the heart of a busy concrete-and-metal city.

A special note about the seats: Get the best you can afford, and at some point try to get seats as close to the field as possible. When I ordered tickets for our family, they would be computer-generated, and thus the seating placement marginal. What I would do to improve our outing was buy an extra seat or two high in the upper deck in the least-expensive non-bleacher area. That way I could take a walk around the stadium and watch the action from different perspectives, and could send our children out to find the other seats and then wave to us from the upper deck. This was always fun, and the baseball park is, in our experience, a safe place for children to do some wandering and exploring on their own.

I DO ENJOY A day at a major league park. In fact, watching any baseball games played by teams that are fairly evenly matched is enjoyable. If your hometown has a minor league team, see some games. If it has a college team, see some games. A Saturday afternoon watching a high school doubleheader is lots of fun, too, and instructive for young players to see, as some of these players may want to give baseball a whirl at that level in their future. But even if your children have moved on to other things, it is interesting for a parent to take in a high school game. The players all just blend together into two uniformed teams trying to play The Game mistake free, and you can sit back and savor the action with none of the emotional attachment or anxiety inherent when your own flesh-and-blood (and likely that of your friends) is involved in the action, striving for moments of glory.

And if you're really feeling ambitious, get on a plane and fly to Japan. The baseball experience there is different and totally enjoyable. Their pros play the game well and their fans are fantastic people. Finding a hotdog at the stadium is not that easy, but there are plenty of bean pods, fried octopus nuggets and noodles, and the beer is delivered fast, cold and often.

Being really, really close to the action on the field at a major league game is quite a treat. For a youth-league coach, it feels as if you are there on the sidelines coaching or managing your own team. I've had excellent seats on a few occasions, thanks to friends or the luck of the draw, and once — for a brief but unforgettable game — I even had the finest seats imaginable. Our family was sitting out in left field at an Oakland A's game one night. José Canseco slugged a line-drive home run right at us. It was his 36th of the season. After a few ricochets, including off the head of one of the Kirst boys, I wound up with the ball. I had not been happy with my computer-generated seats on this occasion, because they were so far from the action, but . . . the baseball gods were looking out for me and had brought the action to me. All very nice!

It was the only baseball I have ever retrieved at a big league park. And it set me to thinking. I wrote to the then-owner of the A's, Mr. Walter A. Haas,

Jr., to vent my feelings about getting seats at his park. Surprisingly, my letter was answered by his staff, and signed by him. This led to a satirical exchange of correspondence that resulted in a baseball-seating miracle, thanks to Mr. Haas.

Two seasons later, Mr. Haas gave me his personal seats for a game, and they were right on top of the A's dugout. Six seats! The game the Kirst clan attended was a big one for the A's. It was televised nationally by ESPN, so it started in the late afternoon. I had brought my boys to the San Francisco Bay area to attend the world's largest baseball-card show, and the A's game was an extra event on our schedule. And was it ever an experience! The stadium was packed. We came with a small group of other youth baseball parents and their players, although they had the "cheap" seats. Still, the kindly A's ushers let me rotate our players and friends into "my" great seats, so everyone in our bunch got to see The Game played at the highest level, in the best possible place other than actually being on the field playing the game.

These seats provided a thrill and an eye-opener for me. The intensity of the players and coaches was much greater than I thought it would be. They were serious, serious, serious about winning the game and doing their best. As I mentioned, it was a very important game, and each team was fighting to make it into the playoffs. To see the tremendous talents moving in and out of the dugout below us and onto their places on the field was wonderful. And to be so close to the action and observe the much greater speed and strength with which The Game was played at that level made an indelible impression. The entire experience was a highlight of my baseball life. Now I had witnessed the entire scope of organized baseball — from Little League T-ball to Major League Baseball, up close and personal. It was just terrific.

Mr. Haas has since passed away and his family sold the A's. But his kind gesture made a real difference to me, my family and our friends. No doubt there is a special place for him in baseball heaven.

IF YOU'RE REALLY AMBITIOUS about your passion for baseball, put Cooperstown, N.Y., on your radar screen and make a visit to the National Baseball Hall of Fame. This town and all it has to offer is so interesting for a baseball fan that making it a trip destination is definitely worth it. It is a must-do for every serious baseball person. And if it takes some convincing of a non-baseball person in your midst, just couch the travel plans along literary lines, saying that you MUST visit the home of James Fenimore Cooper (1789-1851), the first major American novelist, and author of the series of novels known as "The Leatherstocking Tales," which include *The Last of the Mohicans.*

So as your players participate in baseball and grow up, it won't hurt to center some of your vacations around The Game and where it is and has been played. It makes for enjoyable travel with a purpose, and will give your young players a framework for memories of a pleasant past.

# The Pros and I

W hen you're a kid, and even when you get older and are still interested in The Game, you wonder what professional players are really like up close. There are only 750 or so major league players at the start of each season (a few hundred more are called up as replacements during a season or to fill out expanded rosters of non-contenders toward the end of a season), and there are a few thousand more minor leaguers. But you just don't run into pros on the street that often, or anywhere when you can get a good, up-close look at them. To true enthusiasts, the pros are idols, and they're busy nine months of the year training and playing.

I've seen my fair share of pro baseball players at the major league and minor league games I've attended, or as guest speakers at banquets. But I've never had any as next-door neighbors, or friends, or acquaintances. However, I've had face-to-face encounters with three players, getting the chance to talk with them and see what they were like. These encounters happened to me at different ages, and it is interesting how one's perspective changes from being just a kid introduced to a player, to a baseball-crazed kid, to a baseball-crazed adult.

The three pros I met were Ted Kluszewski, the famous Reds slugger; Pete Rose (the major league career leader in hits); and Mark Grace, first baseman for the Cubs. Having been born in Chicago and raised in Cincinnati, I can't ask for a better three to talk about:

• Ted Kluszewski — "Big Klu," as he was known around Cincinnati, and "Big Ted," as he was known around our house — was in business with my dad.

I was very young then but already an avid Reds fan. The Reds of that era had Ted, Johnny Temple, Wally Post, Gus Bell, Frank Robinson, Joe Nuxhall. Names that meant a lot to me (although the typical baseball fan today will probably only recognize Robinson's name).

Big Ted would come over to our home on occasion, and you can imagine what a thrill that was for a young baseball player. My dad was tall — 6-foot-6 — and my older cousins ranged in height from 6-2 to 6-8, so I was used to big guys. But Ted was something else. He was maybe 6-3, but weighed 250 pounds or so, and it was mostly muscle, especially in his shoulders, arms and hands. He had to have a special uniform made with no sleeves on it so he could swing the bat. That's how powerful he was. When he came over and I shook hands with him, his grip would go all the way up to my elbow. Getting to meet him gave me some real bragging privileges in the neighborhood. Quite a thrill for a young guy. I'll never forget it. "Klu" was a dominant player in his day, and he was a powerful home run slugger who rarely struck out.

• I was in business, too busy for baseball, and my boys weren't old enough to be practicing and playing much yet, but it was during this period that I met Pete Rose. I was always a fan of his and admired the way he hustled. He was known, after all, as "Charlie Hustle." I liked the way he played The Game. Also, I was from Cincinnati, and you can imagine how delighted I was with the "Big Red Machine," the powerful franchise the Reds were in the early to mid-1970s, when they reached four World Series and took the championship in 1975 and '76 with such superstars as Rose and Joe Morgan, Tony Perez and Johnny Bench. But I didn't have time to spend at ballparks or poring over the sports sections as I'd had in the old days.

I was running a company, and had a business meeting in Florida, where the Reds had their spring training. One of the company directors said he knew

Pete Rose, and asked whether I would like the director to see if he could get Rose to come over to talk to the guys in the business. I said, "Sure!" figuring I'd never hear about it again.

Well, the next day, right in the middle of a meeting I was conducting, the doors burst open, and into the room walked Pete Rose. What a thrill! Everyone knew who he was, of course, and my friend introduced him. We stopped the meeting, and Rose gave a pep talk to all of us and chatted with everyone, shook our hands, and was really nice. He wasn't as physically large as I thought he would be, but his arms and hands were massive. He was no Adonis, no perfectly proportioned physical specimen, but you could see how he was stocky and very strong-looking, which explained how he was so durable and able to control his bat so well. It was just great to be able to meet Pete Rose face to face and listen to him give a nice off-the-cuff motivational talk to the guys.

Some years later, after his well-publicized off-field problems hit the media and Major League Baseball's commissioner banned Rose from baseball, my boys and I were in San Francisco with another dad and his sons who were friends of ours, to attend another of the world's largest baseball card shows. A number of players past and present were scheduled to appear to sign autographs for a $25 signature fee. Rose was among these, and it so happened he was staying in the same hotel we were in. I was sitting in my room one morning when my sons and their young friends burst in and one of my boys said, "Dad, dad, dad, Pete Rose is in the dining room . . . we're going to go get his autograph. Come on down, go with us."

I said no, I wasn't going to go start ogling and bothering a guy at his breakfast. Just then, my friend came in to see what the commotion was about and where his kids were. When he heard the news about Pete Rose, my friend said he was going to go down to the dining room to meet Pete Rose at breakfast, and if I didn't want to go, too bad. So I said, fine, I still wasn't going.

"I've already met him," I said, very smug. I figured Rose would give this gang of brazen interlopers the brush-off.

Next thing I knew, they were back in the room. They said Rose had agreed to talk to them and sign some autographs after he finished breakfast. They were to come back down at such and such a time. I figured, sure. I knew they were set up for a big disappointment. But they were certainly excited, fully taking the baseball great at his word.

One of my boys saw a sporting-goods store a couple blocks from the hotel, so he ran out and bought some baseballs. My friend kept the other kids in check. At the appointed time they went back to the dining room. Rose was there, as he said he'd be, and signed everything they had brought for him — baseballs, hats, cards, the whole bit. Then he chatted with them for a time and wished them good luck with their baseball and their lives. Couldn't have asked for a bigger thrill for a bunch of starry-eyed kids. Rose did everything but play catch with them. I was happy about that. I knew other "stars" had ducked out the back door and left kids waiting on promised encounters.

So off we went to the card show, and Pete Rose made his appearance. We saw him signing away, with a reservation required and a two-hour wait necessary to get his autograph. He'd taken care of our kids for free and given them a thrill. I'd always told them to play like Pete Rose with his hustle and intensity, and that if they did, they'd have some success in The Game no matter how naturally good they were. Whenever they did heed my advice and bore down with full effort, it paid off. And now, here was the man in the flesh, and actually being nice to them. Great. Baseball can be great.

Later, the kids ran into him again when we were standing on the street corner outside the hotel waiting for a cab, and he chatted with them once more. Good guy. Can't ask for more than that from a star. Helps keep The Game alive.

• Now, Ted Kluszewski was my dad's age. Pete Rose was my age. Mark Grace was old enough to be my kid. Time marches on.

Grace was in town one January as a scheduled speaker for a fund-raiser. A friend of mine was one of the dinner's organizers. He called me that afternoon before the dinner and said, "Jeff, come on over to the house at 6 with the kids tonight. Mark Grace is going to be there, and they can meet him."

At 5:45, I had each of my boys outfitted in a Chicago Cubs hat and we were out the door and over to the friend's house. He let us in and we followed him into the kitchen, and sure enough, there was Grace, sitting at the kitchen table signing his name to some of the items that other children from the neighborhood had brought over. My friend introduced us. Grace looked very young to me. (Again, time marches on.)

He signed every scrap of paper, baseball, hat and program that every kid in the kitchen had brought. Very nice. Then he chatted a little with the kids about baseball and how he'd made it to the majors. Then I got to talk a while, asking him some meaningful questions.

"How good is your eyesight — 20/20?"

He said it was 20/15.

"Did you do any other sports?"

Basketball, but he stopped playing that to concentrate on baseball.

"Can you still walk down the street without people bothering you?"

He could in southern California, but in Chicago more folks were starting to recognize him, although it wasn't bothersome.

"Have you faced Nolan Ryan, and if so, what's it like?"

Yes. You have to start to swing when he goes into his windup.

"How tough is major league pitching?"

Very tough.

"Were you the best player on all your teams?"

No. He was good, but a late bloomer, and didn't come into his own until he was older.

Grace's father had made the trip with him, and was in the kitchen. He explained that he'd given his son good tips while Mark was moving up through youth baseball, but he didn't drive Junior to play or force him to do things. He'd play catch and the like with him, but the one special thing he did was make sure Mark had the best equipment. I knew that was a good point. Good equipment makes a difference, and if a player is going to do his best, he probably should have the best equipment to compete with. Many times, players aren't that adept at figuring out what is best for them.

So that was our visit. I'm a Mark Grace fan. He was nice to my boys and gave them some tips. And I'm a Mark Grace's dad fan, because he gave me some tips, too. The two stayed around for about an hour, before we had to head for the dinner. Mark posed for some pictures, and I got a great shot of my four sons with him. It was a very nice picture of a memorable occasion. And after I got the image developed, I noticed that it had been taken in front of a grandfather clock. Such significance!

The picture shows a professional baseball player with four little players with hopes for the future. And it was taken by me — a relic of the past long forgotten by all but me — with the clock behind ticking away, as time marches on.

# Dreaming of 'The Show'

E very kid in youth baseball knows who the best few players in the league are. And each kid below this all-world level figures that, after the superstars, he's right up there near the top. This belief is particularly strong when players are little. When they get up in the high school range, they can take a look at the talent and realistically determine where they fit in; but those little players are all enthused and they ALL think they're premier talents and heading for the majors. It's only a question of when they get there.

I can categorically state that no player I have ever coached has made it to The Show . . . yet. I've no doubt wrecked many a career in my days managing and coaching. That's youth baseball. So it goes. Many had the talent to go to The Show, but other interests came up and they weren't to be on their way. But I think they will all appreciate The Game after having been on one of my teams.

And what of my career? Well, if I had had better coaching, there is no doubt that it would have been the majors for me. Absolutely. And I can prove it. But for a few breaks . . . blah, blah and blah.

I went to the computer department of one of the world's great universities. There, we input the relevant data of all the Major League Baseball players for my era. Height, weight, speed, batting average and more. One good thing about baseball is the availability of statistics. And we found plenty of info on the backs of old baseball cards. All this went into the computer, along with my vital statistics from what would have been my prime, and testimonials obtained from police files and parole officers: "He ran faster than The Flash when I was trying to catch him. His hands were the quickest I've ever seen when he was counting the money."

The computer worked and worked and worked. Conclusion: .306 lifetime hitter; Gold Glove outfielder; high on-base percentage; few strikeouts; many doubles; few home runs.

So, since we all know computers are perfect calculators — there you have it! A major league career.

So, players, parents and coaches, take the playing advice in this book as gospel! Heed it thoroughly, refer to it constantly. It's your ticket to The Show.

That's why the diamond is called the "Field of Dreams."

# Reaching Your Peak

At some point in your time in The Game, you'll reach your peak. You will go no further. You'll be the knucklehead on the team.

Anyone who sticks with The Game long enough reaches the point where he is the knucklehead, the worst player on the roster, the scrub who puts in the most bench time, the "substitute right fielder." That's one of the reasons you should always be nice to the lesser players on any squad you play on. Someday, you'll be in their cleats.

For me, the end came early. I never really reached my peak, but I did go from starting catcher to substitute right fielder over the course of my career in youth baseball. There's no doubt that, had I stuck with The Game rather than turned to other sports, things would have turned out differently, but that's the way it goes. I guess I allowed myself to be discouraged about continuing in baseball after a little chat I had with a girl I liked in high school. She was the daughter of the baseball coach. She didn't like me, and told me in no uncertain terms that as long as her dad was the coach, I'd never make the cut, no matter how well I thought I could play. Nice girl! So I never tried high school baseball. I continued my swimming career, which turned out to be just fine in every way.

After I was in full-blown adulthood — a husband, businessman and father — I thought briefly of renewing my career. The minor league team in my town of Reno was conducting tryouts. I figured maybe they'd need a novelty player ... and I was a catcher. Teams always need catchers.

Well, I showed up at the tryouts, took a look, and saw that everyone could run fast and was half my age. So I took a pass that day. Then I heard that the local semi-pro league, which had a handful of teams, was holding tryouts. I figured I could for sure make one of those clubs, so I made a few visits to the minor league ballpark where the league played and had myself a look at the level of play. I watched pregame warmups. The better teams were out of the question — loaded with former minor leaguers, college players and ex-high school stars. But a couple teams were desperate to add players. I knew I could make the cut on one of them . . . and keep my dream alive. I was particularly encouraged when I saw one of the catchers. Bigger, fatter and uglier than I. There was my chance!

This catcher was slow. When he squatted behind the plate he had to lift his stomach off the ground to uncover the plate. He was B-I-G. There was hope for me. Then I sat through a portion of one of the games and checked out the pitchers. The best of them were college hurlers, playing in the league to stay tuned up for the college season. No professional contracts for them, because they had a few years of school in front of them. These youngsters were half my age, or even less. They hurled the pearl in the high 80s. Hmmm, hittable by me . . . but no control! With a wife and four sons, and four youth teams to coach, I thought better of it. Couldn't afford to catch a bean ball.

Still . . . my fantasy didn't dissolve entirely. I thought, maybe . . . one of these days . . . if I can just get that knuckler working again. . . .

A FRIEND OF MINE told me how he'd reached his peak. He'd been a real player. All-star in Little League. All-star in Senior League. High school varsity letterman as a freshman. Great high school career. Then a junior-college scholarship.

But at each level, the competition got a little stiffer. He did well in JC and was able to trade up to a four-year university with a top-notch baseball program. And there he hit the wall. He gave it all he had, but the best he could do was platoon at shortstop and second base. And he wasn't the starting shortstop. He just didn't have quite enough talent to put it over the top.

His team made it to the NCAA Regionals, and was one win away from making it to the College World Series. If the team earned a spot to that tournament, only the traveling squad would make the trip, not the deep reserves. The big game began and my friend wasn't in the starting lineup. In the late innings he was called on to pinch hit with runners on base and the game on the line. He got a base hit and his team was off to Omaha. Since he was the hero of the must-win game, he earned the last spot on the traveling team.

In Omaha he sat the bench, as usual. He got one at-bat, and grounded out to short. That was the peak of his career. And the end. Still, he'd gone much farther than most players ever will.

As for me? I knew I was in trouble when, in Senior League, on the regulation-size diamond, my coach asked me not to throw the ball to second at the start of the first inning of one game. No "coming down" throw from me, the catcher? He explained he didn't want the other team to see how "powerful" my arm was right away. At that stage of my career, it was necessary for me to launch the ball high enough to bring down an airliner in order to get it to second on the fly.

But I could still hit, and if you can hit they'll find a place for you to play. And I did go out on top. Sort of.

A more talented catcher was found. I moved to the outfield. Right field. A regular right fielder, but a right fielder nonetheless. I didn't mind the outfield. I had played it from time to time over the years. But it wasn't quite the same as catching. The season ended with me in right field. I'd done all right at the plate. A career? Not quite!

A week-and-a-half or so later, my coach called and asked if I'd be around for the next few days, to which I said yes. He hung up. He called back later to tell me I was on the all-star team. It seemed some of the better players were heading out of town on summer vacation and there was a spot for me to play in the all-star game if I wanted it. I said sure. I was happy.

The all-star game was to be played under the lights at the VFW field. It would be the first game I would ever play under the lights. And the last. I sat on the bench most of the game, but I was glad to be there. When I got to bat, I hit a single. Out in right field, I made a play. But there you have it. A career concluded as a substitute right fielder.

I got a trophy, which I kept for many years, and of course I've got the memories of my active playing days on the diamond and my moments of glory, which get better and better all the time.

SO, ALL PLAYERS REACH the end of the line. It is just a question of when. But we all go into The Game knowing the end will come some day, so enjoy the moments of glory while you can. And as for you coaches, help your players have some pleasant memories when they are at the peak of their game.

# Dads as Coaches

D ads get involved as coaches to participate with their kids and give them the best opportunities possible in youth baseball. But dads also get involved because they simply love The Game. They probably played as kids themselves. It's just a great game. It's fun to train for. It's fun to practice. It's fun to play. It's fun to watch. The Game stays with you your whole life.

It's funny how an adult man can be standing on the infield with the players before a game, and then as game time approaches the man must walk off and sit in the bleachers. There can be a little tug at the heart then, a feeling that, no, I want to stay behind and play!

It's a strange and potent dose of longing. And it shows how deep the roots of baseball can sink into a person, even if those roots are ignored for many years while away from The Game.

So, there will always be a supply of dads ready and willing to coach youth baseball. It's a pleasure to be involved. When Game Day arrives, the feeling of excitement wells up inside. And if you're a manager, you can sit at home in your chair, filling out your team's lineup while a major league game is being broadcast on your television or radio. You feel connected to something larger than yourself.

There are all kinds of pleasures involved in coaching a youth team. The bonding with the players, other coaches and parents. The communal sharing of triumphs and tribulations. Watching players develop. And the unfolding of the games themselves, which are rarely dull. Every at-bat, every play in the field, is a source of unpredictable action.

If there is a price to pay for coaching, it's the sacrifice the family has to make. For 90 days, the dad will put in endless hours preparing and running practices and games. The team is the priority, the season schedule is king. Games cause mood swings: coming home happy and chatty after a victory, or moping around the house gloomy and mum after a loss.

Meals are eaten at the snack bar — steady diets of hot dogs, pretzels, sunflower seeds and Gatorade.

But, inevitably, the season ends. The family no longer feels like it's camping at the ballfields. Who knows? Maybe it's time to take a vacation.

Unless Junior's made all-stars.

PART V

# A MITTFUL OF STORIES

*Baseball lends itself to the stuff stories are made of:*

*• The suspense and tension of competition.*

*• Characters who come to The Game from all walks of life.*

*• Twists of fate when the laws of physics collide with the unpredictable nature of human actions.*

*• Classic plots, including favorites vs. underdogs, championships at stake, unexpected heroics or blunders, moral lessons delivered in ironic ways.*

*• Mini-dramas playing out within grander dramas — such as games within the scope of a season, innings within the scope of a game, outs within the scope of an inning, and pitches within the scope of an at-bat. And a season within the scope of a lifetime.*

*That is all part of the beauty of baseball.*

*The diamond itself is a fertile arena for spawning tales, for each section of a baseball field — the various bases; the nooks, swaths and warning tracks of the outfield; the basepaths and corners; the mound and the batter's box; the foul lines and foul poles; the dugouts and the backstop; the fences and bleachers — has a charm and spirit of its own.*

*Everyone who's ever been passionately involved with The Game has stories to tell of events never to be forgotten. And as the actual events fade into the mists of time, the stories grow even better!*

*In this final part of the book are a few of the stories that materialized during my experience with baseball at the youth-league levels.*

# The Worst Pitch
# Ever Thrown

One of my sons holds the Reno Continental Little League record for the worst pitch ever thrown. It happened like this:

He hadn't had a great deal of pitching experience, but was on the upward swing of the learning curve. He'd walked some, given up some hits, struck a few players out . . . and plunked a few, too. An embryonic pitching talent starting to come into his own.

Soooo . . . in one particular game, he'd pitched himself into a bind. A hit, a couple walks, a pop-up and a groundout. Two down, but the bases were loaded. And, as we know, there is no such thing as a routine play in youth baseball. Anything could happen.

The team I was managing had the first-base dugout. Managers stood outside their dugout in a designated area about a third of the way down the baseline, 20 feet beyond the foul line, near the on-deck circle. So there I was, cheering on our pitcher (my son) and our defense. It was late in the game and the score was tied. My son's older brother was playing first base. That would end up complicating matters.

The son on the mound faced the batter. The first pitch was fouled off, the second was a called strike. Then came two balls to even the count 2-2. The pitcher knew he had to be ready to charge home to cover the plate in case the ball got by the catcher (a typical way runs are scored in Little League). The situation was tense. Frankly, it didn't look good for our pitcher.

The next I knew, either he or his brother had called timeout and were having a powwow midway between the mound and first base. I couldn't hear what they were saying. Just as I started to walk out on the field to see what was going on, the consultation broke up and they returned to their positions. "Play ball," the umpire said. So I didn't get a chance to find out what had been discussed.

If there was any thought to console me, it was that there were numerous ways for us to get that final out to end the inning (that's why I love to have the bases loaded). There could be a popup, groundout, force at any base, or strikeout. I knew we could get out of this jam.

On the mound, my son was really concentrating on his next pitch as he prepared to take his stance. It was an odd moment, as if everything was running in slow motion. The drama was building. He stepped onto the pitching rubber and started to go into a full windup. Why not? The runners weren't going anywhere. (In Little League, a runner can't legally leave a base until the pitch crosses the plate.)

My son's right shoulder dipped down and his left leg kicked high in the air. His knuckles seemed to scrape the ground as he reared back to throw. What?! His motion was sidearm!

His glove was raised up like a shield to mask the deception as he swung forward with an awkward contortion. The momentum of the front leg-kick and his deep sidearm motion caused his body to twist off-balance. The ball rocketed out of his hand.

BUT!!! Instead of heading plateward, it came directly at me where I stood in front of the dugout. The pitch was launched a good 25 feet off target. It cracked right into my shin and settled, spinning in the dirt at my feet. The crowd gasped — an eerie rasping sound. The players' jaws went slack, mouths agape. And I mean ALL the players — fielders and runners. The other team's coaches positioned off of first and third base and in the dugout stood in stunned silence. The crowd went mum. The wind died. There was no noise whatsoever. None. No one moved.

I froze, too. I didn't touch the ball. It was in play ... or so I figured. No one came to get the ball. No runner advanced. Just dead stillness.

Finally, the umpire regained his composure, called time, and asked me to throw the ball over to the catcher. I did, then made sure time was really called. The umpire said it was. I stepped out to the mound and, in as composed a voice as possible, asked my son the pitcher, "What the heck are you doing?"

"It's all right, dad," he said. "It's only a full count now."

"BUT WHAT ARE YOU DOING?"

"Well," he said, "Charlie and I talked about it. And he said, with two strikes on this guy, I could get him with the submarine pitch. So I threw one. I figured I could."

"BUT YOU'VE NEVER THROWN A SUBMARINE PITCH BEFORE!!! YOU'VE GOT TO PRACTICE THAT STUFF BEFORE YOU TRY IT IN A GAME!!!"

The umpire called time in, and I left the little conference on the hill with these final words: "Just throw a regular pitch, and try to keep it low."

He did, and the obviously shaken batter grounded weakly to the second baseman for an easy force out and the end of the inning.

We had just witnessed the worst pitch ever thrown and ever seen at our fields. THE WORST. And I've seen a few bad pitches launched, but usually they are errant into the backstop and NEVER as far out of line as that one into the dugout area.

Is there a lesson in this?

Maybe it's that sometimes if you do listen to your older brother, things may work out?

Or maybe it's that if you are so bad, if you venture well beyond the limits of expected rottenness, you can emerge triumphant?

Incidentally, we went on to win the game. And there were no more submarine pitches thrown that day, by either side.

# Unflinching Eye

Bartholomew Roberts was a big, strong kid on our team, a 12-year-old and our oldest player. As our Little League Minor division team practiced in preparation for the season ahead, our hitters improved their eyes for the ball and their stances and swings. Except for Bartholomew Roberts. He couldn't seem to make any progress at the plate. He just wasn't able to get his bat on the ball.

Although he'd been in the league for a couple seasons and had played in the Farm division, I hadn't had him on a team before. Perhaps his previous coaches hadn't taught him the basics, I thought. But I couldn't seem to help him at all to bat better, either.

I worked and worked with him, pitching him dozens and dozens of tennis balls. He swung and swung and swung, but just couldn't make contact.

It wasn't his attitude. Although he was quiet, Bart was enthusiastic and paid attention. I figured a kid his size should be able to hit the ball pretty far. I was flustered.

I tried to examine every angle. "Are you seeing the ball well?" I asked. He said he wasn't sure.

Bart was right-handed, threw right-handed and batted from the right side. He said he was comfortable from that side of the plate. But I decided to test which of his eyes was dominant. (This test is described in the Part I chapter, "Simply Hitting.") I held my fingers in the shape of a triangle a few inches in front of his face and told him to close each eye in turn, so we could figure out which of his eyes was dominant. Were it his right eye, I'd have him try batting lefty.

"Well, coach, I can't see out of this eye," he said, pointing at his left eye. "I only have one eye. The other one's a glass eye."

"I didn't know that," I said with surprise. "Well, that explains it."

So I had him try batting from the left side, so his functional eye would be facing the pitcher. Of course, I stressed safety with him and emphasized that he must immediately protect himself from any pitch that looked like it was coming at his head.

Turned out he was no better from the left side. He stuck with the right-handed stance.

We kept on practicing, and Bart's hitting did improve a bit as the season progressed. But it's difficult enough to hit a baseball with two good eyes. I admired his determination.


GAME DAY. OUR PLAYERS were seated in the dugout. We had just finished batting in the bottom of the third. I called them to come out and hit the field, take infield warmup before the fourth inning. But nobody budged.

"Pirates, Pirates, you've got to get out on the field!" I hollered.

No Pirates emerged.

I stalked over to the dugout, annoyed.

"Pirates, you've got to get out of there. What are you doing in there?"

"Just a minute, coach, just a minute," a player said. "Bart has his glass eye out and he's showing it to us. It's great."

Bart had his glass eye cupped in a hand, and the players were crowding around, taking turns looking at it. They were fascinated.

That year we had a team of 13 players with 25 working eyes.

BART DID END UP getting some hits that season. Defensively, he played the outfield, where he was no more successful catching flies than he was hitting fastballs. Not his fault. He didn't have depth perception.

I think that season was the end of the line for him playing baseball. I'm glad he had fun at it. He was a good teammate, always enthusiastic. And with no hint of facetiousness, I must say that he really did his best to keep his eye on the ball.

# Notes:

# Lip Fungus Fiasco

O ur star player, "Eddie," had missed two practices in a row. That did not bode well for our Little League team in the Farm division. We had started the season strong. We had good hitters, especially Eddie. In Farm, where you hit off of the pitching machines, the team with the best bats usually wins, since pitching isn't a factor. But you have to field the ball, too, and without the sure-gloved Eddie at shortstop, we were a much lesser squad.

Eddie hadn't called to let me know why he was absent. I chalked that up to him being from a difficult family situation.

Then, without warning, he appeared at our next game. And it was immediately clear why he'd been missing. He had a strange medical condition. It was a lip fungus that looked like something from outer space. The best way for me to describe it is to say that it resembled the greenish, crystallized mold you'd find growing on mayonnaise if you left a jar of it outside for several days in the summer sun.

The fungus covered both of Eddie's lips on one side of his mouth. (As you are no doubt imagining, it was pretty disgusting.)

We didn't know how it had gotten there, but it was there. (Dripping and oozing. Just horrible.)

We could see it. We could smell it. We could see the drops falling from it into the dugout dust.

Eddie said he had seen a doctor about it, and that he was OK. That was scant reassurance for our players and coaches. We were horrified.

We didn't know whether he was contagious.

That lip fungus ended up costing us dearly.

I PUT EDDIE AT his usual position, short. Sure enough, his share of grounders was hit his way. Even though he was under the weather, he fielded them as usual. But the first baseman wasn't eager to catch Eddie's throws. He was tentative. So were the other infielders. They couldn't help thinking about that green fungus dripping on the ball when Eddie touched it. So they kept missing his throws. The ball would bounce away and opponents' runners would advance. Over and over again.

In the dugout, nobody wanted to sit near him. Nobody wanted to touch the team bat.

We lost the game.

Fortunately, Eddie's condition healed up. Fungus-free, he was back to his old self again, and his teammates were greatly relieved. We started winning again. The Green Horror was behind us.

# The Babe Traded for Butterfinger

O ne team I managed had a real mix of ages on it. One young fellow was a little round in the midsection, left-handed, a real baseball enthusiast, and very quiet and contemplative around the older players on the team.

He took his baseball seriously and wanted to do well. He wanted to try pitching, so I let him have some chances. He followed instructions and did a commendable job. His dad was a big guy and also a baseball lover, so you could see that the son might want to stick with The Game and could have some success in the future, being left-handed and all.

However, at this tender point of his career, he was just a little, slightly pudgy guy who needed the usual encouragement about baseball that nearly all young players need, particularly when they are the youngest on a team with older players who seem to be so much bigger and better. He wore his uniform pants very high up, so that the beltline was on his chest. This was due to the nature of his size, the pants' size and our uniform shirts. In all, he looked just like a miniature Babe Ruth. And that's what we coaches called him: "Babe." He took to the name after I explained to him the history of Babe Ruth, and how The Sultan of Swat had started out as an excellent left-handed pitcher with the Red Sox before becoming the famous home run slugger on the Yankees.

Little Babe didn't say much, but he was right in there with his teammates and well-liked — a real part of the ballclub. Everybody was pulling for him when he got his chance to take his licks at the plate, and when he was in the field.

IT SO HAPPENED THAT for a number of games that season I had been bringing Baby Ruth candy bars for our players (and coaches) to eat after the game. One game, I didn't bring the Baby Ruths but substituted Butterfingers, figuring a change of pace might be welcomed by the players and coaches. But I hadn't foreseen the confusion — and despair — this switch would cause.

The unexpected reaction was triggered by the unique way I wrote out the lineup card that I posted on a clipboard on the dugout wall. I always posted the lineup on the wall so that the players could see the batting order and keep one another apprised about who was due up. (Incidentally, I never posted the fielding assignments, as that produced player expectations that could not always be met as the game developed.)

Anyway, at the bottom of the lineup chart, I always scribbled the names of any players who would be absent from that game. The team rule was that if a player couldn't come, he needed to call me beforehand or tip me off at a prior game or practice. To keep things light in the dugout, I'd make up some hypothetical excuse for each missing player's absence and write that next to the player's name. "Alligator wrestling," or, "shark hunting," or, "touring China and the Great Wall," and so forth.

Because on this particular day I'd decided to change the type of candy bar in the dugout, I jotted this down under the names of the couple players who would be missing: "Babe traded for Butterfinger."

That became the source of the confusion!

As our team was finishing pregame warmups, Little Babe walked up to me, and in a hurt voice said: "Coach. Coach. What have you done? What have you done? What do you mean?"

Tears were welling up in his eyes.

"Coach," he continued. "I love this team. What have you done?"

"Well," I said, surprised and concerned. "I haven't done anything. What's the matter?"

"The lineup, coach. Look. Right there. It says, 'Babe traded for Butterfinger.' Coach, I don't want to go. I don't want to be on another team."

The realization switched on in my brain.

I quickly pointed out to Little Babe that in the posted lineup, rather than the player-news area, his name was right there, as usual. He wasn't going to another team. We needed him on this team. We had to keep The Babe if we were going to keep our season going and on track.

"The trade means I'm just giving out Butterfingers instead of Baby Ruth bars tonight."

Then he understood. He wiped his eyes and smiled. He was a happy baseball player again.

And I saw another demonstration of how sensitive youth baseball players can be, and how much their team can sometimes mean to them.

# Notes:

# In Their Cups

F or whatever reason, participants in youth baseball generally avoid uttering the word "cup" when talking about protection, so coaches typically ask their players before a game if they have their "protective gear."

The response from my teams was usually a chorus of "clack, clack, clack," like castanets, as the players tapped between their legs with hands, bats or batting helmets to demonstrate their abidance with the rules. But on most teams, more often than not if a player simply says he's got his "protective gear" on, the coach takes the player's word for it since it isn't something the coach cares to check.

But protective gear is not comfortable to wear, and not all youth players have had enough time on the diamond — or in any sport — to have experienced that breathless, agonizing feeling that results from a shot to the unshielded nards. That's why some players will pretend they are wearing what they are not wearing, and take their chances, despite authoritative warnings that "you'll be sorry" if something unfortunate transpires.

Older, more experienced players don't suffer such shortsightedness. They'll clack on demand, and the clack will be genuine. But the message is never universally received and acted upon — whether the players are pre-pubescent Little Leaguers or Babe Ruth 15-year-olds. So The Game continues with an occasional "Achilles heel" exposed, so to speak.


I WAS COACHING THE Reds in the Babe Ruth division. It was an evening game against another competitive team in the league — the Yankees, if I recall. It was a beautiful, if slightly chilly, night for baseball under the lights. The sun had set. The bright green infield grass glistened with dew. The basepaths and infield around the bases shone the orange they take on when sands are damp and the air heavy with humidity.

The game was close and going well for us, but the Yankees were tough as always and there was little room for error. In a later inning, our opponents threatened to score with men on second and third, but had given up two outs getting them there. Any ball through the infield would bring in two runs. But if we could manage to make the play on the next batter, we'd be in good stead since our big hitters were coming up and we had high hopes of putting runs on the board and taking the lead.

Footing on the grass was treacherous, and several of our players had slipped making plays, but had recorded outs nonetheless with no harm done. A strong right-handed batter came to the plate. He was capable of putting any errant pitch out of the park. He always hit the ball hard, and rarely struck out. All our players knew this and were on high alert.

He took two balls and just missed hammering the third pitch, fouling it off high in the air straight back — a sure sign he was onto our pitcher's best efforts. The batter dug in for the fourth pitch. He was smart and well-coached. He knew our pitcher couldn't afford to hit him and load the bases, so he knew the pitch wasn't coming inside. He also knew our pitcher couldn't waste a pitch and run the count to 3-1, for that would be followed by a fat one down the middle to prevent a walk. Therefore he was looking for a pitch away — something that could be driven to the right side.

He was correct. The pitch came to the outside part of the plate. And drive that pitch he did! He got a full, powerful swing on the ball, and it came off the bat like a rocket. It shot across the infield, a low line drive on a trajectory to the right of our second baseman.

OUR GUY PLAYING SECOND that game was an exceptional fielder who often played third base or shortstop. He knew from experience on the hot corner that all balls must be stopped, and knew from his time at short exactly how to play a ball hit hard to his side and field it cleanly. He was ready for this missile and knew what must be done. The game could be on the line.

The ball hit the wet grass of the infield two feet from the dirt. Instead of taking a normal hop, its contact with the sod caused it to pick up speed like a car with locked brakes swerving out of control on slick pavement.

The second baseman had positioned himself perfectly in the ball's path and was charging forward in a crouch just as it took its screaming skip. It passed by his glove and outstretched forearms and struck him straight on his "protective gear."

The resounding crack was like the thunderclap of a lightning bolt striking very, very close. Our second baseman doubled over on his heels and rolled onto his side, as if knocked over while riding a tricycle. The ball, stopped by the player and his "protective gear," dribbled out onto the basepath sand and stopped.

The stunned fielder, knowing the importance of completing the play, righted himself onto his knees, shook his head, crawled to the ball and made the throw to the first baseman for the third out, just ahead of the batter dashing with long strides toward the bag.

Our intrepid infielder's teammates helped him off the field and into the dugout. There he regained his composure, took some deep breaths and examined the area of his "protective gear." Fortunately, all was in order. Gingerly, he fished downward and finally removed the round, hard-plastic piece that had been splintered and smashed in half by the impact of the batter's drive.

Everyone in the dugout was impressed by our player's fortitude — and sat there with serious contemplations of what might have been but for the "protective gear."

DURING OUR TEAM TALK after the game, I impressed upon our players the value of the graphic lesson they had witnessed about being attired with the proper equipment.

At our next game, when I reminded our players that they should have their "protective gear" in place, the response was a veritable cacophony of clack, clack, clacks. And I am certain we for once had full participation.

# In a Tight Wedge

M y son Rew wanted to pitch on the Minor division team I was managing, and worked hard for a spot in the rotation. He threw at our team practices, and threw at home for even more practice. I put him into a game for two innings, and he responded by regularly getting the ball over the plate. So I gave him more opportunities, which he enjoyed.

My system usually was to throw a pitcher for only two innings per game, thus giving chances to as many worthy players as possible. Rew liked being on the hill, in charge of the pace of the game and at the center of attention. Why not?

One Saturday he was scheduled for an appearance and was, of course, excited. We were in a rush that morning to get out of the house and down to the fields for pregame warmups. Rew was still dressing in the car on the drive over. Fortunately, he'd remembered his glove, cleats, stirrups and hat. He was a bit disheveled, but had a complete uniform.

There's always the thrill of anticipation before a game, but it's doubled when your own kid's going to pitch. Rew had been coming along fine. He'd developed a style that included a leg kick so high that the batter would be looking at the bottom of Rew's shoe, *à la* the great Leroy "Satchel" Paige. Rew could throw pretty hard, but hadn't worked out a curveball or mastered the grip for consistently throwing the changeup. He compensated for these shortcomings by varying the speeds of his fastballs, and hiding the ball from the batter's view as long as possible in his glove and in the backward motion of his delivery. This deception had worked well.

On this Saturday morning, Rew strode out to the mound for the first inning with a smile, shoulders back, brimming with the confidence that well-planned and executed training will give a player. He had completed his warmups in the bullpen, and he threw his six warmups from the mound. Now it was "Play ball!"

Rew pitched fine. He got the ball over the plate as usual, gave up a couple hits but held the opponents scoreless. But I noticed his leg kick wasn't as high at the end as it had been at the beginning. I figured that maybe he'd tired a bit, or was trying something new.

After the third out, instead of dashing off the mound to the dugout, he walked in slowly, funny.

"You did fine," I told him. "You looked good. How do you feel?"

"Dad," he said. "That was the worst. It was awful!"

"What do you mean? It went well. You got 'em out. It was good."

"Dad," he said with a pained expression. "It was terrible! After my second pitch, you won't believe it. My uniform shifted. Do you have any idea how tough it is to pitch with a wedgie?"

Rew was dancing around a bit, tugging at the seat of his pants. He hobbled to the end of the dugout, turned his back to the wall and de-wedged.

I thought about his predicament on the mound.

"Why didn't you call time out and take care of the problem?" I asked.

Rew explained he couldn't just take his pants down out in the middle of the field. And the way the umpires always wanted to move games along, he knew he couldn't just stop for a detour into the dugout with everyone standing there. His only choice was to pitch with the wedgie, as horribly uncomfortable as it was.

That gave me pause to ponder. As a manager you give a player the opportunity to pitch, it goes well, and you still can't have everyone be happy. That's baseball.

I didn't tell Rew then, but let him know later, that managing with a wedgie is darn tough, too.

# Notes:

# Why the Portable Room Must Be by the Diamond

U nusual things happen in baseball from time to time. That's part of the fun of it all.

One of the ace pitchers on the Main division team I was managing was on the hill. He had been hurling a strong outing. Not mowing 'em all down, but keeping the ball low and getting 'em out. The fielders had been doing their jobs and made very few mistakes. Unusual for a Little League game.

We were knotted at 2-2 with our worthy competition. Everyone was interested and attentive — players, fans, coaches and umpires. The pressure and pleasure of a good game when the intensity level rises and holds.

Our hurler, who also was our cleanup hitter, led off the fifth inning with a hit, but we weren't able to drive him in. Despite a couple of good breaks, we stranded him on third base. After the last out he ran into the dugout, tossed off his batting helmet, picked up his glove and hat and headed to the mound, hustling all the way, just as we coaches had taught our players to conduct themselves.

He finished his half-dozen warmup pitches and looked in at the first batter. Our opponents had the heart of their order due up. A few pitches later, the first batter grounded out to short. Our man on the mound started off with a strike on the next batter then ran the count to 0-2. Our catcher tossed the ball back, shouted words of encouragement and pounded his mitt. Our shortstop held up his index finger and reminded his teammates that there was one down and two strikes. Everyone at the field at that moment was thinking baseball. Well, everyone but one person.

As soon as our pitcher caught the toss back from the catcher, he set his glove down beside the rubber, the ball folded into the glove pocket, and raced off the mound, across the infield toward our dugout . . . and then out the fenced exit gate and into the parking lot without a word.

The rest of us were struck dumb. It all happened so fast. The trance of the game was interrupted. The umpire called time.

I headed toward the exit gate myself to see what was up. I spotted our pitcher already vacating the blue portable toilet booth, rushing back toward the diamond, zipping his pants and threading and buckling his belt.

He met me at the gate with a, "Sorry, coach, I really, really had to go, and I couldn't wait anymore."

All I could do was smile and ask, "Did you remember to wash your hands?"

"Huh?" he said.

"Never mind," I said. "Just go back out and pitch."

No penalty assessed by the umpire. A now-relaxed pitcher. A buzz through the crowd.

The game resumed at its previous level.

I think we won.

\* \* \*

AS A FOOTNOTE:

I'm also happy to say that when our league was finally able to afford permanent restrooms, they were built close to the fields — within dashing distance.

# The Snickers King

One season I had the bright idea of giving our players candy bars during the game rather than afterward. I thought the sugar in the system might improve their performance. So instead of bringing chewing gum or sunflower seeds into the dugout, I brought a sack of Snickers bars. They were a big hit with the players, but did not make much of a difference in their play. What's more, it left me with a dugout littered with Snickers wrappers.

Still, I persisted. I decided to try different sizes of Snickers: big, medium, mini. The players gobbled them all, and after a while buzzed around the equipment bag like locusts in a field of grain. They knew where to find the treats. One player sat on the bench wherever I put the bag and just couldn't resist snitching a Snickers. He had chocolate on his mouth, cheeks and uniform, with empty wrappers all over the floor around him, every time I brought the candy. He would ask, "Coach, got any Snickers today?" To me, he became "The Snickers King."

He was not a particularly good player, so he did a bit of bench time; but as long as the Snickers supply was at hand, he was content. He even began to gain a little more weight, and was a hearty soul of a little guy to begin with. Unfortunately, he had real trouble making contact with the ball when he batted. He struck out A LOT, and whenever he did happen to make contact, it was usually a groundout, since he was not much of a runner.

Well, the season progressed and The Snickers King had not gotten a hit — or even a walk. He just did not have the patience to try and wait out a walk. He had a terrible uppercut swing that made contact a matter of luck and divine intervention. I worked and worked with him in practice, trying to correct that uppercut swing, as did several of the other coaches. We began to suspect that maybe he had a hearing impairment and didn't register what we were saying.

The Snickers King lived with his grandparents, and his grandmother asked to see me after one of the games. She said she just could not understand why her grandson could not hit the ball. She said he was a real champion at school on the playground, and could hit with the best of them when the students played softball at recess. In fact, he socked the ball a mile. She also wanted to know why he was eating so much candy during our games and spoiling his dinner. She was nice about all this.

I explained that the uppercut swing was perfect for softball, but that was slow pitch and the swing didn't work in baseball. I explained that we coaches worked with him at every practice on his swing. We used tennis balls, baseballs, the tee and soft toss, but he just did not get it. And the candy? Well . . . since he spent so much time on the bench because he never got on base, he just had more opportunity than anyone else on the team to get into the Snickers. I told the grandmother that I'd have a word with him about the candy and also continue working with him on his swing. I added that I was hopeful he would start hitting in baseball as well as he did in softball, because that would be a big benefit to the team as well as to her grandson.

THE SEASON ROLLED ALONG, and The Snickers King still did not get a hit, and he still sat the bench surrounded by crumpled candy wrappers and with chocolate all over his hands, face and uniform. Now we were down to our second-to-last game, and I was really concerned that The Snickers King might finish the season hitless. He only had a couple more chances at the plate. I took him aside and talked with him at length about his swing. He had to get it level. He had to quit uppercutting at the ball. But I was skeptical whether the words sank in.

Well, that game we faced a pitcher who threw a high arcing changeup. I thought that this might be The Snickers King's big chance. I made sure that he would get to bat against this guy.

When The Snickers King's turn came at the plate, I walked over and talked with him and made sure he had all the chocolate off his hands so he could grip the bat tightly. I also checked that he didn't have any chocolate in his eyes; like many of the players, he darkened the area under his eyes to cut down on glare, but I always suspected he did it with chocolate instead of charcoal. Anyway, I told him to be patient and focus on the ball in the pitcher's hand and get a good hard swing on something over the plate. I purposely didn't mention anything about the uppercut swing or the proper way to handle the bat. This was his chance.

Usually, his at-bat would be three cuts and back to the bench. And after he executed his uppercut swing on a pitch up near his eyes, I figured this was going to happen again. He whiffed fruitlessly at a fastball down the middle of the plate. At 0-2, he was in trouble, and knew it, but by this point in the season he was used to striking out, so at least he wasn't going to be timid about taking a final cut.

From my position outside the dugout, I called out to him to give it full power and get his licks in. I was hoping that the guy on the mound would pull the usual cutesy trick of a changeup to punch out a lesser talent of a hitter, making him swing early, fanning the air.

Sure enough, here came the looping, blooping, slow changeup. The Snickers King let loose with a powerful, wild uppercut swing. His specialty. The arc on the pitch was a perfect match for the swing, and contact was made. And this was REAL contact!

The ball shot into straightaway center field. The Snickers King was stunned — and so were we. We yelled at him to run, and after a moment he took off for first. The ball was hit so hard, it went all the way to the fence, 200 feet away, on the fly and smacked off a sponsor's sign. The center fielder had run out to get the carom off the fence, and missed the ball as it rolled back in.

The Snickers King hit first base and kept on running, heading toward second. Our hearts stopped until we could see that the missed ball would bounce in far enough on the grass, away from the pursuing fielder, to allow our giddy hitter to get to second standing up. And a good thing that, because he wasn't much in our sliding practices.

There was The Snickers King standing on second base with a huge smile on his face. Everybody on our side was cheering. He had his hit — and it was a great one.

Then he reached in his pocket, pulled out a Snickers, tore off the wrapper, and took a big bite.

# Notes:

# GLMs

Having GLMs — "good-looking moms," as explained in the introduction to Part III — as a part of your team's infrastructure can cause an embarrassment from time to time.

A beautiful young mother's son was on one of the teams I managed some years back, near the end of my coaching days. I was one of the older fellows at the diamond in our Little League. The GLM's son and my son were friends at school and had lots of fun together on the diamond and off. They frequently spent the night at one another's houses, and the following day's activities were usually planned by the parents by telephone, with the reconnoitering point for the dispatch or delivery of one boy or the other often the place of an event the children had in common, such as a baseball game or practice.

On one of these occasions, my son was to spend the night at his friend's home. It was Friday, meaning the weekend loomed with no school, and they would depart right after our baseball practice. My wife had packed up my son's overnight things, and after practice I bid him goodbye with his night things. He was off to his friend's house for a good time. His friend's mom was there to pick the two up, and off they drove. This lady was a great GLM and friend. She was stunning, young, beautiful, bright and cheery. I waved goodbye. My son was to be delivered to my wife and me at the baseball park the next day, when we had a game.

The next morning at the park, I arrived early to set up the gear for our team's pregame warmups. Of course, I got there much earlier than my wife, as she only needed to be there by game time. Our son was to arrive at the field at the appointed time with his teammate. The first games of the morning already had been played. On Saturdays there would be as many as six games in a row on each of the complex's diamonds, plus a couple morning games on the T-ball field. So the parking lot was teeming with people, as usual for a Saturday.

As I was walking across the parking lot — in an open spot away from cars but full of players, parents and coaches — to where our team would meet at the batting cages, my son and his friend arrived, chauffeured by the fabulous GLM. She was running a bit late, so she drove her car right through the crowd to the open area where I was walking. The crowd parted before the car, like the Red Sea before Moses at the shore. My son and his friend jumped out in their uniforms, carrying their gear, and ran past me and off to the batting cage. "Hi coach!" "Hi dad!" They raced ahead and were quickly long gone.

I was still walking, having waved goodbye to our friend, the GLM. But she jumped out of the car and hurried briskly toward me. She was dressed in a "form-fitting" red outfit that would certainly draw attention on any woman. Fabulous. And since she was a GLM of the maximum degree, she could really turn — and did turn — heads in the parking area. Then she shouted out to me, "Coach. Coach. Coach. Here are the things from last night. You forgot them."

She was holding the bag that contained my son's toothbrush and toothpaste, but the crowd did not realize this. All they noticed was this beauty in red moving so gracefully across the ground toward the grizzled veteran baseball coach, and talking about "last night."

I took the package from her hand, said thanks, and we parted.

As I heard the clucks from the crowd, I took in the seemingly knowing winks and smirks. My face turned a shade of red brighter than her dress.

I went off to get our team ready for the game, suspecting that I might hear more about this later. There is no such thing as a youth baseball program devoid of gossip and rumors — and the wilder the better.

# Notes:

# Overrun

T he younger players just starting out in The Game sometimes have trouble
understanding the concept of running through first base, and the
additional explanation that if you turn to the right you are safe and permitted
to return to the base at your leisure, but if you turn to the left, the umpire
might just deem that you've made a move to take second and are no longer in
a safe situation but fair game to be tagged out.

Good coaching requires that you explain that a batter-runner hurrying to
beat the throw to first runs through the base at full tilt, and then ALWAYS turns
to the right. It takes some time and practice for this to sink in.

A young player on one of the Farm division teams (for ages 7-9) I was
associated with was just starting out in baseball. He was a quiet kid, tall and
lanky, and could run like a deer with long strides that covered a lot of ground
fast over long grassy stretches ... not the choppy, fast-acceleration-type baseball
strides you often see. He played outfield and could get to and chase down any
balls hit out there. But he was more than a little fuzzy about the rules; and
because he was young and shy, did not ask questions.

He had some trouble hitting the ball early in the season, so he didn't get
on base much. Or at all. Then he got a hit off the pitching machine and dashed
to first. FAST. He ran through the bag, just as he'd been taught, turned to the
right, and walked back to the base slowly as he caught his breath. The first-
base coach congratulated him on his accomplishment and got him ready for
subsequent action.

A groundball was hit toward the first baseman — easily fielded — but our base runner was off like a flash. The only play for the first baseman was to make the unassisted putout at first, which he did. Meanwhile, our runner — taking his base-running lessons to heart — had sped like a streak to second … and run through the bag.

He took a turn to the right, and was catching his breath on a leisurely walk back to second base. Everybody who knew the game of baseball and was on his side of the equation startd shouting, "Get back on the bag! Get back on the bag!" Everybody on the other side of the equation started shouting, "Tag him! Tag him!"

The first baseman had the ball. He tossed it to the second baseman and the shortstop moved toward the bag to help out if necessary. Shortstops in youth baseball, being the prima donnas they sometimes are, called for the ball. But the second baseman wanted to make the tag and moved in the direction of our runner — who by this time was aware that something was amiss. He hurried back toward the base … which was partially blocked by the shortstop. Meanwhile, the first baseman moved down the basepath toward second.

Our runner, seeing three enemy players converging on the base, resembled a startled deer caught in the headlights on a dark night. Then suddenly he sprang into instant action. He turned and took off into left-center field. Youth baseball being what it is, the second baseman (clutching the ball) and the shortstop chased after him into the outfield, with the first baseman in hot pursuit.

Our player ran fast and covered a lot of ground. In the blink of an eye, the three infielders had been joined by the left fielder and center fielder, chasing our guy around the green grass. He turned on the afterburners and sprinted in a large arc across center, circling to get back to second base. The pitcher had by then moved over to cover the bag. Our player saw that and veered off toward right field, with the five fielders madly dashing after him.

It was quite a sight. By this time the umpire had made it to the outfield from his spot near the pitching machine and stopped the play, calling our runner out for being outside the basepaths, much to his chagrin.

Things calmed down, and we all learned a good lesson about base running and the instruction of the finer points.

# Notes:

# Stealing Home

As a season wears on, the players get more confident on the basepaths. Those who have reached base often on hits and walks begin to dream of the thrill of the stolen base, and want to turn that dream into reality. And when it comes to stealing bases, no thrill can surpass the ultimate prize: stealing home.

One of the opportunities to take a base is on a passed ball or wild pitch — in youth baseball that goes in the scorebook as a stolen base. But stealing home in this circumstance is far different from stealing second or third, since the backstop is relatively close to the plate and a pitch that gets by the catcher usually can be retrieved in short order. The runner will need a good jump, superior reflexes and swift legs to hoof it home safely.

One season, my Babe Ruth team was blessed with a speedster we'll call "Bo," who was a star halfback on his high school football team and a star on our team. He was so fast that he could literally steal any base at will, including home, without even needing a passed ball or wild pitch. Bo's only difficulty was getting on base in the first place. The aggressive style he brought with him from the gridiron didn't translate well in the batter's box. But other teams pitched him very carefully, and he would be anxious for action when up to bat. Impatience and an imprecise feeling for the strike zone only helps one's opponents in the field. And while the from-the-heels, massive, fully extended swing occasionally produces a spectacular result, sometimes even a fence-buster, more often it ends in a topped nubber or popup for an easy out.

Bo worked hard at making the transition from a football to a baseball mindset, but he still didn't get on base as often as he liked.

But when he did, he made up for the lost time. He ate up the bases with awe-inspiring steals.

WATCHING BO'S FEATS EMBOLDENED all our players to try the same. Of course, they were often mowed down and sent packing to the dugout with a tear in the eye. There are few Rickey Hendersons. But their base-running skills did improve, and at the three-quarter mark of the schedule, many of our players had enjoyed some success with base theft. My motto about stealing bases was, "If you can make it, take it." That's what our players, and the dads whom I assigned to coach the bases, were counseled.

By this juncture of the season, the tightly packed dirt on the basepaths had been churned up by cleats and slides, and baked by the sun to the point that the areas around the bags were like sand pits. Loose soil. Around home plate, where so much stomping and clomping and twisting and turning takes place, the earth had been ground from hard grains of sand into a fine white powder.

A great player, but not a great runner, on our team had made it to third base. Some of our players were mean, not-so-lean, fighting machines. They were "husky," "thick," "substantial" or "burly." Our runner on third, we'll call him "Franky," was one of these substantial fellows. But he was a gamer. He loved his baseball. He relished participating in The Game. He was usually very conservative on the bases, but this time, his animated crouch and the glint in his eye revealed that the taking of home would be attempted even if opportunity but softly tapped, not necessarily knocked.

Franky took a nice lead off third, standing in foul territory — to avoid any ball that might be hit his way in fair territory — just the way it should be done. He inched a little farther toward home with each new pitch. The pitcher was focusing on the hitter. It was a close game and we could badly use a run from our man on third. Our opponents, of course, just as badly needed an out. The pitcher was working hard, really sweating. And sure enough, after several excellent pitches in and around the strike zone, he let one fly that the catcher was unable to handle — and off to the backstop it did go.

Our man on third saw his chance. Without hesitation he made his move. Off to the races, bound for glory.

THE SANDY BASEPATH didn't do anything to help this dash home. The action unfolded in what seemed like slow motion.

At once, the pitcher alertly charged off the mound to cover the plate, the umpire positioned himself to the side of the plate to make the call, the batter stepped out of the way, and the catcher quickly turned around, knocked his mask off and headed to the backstop to retrieve the ball, either to throw it to his pitcher or make the tag himself.

Franky realized he was in big trouble. It had the makings of an easy out. But unfortunately for the catcher, the ball rebounded smartly off the backstop baseboard and veered somewhere to the left. He couldn't find it.

Franky kept chugging toward home. The gate to glory miraculously, providentially, gloriously reopened.

"There it is!" came shouts from the other team's dugout and stands, along with frantic pointing at the ball's location.

Our player kept chugging toward home.

"Slide! Slide! Slide!" came the shouts from our side, along with arm motions to hit the dirt.

It was going to be a very, very close play. A dramatic confluence of good timing, bad timing, luck, talent, fortitude and a quest for glory all were being watched over by the baseball gods.

The catcher found the ball. With no time to throw to the pitcher, he sprinted and dove to tag the runner at the plate. The runner surged forward with gritted teeth. With immense determination, he launched his body high into the air in a headfirst slide.

Almost immediately, gravity began to do its work. The airborne runner's descent was rapid. His forward motion ceased shortly after impact.

The catcher and runner landed at about the same time in the white dust surrounding the plate. The result was a volcanic-type explosion of talcum-like powder that mushroomed 7 or 8 feet aloft and obscured the play from vision. The umpire's dark blues were turned sheet white. The runner and catcher, extended flat on the ground, resembled bright, white upended snowmen.

As the haze dissipated, it revealed our runner's open hand resting on the front half of the plate, while the catcher's hand clutching the ball was sitting on the pointed bottom half. No tag had been made! The umpire took it all in, thrust his arms out and loudly declared, "Safe!"

Cheers erupted from our side.

Franky rose to his feet and jogged to the dugout, not brushing himself off. Just a big grin, and happy eyes peering out of the solid coating of thick white dust.

An improbable moment of glory to savor forever.

Stealing home.

# A Little Too Tricky

I t was one of those interesting seasons in our local Little League. At the time, the season-ending championship game was a match-up of the winner of the first half of the season against the winner of the second half. The team I was managing was in the hunt for the first-half title, and with it a ticket to the championship contest at season's end.

Weather had played a heavy hand in the season thus far, with several games rained out. That meant the first-half winner had not been determined yet, pending makeup games, and we were well into the season's second half. The makeup games could only be played when a field was available, and this usually meant that teams would have to wait for the early-evening game to end on the unlighted Farm field. To complicate matters further for the first-half contenders, the rules governing the number of innings pitchers could pitch (including required gaps between games and calendar days for pitchers throwing a designated limit of pitches or innings in a previous game) remained constant. In other words, makeup games were treated no differently from regular-season games in the second half, as far as pitch-count rules went, even though making up games could mean a team would have to play three or four games during a week instead of the usual two. It meant a team would have to dig deep into its stable of arms (using players who seldom — or even never — pitched) in order to stay within the rules.

This reality presented a real strategic challenge to managers, for the pitching staffs were not particularly effective after a team's top two hurlers had rung up their allotted mound time for the week. Our team already faced a tough enough task to claim the first-half championship. We had to beat a contender while another team beat yet another contender, and then vanquish the team that was at the top of the first-half standings. All very confusing and challenging.

So our makeup game against this contender began one evening at nearly dusk on the Farm field. The innings went by and the score was tight. We were playing well, but so was the other team. Darkness was gathering, and that meant the game could be called before the six innings were completed. There also was the two-hour time limit to consider. We needed to finish four innings (or three-and-a-half if the home team was ahead) for the match to be deemed official.

It so happened that we were the visitors. Our opponents were up in the bottom of the fourth. We were up by a run. There were two runners on base, and two outs. I desperately wanted to save innings for my top two hurlers for the other games that week, since our bats had come alive by this juncture of the season and we were doing well in the second half. Still . . . I knew we had a shot at the first-half crown. What to do? Whom should I pitch? When should I pitch 'em? Should I keep one of my top arms on the mound, or go with a third- or fourth-level pitcher and hope for the best? How long was the game going to go on? Should I think a game ahead? A week ahead? Think about next season?

My mind was a swirl of thoughts of pitching strategy. Decisions, decisions.

The sun had set; the skies were gray. It was difficult to see. It looked like if we could just finish the inning, we'd have our win and be in possible position to play for the first-half championship. But only if certain things happened in the other makeup games. A chessboard.

What to do? I knew I had to think about THIS game.

The level of excitement on the field was high. The fans were tense. The coaches were strung taut. The umpires knew the game was a big one and were alert and ready for action.

I left my ace in. He got two strikes on the batter. The base runners were ready to roll on the swing of the bat. The sun was now long gone and darkness was minutes away . . . unless the bright moon appeared or they turned on the lights at the neighboring field or . . .

My managerial intellect cranked into high gear. We needed a strikeout, of course. Now, of the three brand-new game balls, shiny and white before the game, one had already been lost, hit foul and never retrieved. Another was gray with dirt and grime. The third was bright and barely used. It was in our pitcher's hand. He was getting ready to throw the critical pitch.

Thinking fast, I shouted out to him to ask for another baseball. He stopped and paused. I strode partway toward home and announced to the umpire that the wet grass may have made the ball slippery, which was true. I was also thinking that the gray ball would be the perfect one with which to get the strikeout, because in the deepening dusk the batter wouldn't be able to see it. The umpire, I figured, wanted to get the game over and would probably call anything close a strike. Stroke of genius on my part!

The pitcher called timeout and tossed the newer, bright ball to the catcher, who handed it to the umpire. The umpire handed over the gray ball and our catcher lobbed it to our pitcher. It was tough for him to catch it in the dim light. I knew this would be our moment.


TIME WAS IN AGAIN. Our pitcher looked in at the hitter, barely visible in the batter's box, and went into his windup. The base runners (no leading off at this level of play) were ready in the running-start position. The ball headed toward the plate. The batter took a limp swing. He could hardly pick up the pitch.

Strike three? NO. He made contact and dinked the ball in the air toward right field. The right fielder charged in, the second baseman back-pedaled. The ball dropped to the grass between them both.

Meanwhile, the runners were off to the races. And just our unfortunate luck — the grass was scheduled to be mowed the following day. In the gray light, with the grass blades high, neither of our fielders could find the grass-stained, gray baseball. It was too well camouflaged. Our first baseman had gone out to help, and our center fielder had charged into the fray, as well. But none could come up with the soiled orb.

The first runner crossed the plate. The game was tied. The second runner rounded third and headed for home. Our center fielder finally came up with the ball. It was going to be a close play at the plate. The ball was fired to our waiting catcher.

He couldn't see it coming in. He couldn't catch it and tag out the runner. The game was called because of darkness. We'd lost by a run.

Defeated by trying to be too tricky. The baseball gods had made their statement. They gave me this hard lesson early in my days as a manager, and it was a lesson I learned well and took to heart.

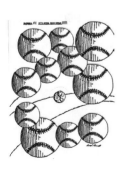
Sadness loomed over our team. But if there was a bright note, it was that we were able to save up some of our good pitching innings for remaining games that week. And the other first-half contenders had to burn up innings in their subsequent makeups. This ended up helping our team's fortunes in the second half —

and we took that title and made it to the championship game.

Certainly, the baseball gods do move in mysterious ways. It is difficult to understand how to appease 'em.

And one thing's for sure: you can't outsmart 'em.

# Notes:

# Terra Unfirma

...................................................................................................................................

Taking care of the grounds is very important. If your league can find a good groundskeeper, that is a blessing. But no matter how hard, as a league official, you try to make things perfect and know what is going on with the equipment and the fields, sometimes things happen. Sprinklers go on in the middle of the night and the teams get to the field the next day only to find a flooded playing area. Lights are left on at night by mistake, to the irritation of neighbors, who call the police to complain. Yes, many things can go wrong.

Once, I was watching an important Saturday-afternoon game. I was one of our league's board members, and that responsibility (self-inflicted) required, in my opinion, being around the fields to keep tabs on what was going on. It was a tight game on a hot sunny day. The pitcher was staring in at the plate, preparing his delivery, when there suddenly was a pause in the action. The batter backed out of the box and the umpire raised his hands and called time. He, the batter and catcher stared at the ground.

The dirt in the backstop area was normally a kind of whitish sand color; but now it had turned a dark reddish-clay hue. The discoloration began to spread, and then the three people around the plate started to sink into the soil. The umpire and catcher vacated the area fast, but the batter was stuck there, trapped in the ooze. The liquefied earth went up over his shoes and started to climb up over his ankles. He was paralyzed with fear. The stunned crowd sat motionless, in that momentary interval before panic set in.

The dark-red color started to spread. It was as if the entire home-plate area was going to be swallowed up by the ground. It bubbled and turned into a quicksand pit. The batter regained his senses and began to slog his way out of the instant marsh. Play was called and the teams gathered in their dugouts. An emergency telephone call was made to the groundskeeper.

It turned out that a city water main just happened to run under the field — in fact, under the home-plate area. The pipe had broken right there, and the sudden release of water and the pressure had created the quicksand pit.

Finally, the water to the main was shut down before the ground had a chance to swallow the snack bar, bleachers and dugouts. Only the home-plate area was in sad shape — a little swamp. It took some time for it to dry, but when it did, and after the main was repaired, that area of the field was firmer than ever.

The only lasting damage that afternoon was probably to one batter, one catcher and one umpire, who may have had some subsequent nightmares about being gobbled up by the ground.

# The Ducks Are Swimming at Second Base

B aseball fields have to be maintained. This is an important part of The Game. Filling holes. Striping baselines. Repairing fences. Properly displaying the sponsor signs. The tasks run on and on and demand a lot of work.

When I was initiated into the youth baseball arena, the dads did all this grunt work, or the league board paid small stipends to people to take care of the duties volunteers couldn't or wouldn't handle. This system worked fine in my book. The fields were kept in playing trim. But one season the board had other ideas, and believed it necessary to bring in a professional for consultation about proper upkeep.

This professional was actually head coach of a local high school baseball team. His background included working in the groundskeeping crew at a major league stadium. After moving to Reno, his expertise had improved both the city's minor league diamond and the field on which his high school team played to the point that they could be considered almost Buddhist garden-like works of art. When he spoke to us amateurs in our youth league, he explained what to do and how to maintain our fields — raking the dirt, mowing the grass, trimming the edges, properly watering the field, keeping the mound and plate areas built up and under protective tarps between games. His knowledge was impressive and made me a believer. One of his tenets was that the players themselves should perform much of the maintenance.

Our board bought into this system. I did, too. The post-game routine was changed to one in which the players — rather than just line up for the handshakes then sit through their coaches' lectures before cleaning out their respective dugouts — grabbed rakes, shovels, tamps, special clay and all the other tools and trappings and dragged the fields and repaired them to be ready for the next games. It was great! The players learned new skills and how to fix up a field. Their toil gave them a sense of accomplishment; and it was no longer necessary for aging coaches with aching backs to work up a sweat after a game.

The players did the work. All they needed was to be supervised.


MY SON CHARLIE WENT through our local youth leagues before the player field-maintenance responsibilities were implemented. Yet he learned the caretaking skills from his high school coach, who had a rugged regimen that produced a field of which everyone involved with the team's program could really be proud. Charlie became proficient enough in the various tasks that he and one of his friends from the summer traveling team associated with their high school team were given the opportunity to work as field-maintenance men for that summer season. They were thrilled. It was an actual job with a paycheck funded by the summer team's budget. They could put to use all the expertise they'd absorbed after games during the high school season.

Charlie and his friend worked hard at their new vocation. As soon as games ended at the high school field during the summer program, the two of them changed out of their uniforms into work clothes and set to putting the field right again. They did a good job. Under their care — and under the tutelage of their high school coach who also directed the summer program — the field looked great.

The summer schedule progressed. In the heart of the schedule was a tournament hosted at the field. After its conclusion, the infield and outfield and the rest of the complex were tattered and in need of plenty of work. The boys' team was off for a few days, but there was no rest for Charlie and his partner. They rolled up their sleeves and set to getting the long job done. This ate up lots of time, and they were exhausted after the raking and dragging and smoothing and tamping and sweeping and chalking and all the rest of the duties. But they also were proud of the results. All that remained was turning on the sprinklers to water the infield and outfield, which sorely needed the moisture. The grass was parched from being played on without respite from the summer heat.

The two weary laborers activated the sprinklers and left the park.

TWO DAYS LATER. CHARLIE and his buddy were relaxing in our back yard, puffing cigars. I'd told my teen-aged sons that they were not allowed to chew tobacco, but that an occasional cigar was permissible. While no tobacco usage is healthy — and indeed should be very strongly discouraged — indulging in a stogie now and then at least was a vice preferable to the constant placing of tobacco between cheek and gum, or — just as bad if not worse — habitually lighting up cigarettes.

So the two idle baseball players were puffing away on huge fragrant cigars on a pleasant, cool, midsummer Reno night, laughing it up, telling lies, philosophizing about life and The Game. I was inside the house. All of a sudden, I heard quite a ruckus out back. Chairs turned over. Feet pounded on the patio. And then the two were charging through the house.

"What's wrong?" I called out.

Their faces looked stunned. Their voices were full of anxiety and remorse. I quickly gathered that some terrible truth had struck them simultaneously during the course of their conversation.

They stammered that they'd left the water running. FOR TWO DAYS.

No doubt this horrific realization had been triggered by some random observation by one or the other concerning "the sprinklers." And then, surely, the jolt of consciousness and the exclamation: "THE SPRINKLERS! OH —!"

They dashed out of the house, clambered into Charlie's car and in an instant were off to the ballfield . . .

. . . Which was, in fact, now an artificial lake. Ducks were swimming at second base. It was a disaster.

The water had swamped the entire infield and outfield, filled the visitors' dugout like a bathtub, flowed down across the practice field and the large soccer field, and even gushed to the side doors of the high school building itself, cascading down the steps like a mini-Niagara into the weight room, which it was slowly flooding.

Fortunately, these two were smart young men (their lazy July absent-mindedness notwithstanding). They assessed the devastation, and realized it was reversible. There was still time before games were scheduled. The stalwart duo set to work with garden tools and slowly but surely got the loose water off the fields. Then they dug a couple trenches for drainage. This arduous task took a long time, but proved effective.

The hot Nevada sun rose the next day and baked the soggy diamond into a playable consistency. Sometimes it is good to play baseball in the desert.

The summer games went on . . . although with a few soggy spots on the basepaths and in the outfield. But this really wasn't so rare in The Game. After all, knowledgeable fans whose memories go back to the 1960s recall that the San Francisco Giants, when playing against the hated Los Angeles Dodgers and their great base stealer, Maury Wills, used to have its grounds crew soak the basepath area near first before the game to slow him down and prevent him from getting a good jump toward second on a steal.

Maybe those accidental wet spots on my son's team's field helped his side roll on to victory in that stretch of the season. I don't really remember. But I do remember that Charlie and his partner kept their summer jobs. And the grass was really green for the rest of that season. A few varieties of wildflowers sprouted, too.

# Notes:

# The Hazards
# of Backyard BP

A s our family started to get serious about youth baseball, it became apparent that no matter how ineffectual, petty or mean a manager and coaches were on one of our son's teams, we could still have some thrills if our child could hit the ball.

So I embarked on backyard batting practice. The initial efforts did not go so well. Hitting hardballs around the back yard, in close quarters, produced dented siding, shattered windows and loosened roof gutters — to say nothing of the tears from a son about being hit with the ball, and the frustration of losing expensive baseballs in the bushes or nearby irrigation ditch, or to the ruinous effects of the sprinkler system if the balls were left out at night.

It was obvious that we needed to do better, so I came up with my tennis-ball system for practicing hitting (as described in the chapter, in Part I, "Better Batting through Tennis Balls"). Initially, the young players of our family were not so strong or good at hitting, so it was possible to use a tree as a backstop, and the fence behind the tree to contain the fouls and missed balls, and the fence across the yard as a catchall for the hits. But as our sons improved and began to hit the ball more often, and harder, the fences proved to be problematic as a defense for the neighbors, and to keep our treasure trove of tennis balls in our yard.

The family to one side of us had children somewhat older than ours, and they were not baseball people. As we hit more and more home runs in batting practice, we put more and more green tennis balls into the neighbors' yard. Fortunately, they were very nice about it, and threw them back when they found them. Their yard had quite a bit of thick, vegetative landscaping, so many balls ended up deep in the jungle and had to be fetched stealthily by our sons on recovery missions. These missions entailed climbing the fence and then digging through the landscaping and pine bark. All fine, but it was best not to disturb the neighbors (and further test their goodwill). And even more critical — their dog, Duke, must not be aroused.

Duke did not like having intruders in his yard. But he did like chewing on tennis balls. So to preserve our arsenal, the recovery missions had to take place fairly frequently. Although tennis balls were superior to baseballs in that neither evening dew nor overnight sprinkler watering could ruin them, they could be rendered into fuzzless, slobbery uselessness by the earnest jaws of a canine.

On quite a number of occasions when one of our young men went over the fence, rooted for tennis balls in the neighbors' underbrush and tossed them back into our territory, Duke would go wild inside his house. Our neighbors, not knowing that the ball-retrievers were loose in their yard, would let him out. This resulted in a number of very close calls in scrambling back over the fence, a couple of torn pairs of pants, and some fang marks on a calf. But that's the way it goes when you're hitting home runs and have to bring them back yourself.

One day, when we had a social gathering with our neighbors on that side, I learned that the husband had initially thought he was going blind with seeing all the green tennis balls in his back yard, thinking they were floaters in his eyes. Then he decided his yard was suffering from a rare and troublesome grass fungus or some infestation of mushrooms. His family were very nice neighbors, but moved away before we finished our baseball days.

On the other side of our yard, in the early days, we were blessed by kindly neighbors who did not mind the tennis balls going over into their yard. These balls were usually fouls, but sometimes we would switch sides for home plate and their yard would become the depository for the homers. Their swimming pool experienced a few instances of balls clogging the leaf catcher, and one or two times I know that homers hit the satellite dish and caused reception problems.

But, again, these were nice, nice neighbors. They did not have children, but did have cats, and the cats never attacked on our ball-recovery missions.

AS OUR SONS MATURED and got even stronger and better at hitting, it was apparent that we needed a way to restrain the tennis balls. Thus, my homemade design for a backyard batting cage (described in Appendix A). The batting cage saved thousands of balls from leaving our yard; but every so often, the netting would part at just the spot the ball was hit, and zoom . . . into the neighbor's yard. Never really a problem, except one time.

We had new neighbors on the south side (Duke and his family had moved away). The new neighbors were having an outdoor barbecue. I was pitching to one of my sons in the batting cage. The pitch was right down the middle of the plate, and he hit it with full force. It blasted through the bird netting, ricocheted off one of the fence posts and flew high into the air. Very, very high. Into our neighbors' airspace. As gravity took over, the ball plummeted straight down. It landed right on the hot grill loaded with sizzling steaks, with the party guests surrounding it with their plates.

It was a surprise to all. Because of the steep angle of the drop, the guests must have thought that the green ball had fallen from an airplane on the

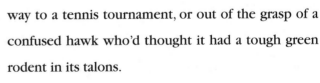 way to a tennis tournament, or out of the grasp of a confused hawk who'd thought it had a tough green rodent in its talons.

That concluded our BP for that day. We put the bats and gloves down and slinked quietly back into our house. Nothing was ever mentioned from our

side of the backyard fence about the uninvited tennis-ball dinner guest, and our neighbors never brought the subject up, either.

But from then on, we were very careful not to practice hitting in a southerly direction when the neighbor's barbie was in use.

# Notes:

# Waiver Surprise

............................................................................................................................

As president of a youth baseball league, you can grant a waiver of the sign-up fee to families in need. This is all well and good, but such a grant is best kept confidential to prevent embarrassment and finger-pointing at the ballfields.

Usually, the family granted a waiver is thankful and asks what they can do to help out the league. After all, a league needs fees to operate. It must pay for uniforms, insurance, baseballs, equipment, groundskeeping, umpires and other costs that arise during the course of a season. So, waivers must be given only after careful consideration of a family's financial situation — and they must not be handed out very often.

Now there are many advantages to being in a youth baseball program, just one of which is childcare. According to my back-of-the-envelope calculations, youth baseball is the cheapest form of childcare, even when full fees are paid. When it is free, and your family budget is tight, all the better. An even greater attraction.

I'd heard about one league president who'd granted several fee waivers. The word went out that you didn't have to pay to play baseball or be part of the program, with its ancillary benefits, and the league was inundated with non-payers and went out of business. So waiving fees is a policy that needs to be implemented with great judiciousness.

When I was league president, a man and his wife requested a fee waiver. I reviewed their circumstances and granted the waiver so that their young fellow could play. The season went along, and neither the father nor mother ever did one single thing to help the league. They came to all the games, were visible at the fields, and appeared to be having an enjoyable season. It disturbed me that I had granted them the waiver and had explained to them that there is always something that needs to be done by volunteers to put on a baseball season. The list is endless. All help is welcome. But this couple never called me, or made a comment at the park to offer their help.

I decided to remain silent and let things take their course, even though board members asked me once or twice how the fee waivers had gone that season. Silence, I determined, was to be my position. Cordial silence. Irritated silence. But silence.

To see the man and woman at the ballpark so often, and have that kind of thought on my mind, was the sort of thing that gets under one's skin and can sprout resentments and unkind thoughts about one's fellow humans. But, still, I maintained my silence.

In the end, I was rewarded for my reserved approach. On the final day of the season — when all the league's families would be scattering to the wind, and all forgotten about the season and nothing said about the waiver — what do you know? The father came up to me.

He handed me a money order for the full sign-up fee and said, "Thank you very much for the help." He said his son had had a very nice season.

The league now had its money, and I had a nice lesson in the virtues of patience and keeping potentially hurtful information about others to myself. I can still see the face of the father who paid the bill for his son's good time, and the satisfaction he showed in paying his bill and having a good experience with baseball, that grand old game.

## Appendix A

# How to Build a Backyard Batting Cage, Cheap!

After some years in youth baseball and learning how important being a good hitter is for a player to obtain satisfaction from The Game — and also learning that practicing hitting regularly pays BIG, BIG dividends — my thoughts turned to having a home batting cage to further the prospects for my boys.

When they were little, it had not been so much trouble keeping tennis balls in our back yard during batting practice ("BP"); but as the boys grew, it became tougher and tougher to keep an adequate supply together. As mentioned in the Part V story, "The Hazards of Backyard BP," we were forever climbing into the neighbors' yards . . . or dipping into the irrigation ditch or scouring the street. And when we headed instead to the public fields to practice, it meant waiting a good while for our turn to set up equipment and use the field, or to take a turn in the batting cage. Meanwhile, the cages at the local sporting-goods store were usually booked solid and far in advance, and were expensive to use, as well, in the 30-minute or 60-minute blocks. Something had to be done.

The solution seemed clear: buying a batting cage of our own for the back yard. But as I investigated cages in those days, there was not much commercially available in ready-to-assemble form. And what was available was expensive and required permanent installation. None was right for me.

As I contemplated The Game and the societal ramifications of baseball and the quest for moments of glory, I dreamed of how nice it would be for EVERYONE to have the opportunity to practice batting at his or her leisure and let that translate to success and good feelings on the diamond — instead of the all-important BP being accessible only to the lucky few with either the financial wherewithal to own a personal batting cage, or the connections to frequently use such a facility. It seemed to me that the world would be a better place if there existed a type of removable batting cage that everyone could own for under $100.

My mind was at work at this for quite some time . . .

MY WIFE AND I took a trip to Europe. We happened to be in Paris — a stunningly beautiful city, but not a good baseball town. We were having a wonderful time, and one evening booked seats on the late-dinner cruise on a pleasure boat of the glass-decked Bateaux-Mouche line, which serves sightseers by cruising the Seine in the heart of the city.

It was a fine evening. A ship filled with people laughing, drinking, dining, listening to music and song and cruising on the famous river taking in the fantastic sites as their twinkling lights glinted in the twilight. As the cruise drew to its conclusion, our Bateaux-Mouche pulled up near Notre Dame cathedral. The lights inside the ship were dimmed, and the vessel paused there in the Seine, spotlights directed at the enormous cathedral's majestic 700-year-old architecture. The heart-wrenching strains of Ave Maria from the ship's sound system filled the night. As I looked at fabled Notre Dame — its Gothic archways and soaring spires, flying buttresses and gargoyles suffused in illuminating rays — with the timeless hymn serenading the moment, powerful emotions surged through me. And I had a Vision. Yes, a vision with a capital "v."

The Vision of the Batting Cage. Clear. Brilliant. Divine. I now knew what to do: I would build my own cage. I was consumed with joy!

My wife and I continued on our European journey, but I could not wait to translate my vision into reality on our return to the Good ol' U.S. of A.

Back in Reno, I went to a home-supply store and procured the materials necessary to construct my architectural masterpiece. It would have appealing curves, towering arches, flying buttresses. I even contemplated including a few gargoyles to guard the upper extremities, but restrained myself. This was baseball, after all. Once the cage was finished, I tested it with my sons. IT WORKED! I had created a batting cage for the common man. Now one and all could enjoy the benefits of improved hitting success on the diamond.

Then disaster struck. Reno, Nevada, is known for a particularly vicious weather condition called the Washoe Zephyrs. These high-gusting winds come strong and howling off the Sierra Nevada range and have been known to carry off trees, coyotes, and even rattlesnakes curled beneath their boulders. Sometimes, the boulders, too. Sadly, a Zephyr whipped out of the mountains one night and reduced my batting cage to a twisted pile of PVC pipe and polyurethane netting. My heart was broken.

BUT NEVER SAY DIE. The cage had worked for a time. The vision had been true. The costs had been right. I would go back to the drawing board. Indeed, I did, and the result — while not very pretty — ended up serving us for many seasons, and, in fact, proved beneficial to the Kirst brood all the way through their high school baseball years.

(You can see how to build one yourself at the end of this Appendix A.)

Yes, our backyard batting cage worked great. The neighbors never complained (even after the barbecue incident recounted in the aforementioned chapter in Part V), and I suffered only one investigation from the deed-restriction Gestapo into whether my cage was a permanent structure (it was found not to be). Of course, to me, the cage was an object of beauty that only became more beautiful with every additional pitch and home run swing.

When the birdnet weakened from exposure to the sun, it was only necessary to throw over another layer of birdnet. When the winds made the birdnet sag, it was only necessary to tighten up the bailing wire and add more duct tape. Along with its delicate beauty, the cage possessed a simple durability. Yes, it was a wonderful baseball tool. Only for tennis balls, I must hasten to add, as the netting and structure were much too flimsy to restrain a flying baseball more than just a few times. Still, its practicality was beautiful in and of itself.

Whenever one of my sons wanted to "hit a few," it only required that I take a few steps out into the back yard and throw some pitches. This led to much more BP. Any of my sons could take his cuts several times in an afternoon or evening if he wanted. The boys often did, and I, in my fatherly coaching mode, rarely had to ask them if they wanted to get BP in. They were asking me. It was nice. And as they improved, and matured in size, their need for faster pitches was solved by my moving closer and closer to the plate. By the time they were of high school age, I could move up to about 12 feet away and throw as hard as I could to try to get the pitches by them. Yes, 50 or 60 mph from me at that distance with a tennis ball was all they needed to keep their hands quick and still see the live pitching motion.

It worked out really, really well for the Kirst family, and for a long time.

I HIGHLY RECOMMEND PUTTING up a backyard batting cage. You'll find that going into the cage more frequently for shorter sessions (say, 30 pitches), rather than less frequently for one long session (say, 100 pitches), is much better for improving skills. If a batter really gets on the pitches by the 25th throw, that's fine; but in a game he'll have to be on it after just two or three pitches. Therefore, all BP needs to be conducted with this fact in mind.

As for the benefits of using tennis balls instead of baseballs — well, that's obvious, isn't it? (If not, refer to the Part I chapter, "Better Batting through Tennis Balls.") As your player becomes bigger, stronger and quicker and can really pound the ball, a whack on the shin with a tennis ball, even from 12 feet away, won't faze you. No pitching screen is required with the tennis-ball system of BP. Yes, a backyard batting cage can really add joy to your baseball lives.

AT THE END OF the fall baseball season it is time to take the batting cage down. I recommend you don't neglect this task. It will be a sad endeavor, because you will have had fun practicing with your children and their friends. But it is best to take a rest. You'll need it. Your arm will need it. The grass will need it. The neighbors, probably, will need it. (Think of the sounds associated with BP.) Your spouse will need it, and be grateful for an uncluttered view out the back windows. Yes, very grateful!

Then around February, when talk turns to spring training in the major leagues, and your youth leagues have their sign-ups beginning, you'll start to hear, "Hey, dad, when can we put up the cage?" And that construction project with your children will make for great fun, and give them a nice sense of accomplishment when they see it finished and ready to use.

I left our cage up one winter, just to see what would happen to it. We did get some very interesting ice formations in the netting. And having left it up, it was so much easier to get it in shape for our own spring training. But the best times were when we put it up and took it down and let it rest . . . outside . . . until baseball season arrived in spring.

SO HERE ARE THE materials you'll need to build your cage:

- White PVC pipes, 10-foot-long, 1 1/2-inches in diameter.
- White PVC T-connecting pipes, 1 1/2-inches in diameter.
- Baling wire (tiewire) spools.
- Duct tape rolls.
- Clothesline roll.
- Rebar stakes.
- Birdnet packages.

Material notes:

- The PVC pipe of the recommended diameter is just right. Smaller size is too flimsy, while the 2-inch pipe is too heavy.
- The number of pipes depends on how many sections you want in your cage.
- Spools of baling wire have about 328 feet length of wire. A couple of spools are nice to have around.
- The T connectors hold the pipes in place. If they are glued to the pipes, it is impossible to take the cage down at the end of the season. The number of T connectors depends on the number of sections desired in the cage.
- A couple rolls of duct tape should do the trick.
- One package of clothesline, about 200 feet long, will get the job done.

Cotton rather than synthetic is best to prevent slippage.

- Rebar stakes are inexpensive and work well. The 2-foot-long ones work fine. Other stakes work, too. Even sticks and branches will work.

- Birdnet comes in a variety of sizes and shapes: 28 X 28, 14 X 45, 14 X 14, 7 X 20. You need enough of this to cover the size structure you have chosen to build. The birdnet should drape loosely over the frame. It deteriorates in the sun and weakens, so it is best to have spares to throw over the top if a weakness in the netting develops. It lasts a long time but needs to be monitored.

Tools:

- Saw, to cut some of the pieces of PVC pipe.
- Pliers, to snip the baling wire.
- Knife, to cut the duct tape and clothesline.
- Foldout ladder. A regular ladder cannot be leaned against the batting cage structure. Two ladders are helpful.

Maintenance tip: Tighten the baling wire from time to time. Add additional duct tape when the initial tape becomes weathered and loses sticking power.

See diagram for how this looks when it is put together. The batting cage is not difficult to construct.

Diagram of backyard batting cage.

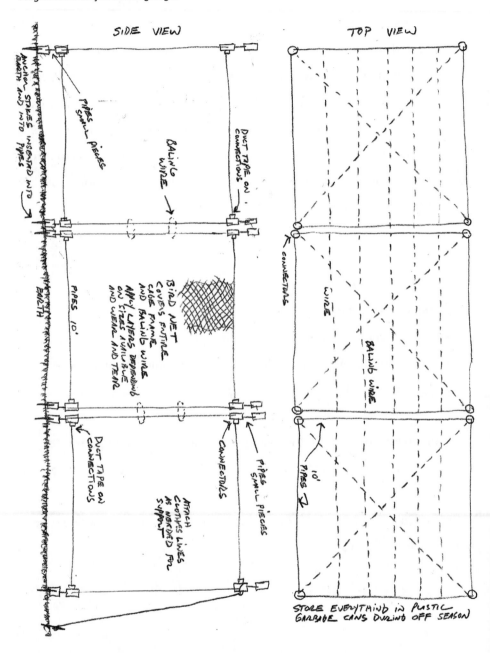

For those of you who'd rather purchase a backyard batting cage, steel-and-nylon models can be found online, with some sold with L-shaped screens for the pitcher to stand behind. The cost of these cages generally ranges from $500 to $1,200.

←First section of frame.

View of an upper corner. ➤

←View of a lower corner.

The finished product — complete with
batter honing his eye.➤

# N⚾tes:

# Appendix B

# League Newsletter

I found that a newsletter is a nice way of communicating with a league's participants. Three letters per season is probably ideal: one distributed at schools and mailed prior to signups; one at season's midpoint; and one mailed to all as a season recap.

Communication is essential to having a smooth-running league. Communication keeps people interested, and uncovers those who might like to be involved but are too timid to come out front and center and ask.

Here is a sample of one of the newsletters I produced while league president.

RENO CONTINENTAL LITTLE LEAGUE NEWS

SO DON'T COMPLAIN ABOUT THE WEATHER, ALREADY. On bended knee your President risked zapping by thunderbolt and presumptuously asked for not just good, but outstanding, weather for Tryout Day, Opening Day, and Picture Day. Just reflect back and realize that with the snow, rain, sleet, hail, sub-freezing temperatures and generally nasty atmospheric stuff we've all endured during the first half, on those three very important days for this league, you witnessed minor miracles. Cloudy skies parting for a few hours, warmth, and the sun shining through. Be thankful and count your blessings. Plus, open your shades. I've got the weather looking a little better now anyway.

Polls say that 67% of the population in America is BORN TO COMPLAIN. Luckily for all of us the percentage of complainers in Reno Continental Little League is far lower than that. I won't bore you with the f-a-s-c-i-n-a-t-i-n-g details of the dozens and dozens of calls I've fielded this year (why, I've had complaints from as far away as Bakersfield, California). But just remember, on a scale of 1 to 10 your Reno Continental Little League is a TEN PLUS. Folks, I've looked around a lot, and this program is as good as it gets. Be proud of what you have here, and take an active part in helping to keep it topnotch for you and for those families coming up the ladder. RENO CONTINENTAL IS A WINNER ALL THE WAY.

Congratulations to the Main-METS, Minor-ORIOLES, Farm-A's, and the Tee Ball (oops, we don't keep track in Tee Ball) for winning their divisions in the first half. Now let's the rest of us get with it and take these guys down a peg or two here in the second-half action.

All MANAGERS, COACHES, and OTHERS interested in managing or coaching next year or in the Fall Baseball Season need to throw their names into the hat. Decide what you want to do now so you can be considered for a position. Call me so I know your interests.

Ray A____ was elected to be your District Administrator for another three-year term. He's done a grand job and it is great to have him back. If you missed the balloting for this $275,000-a-year, big bucks job, don't feel bad. You weren't supposed to vote anyway. And in the fine Cook County, Illinois, fashion, the election was held secretly, at midnight, in a snowstorm, in the basement of an unmarked building. For all who want to reach Ray, his telephone remains unlisted and his address unknown.

And BASEBALL IS A DANGEROUS GAME. Remind your players to THINK SAFETY. Do not swing bats near people. Don't walk within 7 feet of someone with a bat in his hand (even if he's not swinging, you don't know when he will). Never throw a baseball at someone unless you KNOW he's looking. ALWAYS WEAR PROTECTIVE GEAR!!!!!!!!!!!!!!!!!!!!

Speeding in the parking lot: Let's back off on the throttle when driving near the baseball fields. Children are everywhere. Use CAUTION!!!! …And to help you slow down, photo surveillance devices have been installed to record speed, license plate numbers, and video footage of drivers and automobiles. All arrests for speeding infractions during the season will be made at the homes of offenders on September 16. So slow it down now, or you'll be hearing a knock on your door later.

@#$%$ %¢&) (&&*¢%$ @#$!!¢&* !!!!!! SAY WHAT !!!! @#$#@ %%$$**% +#$$## !!!!

Yes, you've heard it before, and I'm sorry to report that Bad Language has been used on the baseball fields this season. Muttering obscenities under your breath, to yourself, is one thing. Shouting them out is quite another. Such conduct will not be tolerated. Players using offensive, hostile, threatening language will get themselves suspended from games. Adults, banished from the ballpark.

If you feel a regurgitation of vile verbal profanities brewing biliously in your bile-bloated belly, take a walk. Blow off some steam, alone. Don't embarrass yourself and those around you by being a jerk. There are enough jerks on this celestial ball already. Why add to the problem?

BOOSTER CLUB information and merchandise is available from Jim L__

____, 555-6636. Shake loose some change and buy something if you haven't already.

BONNIE C____ is Reno Continental's "Volunteer of the Year." Take the time to meet Bonnie. Seek her out. She is indeed a shining star. A real doer. This league is so very fortunate to have her.

All our best to Sharon B____, who has been ill for a time. We hope to see her out at the baseball fields one of these sunny days soon.

The league is short a few sponsorships this year. If you are a manager who has not yet delivered a team sponsor, better put some effort into it ..... TODAY!!! Time is running out. The league needs the sponsors, and not finding one will affect who gets the opportunities to manage next year.

I know it's not pleasant going around clanging a tin cup making a nuisance of yourself asking for money ... BUT IT MUST BE DONE. If you want Reno Continental's quality baseball program to continue, twist some arms, hammer some heads, beg, plead, cry, and bring in that sponsorship. Call RIC N____, 555-9062, and talk about it N-O-W.

A tip: Review your team rosters and communicate with your players' parents. You'd be surprised at how many "Lifestyles of the Rich and Famous" kinda folks are on your team or are friends with someone who is a Fat Cat. Check it out. Ask. You'll find an open wallet. Sponsoring Little League Baseball is a kind and generous thing to do. Those who have had some lucky breaks and a little prosperity in their lives are willing to help, but need to be asked.

No one is gonna send you cash out of the blue (unless you win a MacArthur Scholarship). Ya Gotta Ask For The Order. Let's get with it on these final sponsorships. Build this league's bank account.

Construction will NOT begin on the DOMED STADIUM during this Administration. The league will not commission a $125,000 feasibility study of such a project. Keep this baseball simple.

The start of the Casey Stengel Baseball School is just around the corner. June 17 to be exact. Call Mike R___, 555-7763 for DETAILS.

Fall Baseball will be a go again this year. Ask me about it if you are interested in playing, managing, coaching, umpiring, or participating in other ways. There will be a player sign-up mailer out before long. Space is Limited.

Thanks to Suzanne at Channel 55 for giving Reno Continental 200 discount Reno Silver Sox Tickets . . . . . Distributed FREE at our Concession Stand.

. . . . . . And speaking of the Concession Stand. Remember, pulling a shift is a mandatory part of being in the league. Don't miss your time. You are counted on to do this job. Records are being kept of who lets the league down. DON'T get yourself on that list !!!!! You'll be sorry at Halloween. Seriously . . . . . . . DO YOUR DUTY. It is important.!!!!!!!

Don't forget Reno Silver Sox Little League Day, coming up June 9. The Silver Sox office has the facts. 555-8760.

Parents and Managers: Your league made a major investment in equipment and uniforms this year. All of it must be returned promptly at the conclusion of the baseball regular season. If you don't want to see your player running naked in center field chasing after imaginary baseballs next season, turn the equipment and uniforms back in . . . and PRONTO!! THIS IS A PRIORITY THIS YEAR. Don't forget it. Our generous sponsors deserve to have us take care of the first-class gear their cash helps us buy.

And with weather improving, spectators are present at the ballpark in the stands. No longer locked warmly in their cars during games. Please remember that in our league, THE UMPIRE IS ALWAYS RIGHT, even when he's wrong. We are lucky to have a good crew of umpires. Keep the abuse of the men (and lady) in blue to a minimum. They are doing their best. A little good-natured ribbing is OK, but save the hostilities and unpleasantries for your trips to the Bay Area Giants and A's games. Those umps can take their lumps. Ours deserve to be treated with respect.

This year, Reno Continental is serving over 500 players and their families. Your league operates because people put a great deal of effort into making it go. Do your part and become an active Reno Continental volunteer.

Join a committee. Manage or coach. Look into serving on the Board. Many, many things need to be done to keep the league functioning. NOW is the time to put your name in for the areas you can help with next year.

CALL ME . . . . . We can talk about it. I will get you placed. ACT!!!!!!!!!! If the league operating burden is spread over many shoulders, no one need be crushed by trying to do it all alone.

Call me up, or chat with me at the ballpark. Take part.


Jeff Kirst, President                    555-7876

## Appendix C

# Letter to Bob

I wrote the following letter to a friend named Bob, in response to his query about the path his grandson should take in baseball:

BOB:

First. HAPPY BIRTHDAY!!!!!!!!!!!!!!! 80 is a big one. I think the next two big ones for you will be 95 and 100. A week or so ago on the radio I listened to a program in which a few of the tens of thousands of people in America over the age of 100 were interviewed. They had good things to say, were enthused about life, and I found the program to be quite uplifting. Time being what it is, you'll make the Century Club before I do, but heck, I'm looking forward to those times after listening to what all those people in their early 100s had to say.

Baseball. While I do not consider myself to be a baseball nut, I am an enthusiast and in some respects an expert. I'll ramble on here about some of the things I know relating to your grandson's situation. My knowledge came from trying to help my sons with their athletic endeavors. Excuse the typing errors, any bad grammar, and spelling problems. I want to get this into the mail to you, and I ain't got a lotta time.

By the time a young player is a senior in high school, he needs to decide if he wants to try and take a shot at making a living playing baseball or if he is just playing for sport. Realistically, a spot in the majors is hard to get. At any given time there are only about 800 players on the major league rosters. Professional baseball in the minors is great, but not lucrative. Coaching at the college level can be a real moneymaker if you are adept at running camps and developing a winning college team, but the REAL money in baseball is making it to the major leagues. If you've got a chance, take the chance.

Most college players don't make it to the majors, let alone even the professional level. Talent in baseball often blooms early, and the scouts sign players to contracts right out of high school. If the offer is good enough, take it, and go to college later.

Around here, the best we've seen in recent years was an opponent of my son's. He was an unenthused student, from what I heard, and while offered a full-ride scholarship to college, did not want to go and turned pro. The word was he got right around $300,000 to sign, and then is paid minor league wages as he works his way through the system. He was really good. He pitched and played shortstop. He threw about 88 mph, with a 76 mph curve. My son faced him a few times, did well, and said he was a tremendous player.

He would routinely get 12 to 15 strikeouts when he pitched a seven-inning game. Anyway, that player was good. I think he also came within 1 home run of tying Ken Griffey, Jr.'s high school home run record. He could hit, too. Now he's playing third base and left field. He batted .260, I think, and is improving steadily.

Another player from my son's playing days was in Vegas. He was All-World, and gave up a full scholarship to the University of Miami to sign for a million bucks and turn pro. Others have signed from around here, but it is rare. It makes the newspaper.

Of the players I've coached, some have continued on in college. They have played at junior colleges, state universities, and private colleges.

My son had some offers from junior colleges, but after following the results of some of the players I coached or whose careers I tracked, we decided that was not a good way to go.

Scholarships are hard to come by in baseball. The teams are allowed to give 11.5 scholarships. Six usually go to pitchers, five to position players. But schools divide up the room, board, tuition, books, etc., to use it to the best advantage in recruiting the talent. If you can pay the tuition, that is a plus in finding a place to play or in being recruited. Left-handed pitchers are always in demand. They're the most sought-after players. And if you can hit ... they'll find a place for you to play.

When you join a college baseball program, count on taking extra time to get through school. You've got fall games and training, and then when the season starts, you've got to play some 55 games, half of which are on the road. It takes up all your time and it does have a big effect on grades.

The coaches at the college level are expected to win, and the players fit in as athlete-students, rather than student-athletes, at the Division I and junior college levels. Division III is a different deal, as is the Ivy League.

Division III schools cannot offer athletic scholarships. Ivy League schools cannot offer athletic scholarships, either, and they cannot recruit players unless they reach a certain threshold of academic achievement, calculated as a combination of high school grade-point average, the SAT I Verbal and

Math scores, and the scores on three SAT II tests. I can fill you in on that if you want.

When my son and I discussed it, we concluded that it is a difficult decision on whether to sacrifice grades and the student social life side of the college experience for baseball. At the Division I level, it is that choice. On the plus side, you're part of a team and it is the thrill of glory and a continuation of the joys of achievement from the high school years. It is a hard choice, because there is only so much time in a day.

None of the players I know who played baseball in college have done really well academically. It is hard to do it all.

My son was torn, and it was very tough for him. He saw what those who went before him did. We added it up and figured that at the current rate of tuition at a private school, it cost approximately $500 per game to be part of a baseball program. He also looked at the alternatives. He knew he was good enough to play at the college level.

His teammates had played. He had gone to college camps on several occasions, and knew he could compete with the best. It was a tough choice for him.

He decided that he would continue with his baseball after the summer of his first year in college. His great high school coach gave him an opportunity to play on the traveling team. He played and was better than ever that summer. A year layoff had only made him better. But the true passion for The Game had left him at that point, and he was happy moving on to other things. Every player is different.

He may still give it another whirl. He's only 21. But for now, he is happy with the choices he made. He played from ages 5 to 19.

My son the swimmer is doing athletics at the college level. He worked out at swimming 25 hours a week when in high school. He works out four hours a day in college. It is tough to keep it all going if you are involved in a sport. His grades are good, but not all A's. It is a difficult time for young people when you go to college, with or without a sport. In his case, the sport has helped him, because he has met nice people through the team, and training has given him the anchor activity he needs to stay organized and manage his time.

Call the coaches of schools you may like to attend. I repeat. CALL THE COACHES OF THE SCHOOLS YOU MAY LIKE TO ATTEND. Call them at least 10 times before you get disappointed in them not calling you back. They are busy. EVERY parent and player is calling them, and most are ignorant of the athletic facts of life at the college level. CALL THE COACHES. Talk to an assistant if the Head Coach is not available. Often, an assistant does the recruiting.

In the old days players came to college unpolished, and the coach could add much to their game by showing them the finer points. Today, players from good high school programs already know the finer points. My son played 100 games a year for several years while in high school, plus hours and hours practicing.

Tell the coach your grandson's 6'5 size and lefty status. That is impressive. A coach would figure that he might have something to work with there. A professional scout would KNOW that he had something to work with there.

Find out what positions are open on the team you aspire to. There is little sense going to a place where you'll sit the bench for a couple years behind someone who is ALL-WORLD. Talk to the Coach. Ask him to tell you the composition of his team. And remember, a good college coach in a good program has his eyes on talent in high school a couple years before it is time for them to go to school.

Great pitchers are often burned out in college. In the college game, the best pitchers have already been recruited by the pros and signed by the minor league teams. Everybody needs pitching. So if you are a college-oriented great pitcher, you will be overused. Plenty of glory, but your arm will be shot. Young people think they are indestructible. And they are for a time. But in the long run of a baseball season, they are not. Is the coach or your prospective college team sensitive to the over- and under-use problems of athletes?

In Division I baseball, a player has five years to play out his four years of eligibility. An injury might lengthen that time if handled in the right way. Transferring schools is difficult. It entails releases from athletic departments, sometimes sitting out a year, and problems. Try to make a good choice in the first place.

Coaches move on. Ask the coach who recruits you what his plans are. If the program is losing games, the coach might not be around because of it. Ask. You don't want to be stuck with people you didn't discuss the future with when you signed up.

That's about all I can think of for now, plus, my fingers are tired.

I'll call you.

It will be two more years before I have to go through this stuff with my youngest son. If he is still involved in sports. He plays baseball and water polo . . . for now.


Jeff

## Appendix D

# Words of Wisdom from the Ancients and a Couple of Others

*The following words are from Polybius (203-120 B.C.), Greek historian and author* of The Histories of the Rise of the Roman Empire, *in his writing* The First Punic War. *Polybius' points apply to the value of a book such as this for those who participate in youth baseball, since by absorbing the lessons of this book, they won't have to learn those lessons through — as the Greek scribe would have phrased it — "their own calamities":*

"I have recorded these thoughts with a view to the improvement of the readers of my history. There are two ways open to all men of changing their ways for the better — one is through their own disasters and one through those of others; that involving one's own calamities is the more vivid, but the one involving those of others is less painful. Therefore the former method should never be chosen voluntarily, since it affects its improvement along with great labors and risks; but the latter method should always be sought out, since in it we can see the better course without being injured. Basing our conclusions on these facts, we must agree that the experience accruing from a study of serious history is the best education for actual life: for such experience is the only kind that, without injuring us, makes us true judges of the better course of action on every occasion and in every set of circumstances. So much, then, for my opinion on this subject."

\* \* \*

*The following words are from Hsün Tzu, an advisor to King Hsiao-ch'eng of Chao, who reigned in China 265-245 B.C. While they describe the effect of leadership on military success, they apply equally well to a manager's leadership of a baseball team, and to the administration of a league:*

"He who treats his officers well will be strong; he who does not will be weak. He who loves his people will be strong; he who does not will be weak. He whose government decrees are trusted will be strong; he whose government decrees are not trusted will be weak. He whose people are unified will be strong; he whose people are not unified will be weak. He whose rewards are generous will be strong; he whose rewards are meager will be weak. He whose punishments are held in awe will be strong; he whose punishments are regarded with contempt will be weak. He whose supplies and armaments are complete and efficient will be strong; he whose supplies and armaments are crude and inefficient will be weak. He who uses his soldiers with caution will be strong; he who uses them rashly will be weak. He whose strategies proceed from a single source will be strong; he whose strategies proceed from several sources will be weak. This is the abiding rule of strength and weakness."

\* \* \*

"For when the One Great Scorer comes to mark against your name, he writes — not that you won or lost — but how you played the game.

— *Grantland Rice*

\* \* \*

"When a true genius appears, you can know him by this sign: that all the dunces are in a confederacy against him."

— *Jonathan Swift*

\* \* \*

"This blessed plot, this earth, this realm, this baseball's Field of Dreams."

— *William Shakespeare,* Richard II, Act II, Scene 1 (more or less)

\* \* \*

"If you don't think too good, don't think too much."

— *Ted Williams*

\* \* \*

"If the world were perfect, it wouldn't be."

— *Yogi Berra*

\* \* \*

"Growing up is a ritual — more deadly than religion, more complicated than baseball, for there seemed to be no rules. Everything is experienced for the first time. But baseball can soothe even those pains, for it is stable and permanent, steady as a grandfather dozing in a wicker chair on a verandah."

— *W.P. Kinsella, in the novel,* Shoeless Joe, *from which the movie* Field of Dreams *was adapted*

# A Partial List of Suggested Reading and Viewing

**Books on the Little League experience:**

Brown, Paul B., *My Season On The Brink: A Father's Seven Weeks As A Little League Manager*, St. Martin's Press, 1992.

Burroughs, Jeff, and Hennessey, Tom, *The Little League Team That Could: The Incredible, Often Whacky Story of the Two-Time Little League World Champions,* Bonus Books, 1994.

Dunow, Henry, *The Way Home: Scenes from a Season, Lessons from a Lifetime,* Broadway Books, 2001.

Fortanasce, Vincent, *Life Lessons from Little League,* Image, 1995.

Geist, William, *Little League Confidential: One Coach's Completely Unauthorized Tales of Survival,* Dell Publishing, 1999.

Hohenstein, Kurt, *The Rules Of The Game: Simple Truths Learned from Little League,* Thomas Nelson, 1996.

Mitchell, Greg, *Joy in Mudville— A Little League Memoir,* Pocket Books, 2000.

Newkirk, Jay, *Hey Batter! The Little League Season: A Manager's View,* H.R. PR, 1996.

**Other books on Little League:**

Frommer, Harry, *Growing Up At Bat: 50 Years of Little League Baseball,* Pharos Books, 1989.

Martens, Rainer, *Parent Guide to Little League Baseball,* Human Kinetics Publishing, 1993.

**Books on baseball skills:**

Bartlett, Brett R., *The Perfect Season: How to Practice and Play Youth Baseball,* Whirlwind Press, 2003.

McIntosh, Ned, *Little League Drills and Strategies: Imaginative Practice Drills to Improve Skills and Attitude,* Contemporary Books, 2003.

Monteleone, John J., *Little League Baseball Guide to Correcting the 25 Most Common Mistakes: Recognizing and Repairing the Mistakes Young Players Make,* Contemporary Books, 2003.

Van Auken, Lance, and Van Auken, Robin, *Play Ball: The Story of Little League Baseball,* Penn State University Press, 2001.

Vorhees, Randy, *Coaching the Little League Pitcher: Teaching Young Players to Pitch With Skill and Confidence,* McGraw-Hill, 2002.

Vorhees, Randy, *Making Little League Baseball More Fun for Kids: 30 Games and Drills Guaranteed to Improve Skills and Attitudes,* McGraw-Hill, 2002.

Williams, Ted, and Underwood, John: *The Science of Hitting,* Simon & Schuster, 1970 (revised, 1986)

**Instructional video on baseball skills:**

*Baseball the Pete Rose Way.* This was produced for Embassy Home Entertainment in 1986. Copies may be hard to find. A later instructional product is the 2002 DVD Pete Rose: *Playing to Win,* from Image Entertainment (check with Amazon.com).

**Classic books about baseball:**

Adair, Robert K., *The Physics of Baseball,* HarperCollins, 1994.

Anderson, Sparky, *Sparky!,* Prentice Hall, 1990.

Honig, Donald, *Cincinnati Reds: An Illustrated History,* Simon & Schuster, 1992.

Lasorda, Tommy, and Fisher, Andy, *The Artful Dodger,* Avon, 1985.

Rickey, Branch, *Branch Rickey's Little Blue Book: Wit and Strategy from Baseball's Last Wise Man,* Macmillan, 1995.

Will, George F., *Men at Work: The Craft of Baseball,* Macmillan, 1990.

**Classic books on politics and human nature:**

Cervantes Saavedra, Miguel de, *Don Quixote de la Mancha,* Oxford Paperbacks, 1998 (reissue). Translation, by Charles Jarvis in 1742, is of the landmark comic novel first published in Spanish in two parts, respectively, in 1605 and 1615.

Machiavelli, Niccoló, *The Prince,* Penguin, 1999 (reprint). Translation is of the political-advice book first published in Italian in 1531.

Tzu, Sun, *The Art of War,* Oxford University Press, 1971 (reprint). This is one of the many translated versions of the original 7,000-word treatise in ancient Chinese. Sun Tzu's essays are some 2,500 years old.

**Television documentary:**

*Small Ball: A Little League Story.* This documentary was produced for PBS and covers the 2002 run to the Little League World Series by a team from Aptos, Calif. It is available for purchase as a video or DVD.

**Motion pictures (available on DVD):**

*The Bad News Bears* (the 1976 original or the 2005 remake), Paramount. Walter Matthau and Tatum O'Neal star in the original and Billy Bob Thornton stars in the remake of the classic story about youth baseball and the relative importance of winning.

*Bang the Drum Slowly,* Paramount, 1973. Robert De Niro stars in the tear-jerker about a professional catcher secretly stricken with the terminal Hodgkin's Disease, but playing a final season.

*Field of Dreams,* Universal, 1989. Kevin Costner stars as an Iowa farmer who turns a cornfield into a diamond for ghosts of legends, heeding a whispered voice that says, in reference to the late, great "Shoeless" Joe Jackson, "If you build it, he will come."

*A League of Their Own,* Sony, 1992. Starring Geena Davis, Rosie O'Donnell and Madonna, set in 1943 and based on the All-American Girls Professional Baseball League.

*The Natural,* Columbia/Tristar Studios, 1984. Starring Robert Redford as an aging player making a comeback after being shot by an obsessed fan.

*The Rookie,* Walt Disney, 2002. Starring Dennis Quaid and based on the true story of Jim Morris, whose minor league pitching career was ended by an injury. Morris becomes a high school teacher and coach, and 12 years after retiring from The Game, attends a major league team's tryout and ends up in The Show.

*The Sandlot,* Twentieth Century Fox, 1993. Set in 1962, about a group of kids playing baseball the old-fashioned way: on their own!

**Broadway play:**

*Damn Yankees.* Recordings of the 1955 original production and the 1994 version are available on CD through Amazon.com. The 1958 Warner Bros. movie version is available on DVD. Based on a novel, *The Year the Yankees Lost the Pennant,* the plot concerns a deal with the devil made by a hapless Washington Senators fan to become a 22-year-old slugger who helps his team beat baseball's elite squad. Classic songs include *(You Gotta Have) Heart* and *Whatever Lola Wants.*

# Notes:

# About the Author

Jeffrey J. Kirst is a graduate of the University of California, Berkeley. He lives in a walled compound in Reno, Nevada. *Screwballs, Curves and Knuckleheads* is his first book, but he warns that it may not be his last.